By Calvin Trillin

THE
LEDE

THE LEDE

Dispatches from a Life in the Press

CALVIN TRILLIN

RANDOM HOUSE
NEW YORK

Published in the United States by Random House, an imprint and division of Penguin Random House LLC, New York.

RANDOM HOUSE and the HOUSE colophon are registered trademarks of Penguin Random House LLC.

The pieces in this book first appeared in the following publications: *The New Yorker, The Nation, Time, Brill's Content, The New York Times,* the Toronto *Globe and Mail,* and newspapers through distribution by King Features Syndicate. Some of the obituaries were delivered at memorials.

Library of Congress Cataloging-in-Publication Data
Names: Trillin, Calvin, author.
Title: The lede: dispatches from a life in the press / Calvin Trillin.
Description: New York: Random House [2024]
Identifiers: LCCN 2023015611 (print) | LCCN 2023015612 (ebook) |
ISBN 9780593596449 (hardcover) | ISBN 9780593596456 (ebook)
Subjects: LCSH: Journalism—United States. | American wit and humor.
Classification: LCC PN4725 .T745 2024 (print) | LCC PN4725 (ebook) |
DDC 071/.3—dc23/eng/20230830
LC record available at lccn.loc.gov/2023015611
LC ebook record available at lccn.loc.gov/2023015612

Printed in the United States of America on acid-free paper

randomhousebooks.com

2nd Printing

FIRST EDITION

Book design by Ralph Fowler

In memory of Edward Koren—
artist, firefighter, mensch

Contents

PART I
The Trade

"Burt Bernstein, for instance, worked for untold hours on a palindromic casual. It was in the form of a play called 'Look, Ma, I Am Kool!,' and it had characters delivering lines like 'Nail a timid god on rood. Door no dog, dim Italian.'"

PART II
Reporters and Reporting

"Covering the cops is often something a reporter does early in his career—an assignment that can provide him with enough war stories in six months to last him through years on the business page."

PART III
Big Shots

"His reputation for both acquisitiveness and devotion to great historical figures has been such that his assistant in London once had to state formally, in response to press inquiries, 'The proprietor of the Daily Telegraph would like to go on the record to say that he does certainly not own Napoleon's penis.'"

PART IV
R.I.P.

PART V
Controversies

"What, exactly, does the film critic of a main-line American daily news-paper do about movies like The Night Evelyn Came Out of the Grave?*"*

PART VI
Niches

"Reading that the best barbecue in Texas was at a place I'd never heard of, I felt like a People *subscriber who had picked up the 'Sexiest Man Alive' issue and discovered that the sexiest man alive was Sheldon Ludnick, an insurance adjuster from Terre Haute, Indiana, with Clooney as the runner-up."*

PART VII

Closings

"I knew all the verses to 'We Shall Overcome.' My expense account in-cluded items like 'trousers torn in racial dispute' and 'after prayer-meeting snack, Tuskegee, $3.75.'"

Introduction

n the pre-Google era, when someone in my family needed to find, say, an obscure fact or an unlisted telephone number, one of my daughters was likely to say, "Let daddy do it; he's practically a trained reporter." When the task was something like composing a note to a teacher, I got what some would consider a slight upgrade, although it, too, included a qualifier: "Daddy can do it; he's nearly a professional writer."

I think "practically a trained reporter" sums it up neatly—that is, if you include my training at Sarachon Hooley Secretarial School, where, according to *The Kansas City Star,* Anne Sarachon Hooley spent thirty-seven years "training Kansas City women to be valuable secretaries."

When the Kansas City public schools closed around April one year because of lack of funds, my father decided that my sister and I should use that early release from high school to learn typing. In those days, it was routine, of course, to train girls to be "valuable secretaries." But why me? I've often said that my father's aspirations for me were clear early on: he wanted me to be the president of the United States, and his fallback position was that I not become a ward of the county. Neither of those positions requires typing. I like to think that journalism struck him as a conceivable middle course. Reporters do type—although, from what I've gathered from old movies, in those days many of them did not devote more than two fingers to the task.

I bring this up because I think it's incumbent upon anyone writing about his own field to reveal his predilections and experience in that field. For instance, I should mention that my own reporting for the past five or six decades has been overwhelmingly for magazines, and that magazine reporting is, compared to newspaper reporting, a lackadaisical calling. For fifteen years, I did a three-thousand-word piece for *The New Yorker* from somewhere in the United States every three weeks. When magazine writers heard that, they'd say, "How do you keep up that pace?" Newspaper reporters would say, "What else do you do?"

I did work on the college newspaper, where I learned one version of objective journalism: we were equally inaccurate about both sides. I later learned another version from a photographer on a Little Rock paper. He said when he had an assignment to take someone's picture, he'd stop at the city desk and say, "Do you want him gazing out at the sunset or picking his nose?"

The disparate nature of these pieces—some serious reporting pieces, some short pieces that are meant to amuse (what writers and editors at *The New Yorker* used to call casuals), some pieces that are somewhere in between—can be explained simply: I never got my act together. If I was working on, say, the sort of piece that *The New Yorker* runs under a rubric like "A Reporter at Large," I could imagine a caricaturist depicting me with the type of hat reporters wore in those old black-and-white movies—a fedora that has a press pass jutting out of the hatband. The next day, writing a casual, the caricature shows me fully encased in a clown costume, big floppy shoes included. Some other day, I'm in an incongruous outfit: the clown costume topped off with the fedora.

I've been writing about the press almost as long as I've been in the game. In the early sixties, when I had a day job at *Time,* I was writing on the side for *Monocle*—a publication, I might mention, whose pay scale was so low that they once sent me a bill for a piece of mine they'd published. In a *Monocle* feature called "Letters to

Other Editors," I propounded a theory that *The New Yorker* pur-
posely included in each issue one cartoon that wasn't funny at all,
so that the reader would assume that he must be witnessing "sub-
tle humor beyond his power of perception, and that *The New
Yorker* is therefore even more sophisticated than he thought."

Some years later, after I'd moved to *The New Yorker, Monocle*
had been replaced as a sideline by *The Nation,* where I wrote a
column and, eventually, contributed what we called "Deadline
Poetry." *The Nation* was joined for a while by a magazine on the
media called *Brill's Content,* where I wrote a column called "The
Wry Side." (That title was not my idea. As someone who has often
been referred to as wry by reviewers who are trying to be kind, I
long ago decided that "wry" means "almost funny.") During the
Brill's Content period, some prominent reporters and columnists
on major papers were revealed as having played fast and loose
with the facts, and I suggested that the Columbia School of Journalism might want to have etched in stone over its front entrance
the motto "Too good to check."

Meanwhile, at *The New Yorker,* I regularly found myself writing
about the press—a profile of a prominent homicide reporter here,
a casual parodying newspaper correction columns there. At all of
these publications, I had the freedom to write about what engaged
me—which is why I've written about *Beautiful Spot: A Magazine
of Parking* but not about, say, the broader cultural implications of
TikTok's appeal to American teenagers. At some point, it occurred
to me that disparate pieces from various places in various styles
amounted to a picture from multiple angles of what the press has
been like over the years since I became a practitioner and an observer. I hope that is what this book provides.

Part I
THE TRADE

The Lede

t's said that when James Thurber, as a young newspaper reporter, was told by an editor that his story's first paragraph, what newspaper people might refer to as his lede, suffered from wordiness, he handed in a rewrite whose opening paragraph was, in its entirety, "Dead."

There followed a second paragraph: "That's what the man was when they found him with a knife in his back at 4 p.m. in front of Riley's saloon at the corner of 52nd and 12th streets."

Like that editor, I admire those short, punchy ledes often employed by crime reporters. But I also admire the ambition of those long ledes which you often see in the obituaries that appear in *The New York Times*—ledes whose first sentence manages to stuff the highlights of an entire lifetime in a clause between the decedent's name and the fact that he has expired.

You might say that I'm a collector of ledes. I assume that's why my friend James Edmunds, who lives in New Iberia, Louisiana, sent me an article that appeared in *The Advocate* of Baton Rouge on September 23, 2019. If the function of a lede is to engage the reader, this article's lede seemed to me remarkably effective. Here it is:

> A veterinarian prescribed antibiotics Monday for a camel
> that lives behind an Iberville Parish truck stop after a
> Florida woman told law officers she bit the 600-pound
> animal's genitalia after it sat on her when she and her
> husband entered its enclosure to retrieve their deaf dog.

Notice how the reader is drawn in with a single unpunctuated sentence that starts slowly and gradually becomes an express train that whistles right by the local stops without providing an opportunity to get off. A veterinarian is summoned to administer antibiotics to a camel—routine stuff so far. Yes, the camel lives behind a truck stop, which is an unusual domicile for a camel but probably not unprecedented. It wasn't that long ago that gas stations along highways like Route 66 lured travelers with roadside zoos that were advertised by signs like "See Albino Raccoon" or "Live Two-Headed Goat." And this takes place in Louisiana, where animal stories that might be considered unusual elsewhere are commonplace. In 2007, when Louisiana finally banned cockfighting, the last state to do so, a state senator from Opelousas fought to exempt a less lethal version of the sport he called chicken boxing. Louisiana once tried to eat its way out of an environmental crisis caused by the nutria, an invasive rodent that devours marshland, by encouraging some of the state's celebrated chefs to invent tempting nutria dishes with names like Ragondin a l'Orange.

And then we come to the woman who bit the camel's genitalia and is talking to law officers, perhaps claiming self-defense as a way to wiggle out of a cruelty-to-animals charge. Identifying her as a "Florida woman," as I interpret it, suggests that we're dealing here with what Newfoundlanders would call a come-from-away and New Yorkers would call an out-of-towner. The tantalizing implication is that a local woman would have known that you could give a truck-stop camel an infection requiring antibiotics by biting its genitalia.

While the veterinarian was caring for the camel, was anyone attending to that Florida woman? She had, after all, been sat on by a six-hundred-pound camel, an experience that must be at least uncomfortable and probably injurious. A reader has to wonder if she had some broken bones or some cracked ribs or at least a nasty taste in her mouth.

And we still have the deaf dog to deal with. The Florida woman and her husband (presumably a Florida man) may have tried to call him back ("Here, Fido! Here, Fido! Come out of the camel's enclosure, Fido") even though they knew that, because of his deafness, they might as well have been singing the FSU fight song, or whatever Florida people do when things don't seem to be going their way.

As I see it, the Florida woman and the Florida man have no choice but to enter the enclosure. The Florida woman is still shouting at the deaf dog to follow her out. Her husband has tried to calm her down by saying things like "Hush, Florida woman, or that camel is going to lose his temper and take it in his mind to sit on someone." The camel has, in fact, been getting a bit riled. He has decided to sit on the Florida woman, but, in his excitement, he fails to do so in a way that evolution has taught him to sit on an enemy without exposing his genitalia to retaliation.

At that point, as if a shutter had clicked, it becomes a tableau vivant—one that I have carried in my mind ever since. The Florida man looks alarmed. The dog looks puzzled. The camel looks pained—even more pained than camels normally look. All we see of the Florida woman is her legs extending from underneath the camel. Talk about engaging the reader! I was so engaged that I felt no need to read the rest of the story. The lede is sufficient. It's now in my collection.

Class Acting

1998

One day, a friend of mine who was working for a newspaper in Washington spent a couple of hours trying to get people on the telephone so they could lie to him about a particularly boring hearing he had covered. Pausing between calls, he glanced around at all the other reporters in the newsroom who were similarly occupied, and suddenly wondered, "Is this a job for a college graduate?" That was thirty-five years ago, and I still don't know the answer to his question. I've been making do with "not necessarily."

Although a reporter is no longer thought of as a coarse man who wears a shiny suit and probably keeps a bottle of cheap bourbon in the bottom drawer of his desk, it still isn't clear where he fits into polite society. Network anchors, for example, are now national celebrities who make millions of dollars a year. But when an anchorman interviews an obscure member of the House of Representatives on camera, the anchorman addresses the representative as "Congressman" and the representative calls the anchorman by his first name. The only guests a network anchor feels free to call by their first names on camera are his fellow newsmen, many of them millionaire celebrities themselves.

English journalists, who are candid enough to call an anchor a "news reader," seem to have a clearer idea of where they stand. In the early seventies, an English reporter I knew who had been assigned to New York was about to bring his family from London by ocean liner, and I asked him which deck they'd be strolling around. "Cabin class," he said, naming the undramatic middle option that existed on transatlantic ocean liners between first class and Leonardo DiCaprio's mob in steerage. And then he added, in the matter-of-fact voice he always employed to instruct me on some elementary rule of cricket, "Journalists travel cabin class."

I suppose class is what I'm talking about here—which is to say that in this country, I'm talking partly about money. When I was a boy, it was sometimes said that what reporters got out of the game was a decent obituary. Reading the pinched little C.V. his paper ran to mark the passing of a biologist or a banker, a reporter having some trouble with the mortgage payments could at least take satisfaction in knowing that he himself might be piped off to the next vale with a ripe eulogy that ran a full column and might include a sentence that began, "Known to his colleagues as a warm and witty man. . . ."

When I started out, reporting was seen as a poorly paid and faintly déclassé calling that might offer someone—usually someone from a modest background—an occasional spurt of the high life on someone else's money. Even then, journalism had a sprinkling of people from families that had always taken first-class crossings for granted, but I tended to associate them with a special corner of the field in Washington—a view that resulted in my experiencing my own telephone epiphany in Newark.

On a very cold day in 1972, while covering some trouble between black and Italian residents in the North Ward of the city, I was trying to make a call from a grimy pay phone tacked to a building in the disputed territory. Finding myself put on hold by an obdurate secretary, I tried blowing on my hands for warmth, glanced around to make certain nobody was throwing any bricks in my direction, and heard myself say out loud, "I wonder what Joseph Alsop is doing right now." I pictured the elegant and well-born Mr. Alsop in the richly paneled dining room of a Washington club, selecting the wine with great care, while his luncheon guests, an ambassador and the director of central intelligence, waited patiently. It occurred to me that I was in the wrong end of the business.

One year, on behalf of all reporters everywhere, I suggested that Roy Reed be given the Pulitzer Prize for managing to convince the poohbahs at *The New York Times* that New Orleans, a backwater in just about every human endeavor except the enjoyment of life, rather than Atlanta, the Babbitt-ridden commercial center and air hub of the South, was the logical place for the *Times*'s Southern correspondent to make his headquarters. The true high life on someone else's money, though, has traditionally been available in foreign postings. In the fat days of Time Inc., I never passed an impressive mansion in a foreign capital without thinking, "It's either an Arab embassy or the home of the *Time* bureau chief."

You could argue that reporters, no matter how much money they make, forget at their peril that they are essentially cabin-class people traveling first class on an upgrade. They are, after all, engaged in a trade that involves rude questions, snooping, and a tendency to wander into gatherings they might be asked to leave— behavior that is outside of polite society. When reporters invite the people they cover or flashy movie stars to fancy banquets, they tend to look silly, as just about everyone involved in the White House correspondents' glitzfest this spring seemed to realize. When they acquire protective feelings toward the important people they enjoy seeing socially, they tend to get scooped.

Still, it's tempting for people in our trade to pretend that we're at the gala as a legitimate guest, rather than as somebody who's somewhere between a guest and the person who may be wearing a tuxedo but is actually in charge of the valet parking. About ten years ago, I published a travel book—most of the traveling having been underwritten, it almost goes without saying, by magazine expense accounts. One reviewer criticized it for being about trips that were possible only for upper middle-class travelers like the author. I phoned my sister in Kansas City. "Guess what," I said. "We finally made it."

This Story Just Won't Write

Time Warner, whose profits now come from cable and film, has announced that *Time* magazine is about to be "spun off"—a phrase that to me has always conjured up a business enterprise caught in the final cycle of a giant washing machine, with desks and office machines flying through the air and middle-management types being blown away, head over heels, like so many tumbleweeds. *Newsweek* has ceased to exist as a print magazine. For a long time now, of course, newsmagazines have borne little resemblance to the sort of publication that was invented at *Time* in 1923 and loosely replicated at *Newsweek* ten years later—a magazine designed to present the week's news succinctly to "busy men" who were too involved in their important endeavors to spend time wading through a lot of newspapers. Starting as strictly a rewrite operation, *Time* eventually had reporters and stringers around the world. They sent "files" to an operation called Time Edit, in New York, where writers, drawing on those files and the material that researchers had dug out of the library and whatever could be lifted from the *Times*, composed tight narratives that were conveniently compartmentalized into sections like Sport and Medicine and Religion and Show Business.

That system, which for decades was the formula for producing a newsmagazine, went by a name that had the communal ring of a town picnic or a Tupperware party—group journalism.

In the early sixties, in the heyday of group journalism, I spent a year as one of the writers in Time Edit. I'd previously spent a year as a reporter (or "correspondent," as the masthead had it) in the Atlanta bureau, covering the civil rights struggle in the South, and six months in the New York bureau—a misfit operation in the group-journalism scheme of things, staffed by two or three reporters who sometimes compared themselves to Transit Authority policemen assigned to the tunnels. For half of that year in Time Edit, I was what we called a floater—a utility infielder who was brought into a section when, say, the person who wrote Sport was home with the flu, or when one of the World writers was on vacation. Since writers were listed on the masthead as associate or assistant editors, I've assumed ever since that I could justifiably refer to myself, on occasions when credentials are called out to add weight to a point of view, as the former Art editor of *Time* (four or five weeks, at various times) or even the former Medicine editor of *Time* (two consecutive weeks, although I must admit that the section was killed both weeks).

There were some enjoyable aspects of being a floater. When I settled into the desk chair of, say, the Education writer, someone who presumably pored through the education quarterlies and lunched with school reformers and kept abreast of the latest disagreements about how best to teach reading, I could feel myself imbued with the authoritative tone favored in those days at *Time;* I called that "instant omniscience." I had become adept at using one of the tools employed to assert *Time*'s authority—what I thought of as the corrective "in fact," as in "Democrats maintain that the measure would increase unemployment. In fact. . . ." There were no bylines in *Time* then, so the readers had no way of knowing whether the Art section's critique of the new Coventry Cathedral had been written by someone steeped in the history of church architecture or by a floater who'd moved in after a short stint in Medicine that had left him with no words in the magazine for two weeks and a more detailed knowledge of loop colostomy procedures than he'd ever hoped to have.

I liked the frequent change from section to section. In the South, my movements had been so constant and unpredictable that I'd kept a packed bag at the office. As a floater, I at least might get a change of subjects from week to week, even if I never left a building on Sixth Avenue. In 1980, long after I'd left *Time,* I wrote a comic novel that was set partly at an unnamed newsmagazine— the novel was called *Floater*—and I admitted in the flap copy that I was the restless floater referred to in passing as having tried to get out of an overlong stay in Religion by writing "alleged" in front of any historically questionable religious event. The senior editor whose responsibilities included Religion simply crossed out all of the "alleged"s. If there was anything *Time* was experienced in dealing with in those days, it was smart alecks.

Back then, a newspaper reporter covering anything that involved *Time* rarely seemed able to resist the temptation to write his story as a parody of what he thought of as Timestyle—although the parodies actually tended to resemble the style used by Wolcott Gibbs, a quarter of a century before, to parody *Time*'s backward sentences in a *New Yorker* profile of its co-founder, Henry Luce. ("Doomed to strict anonymity are *Time-Fortune* staff writers.") By the time I was working in Time Edit, just about all that remained of the style Gibbs had lampooned was the use of phrases like "says he" or "said she" to introduce a quotation, plus a number of constructions that must have grown out of the pressure *Time* writers were under to write as compactly as possible—saving a few words by referring to the writer of a new novel, for instance, as "gap-toothed author Smith." (In the eighties, *Spy* magazine, both of whose founding editors had been writers at *Time,* paid a sort of homage to those leftover tics by using phrases like "short-fingered vulgarian Donald Trump.") It was largely because of the constant pressure to compress that *Time* prose struck me as more difficult to write than to parody.

A common complaint then among *Time* writers who found themselves stuck on a story was "this story just won't write"—as if the story had a will of its own and was using it to resist being shaped into a coherent narrative. I may have used the phrase from time to time myself. The problem was mostly space. There on my desk was the raw material for one of the three or four stories in my section: a fifteen-page file from the main reporter on the story, a five-page file from the Washington bureau on the federal angle, three books that the researcher thought I might find useful, a fistful of previous *Time* files, and, of course, some clippings from the *Times*. From this, I was to produce a seventy-line piece that had the arc of a story rather than the "inverted pyramid" structure that was then the template for newspaper articles. (Since the news sometimes failed to conform to *Time*'s printing schedule, the paragraph containing the denouement of the story often began "At week's end.") Given the density of the seventy lines and the imperative to keep the story moving, there often seemed to be at least one highly relevant fact that simply didn't fit. I pictured that left-out fact darting around to find an opening and being rebuffed by every paragraph it tried to squeeze into—like someone trying door after door in a desperate effort to board a thoroughly stuffed rush-hour subway. Sometimes, if I had until the next day to turn the story in, I'd head home, finding that the knot in the narrative came loose with the rhythmic clacking of the subway train.

Writing the story at seventy lines didn't mean the compressing was over. At week's end, as we would have put it, the makeup people would invariably inform us that the story had to be shortened to fit into the section. Since words or passages cut for space were marked with a green pencil—changes that had to be made because of something like factual error were in red—the process was called greening. The instructions were expressed as how many lines had to be greened—"Green seven" or "Green twelve." I loved greening. I don't have any interest in word games—I don't think I've ever done a crossword or played Scrabble—but I found greening a thoroughly enjoyable puzzle. I was surprised that what I had thought of as a tightly constructed seventy-line story— a story so tightly constructed that it had resisted the inclusion of that maddening leftover fact—was unharmed, or even improved, by greening ten percent of it. The greening I did in Time Edit convinced me that just about any piece I write could be improved if, when it was supposedly ready to hand in, I looked in the mirror and said sternly to myself "Green fourteen" or "Green eight." And one of these days I'm going to begin doing that.

When I worked at *Time,* all editors and writers were male and all researchers were female, as a matter of policy. No one took much notice of this. One researcher, Johanna Davis, was so clever that the senior editor in charge of the section she worked in, Show Business, allowed her to write some stories. But that arrangement was off the books. Josie Davis was listed on the masthead as a researcher, and I assume that on stories she hadn't written she continued to do the job of a researcher—sending out queries to reporters in the field, gathering material for the writer from the library, and fact-checking copy as the section closed. Fact-checking was the main task of a researcher. On each story that had been approved by the senior editor, she met with the writer to thrash out questions of where his prose strayed from ascertainable facts. There was considerable thrashing. The writer's incentive had been to get the senior editor's initials on the copy, which meant that he might have an expansive view of a fact that, if taken absolutely literally, could easily have ruined a transition. A writer at *Time* lived and died by his transitions. The researcher's incentive was to put a red check above each word that seemed solid enough to keep her from being on the receiving end of an "error report." I once read a biography of Briton Hadden, the co-founder of *Time,* who was credited with inventing the fact-checking system as well as much of the *Time* prose style. (He was generally thought to be of a much more playful temperament than his partner, although it would not have been difficult to be more playful than Henry R. Luce.) According to the biography, Hadden designed the fact-checking system with the thought that putting a male writer and a female researcher together in a quasi-adversarial situation would create a sexual dynamic that could lend energy to the process. I don't know if that was what Hadden had in mind, but I know that tears were not unusual on closing nights.

It wouldn't have taken any special planning to make Time Edit a work environment that was highly charged sexually. Instead of being out reporting, as would have been the case at a newspaper, the employees were always inside an office building, with not much to do at the beginning of the week and too much to drink at the end of the week. (Closing the section required a catered meal or at least a few bottles in the senior editor's office late in the evening.) There was constant interaction in story conferences and fact-checking conferences and closing-night gatherings; whoever said that writing is a lonely craft had never worked as a writer in Time Edit. Often, the couplings that emerged from these interactions were discreetly handled, so that the first hint that the two people involved were any more than casual office acquaintances came with a wedding announcement or an ugly scene in the hall. What would now be considered sexual harassment was a subject of anecdotes rather than outrage; one editor, a man with an unfortunate shape and a reputation for chasing researchers around his desk, was known, behind his back, as the Horny Avocado.

In an issue of *Time* in that era, the place where group journalism could be seen shining in all of its glory was in the Letter from the Publisher—a weekly offering that was not, it almost goes without saying, written by the publisher. During my employment at *Time*, the "publetter," which was meant to be a report on *Time*'s inner workings, was also the only place other than the masthead where, as Wolcott Gibbs might have put it, "mentioned were the names of *Time* writers and reporters." Reporters and writers were not only mentioned, they were mentioned in heroic language. As the publetter told it, group journalism was a staggeringly efficient machine: in India, Delhi bureau chief Jones caught the last plane to the scene of the disaster, leaving photographer Johnson to make his way by bus and motor scooter and yak cart, while Smith, in Washington, tapped his sources in the defense and intelligence communities in time to allow veteran World writer Thompson to incorporate the foreign policy implications into a fast-breaking cover story that included files from bureaus in London, Paris, Chicago, and Calgary. There were occasions when the machinery did work that efficiently. But most employees of *Time* in those years would have described group journalism in a simpler way: some people work in the first half of the week and some people work in the second half of the week.

I have sometimes wondered whether having to pay all those people for half a week's work helped bring about the demise of group journalism. But there were more serious problems. Essentially, power over a story grew in direct proportion to distance from the event it described—the least power being in the hands of the reporter who had actually been present. With the best of intentions, a writer was likely to put a different spin on the story by presenting it as a sixty-line narrative. There were writers who seemed to use files mainly to pluck out punchy quotes or the details *Time* loved to include in order to bring the reader closer, like what the school board president had for breakfast on the day of desegregation. One writer was said to believe that using an entire sentence or paragraph from a file was tantamount to plagiarism. The senior editor of a section—who might not have even read the file thoroughly, since he had a growing stack of files from his other sections to worry about—could, after asking for a couple of new versions that still didn't please him, completely rewrite the story. (*Time* senior editors tended to act less as editors than as promoted writers.) The managing editor might toss in a paragraph of his own here and there. The finished product could be almost unrecognizable to the reporter who'd begun the chain; the first time he'd see it would be when he read it in the magazine. In one real-life exchange that I later transmogrified for *Floater,* I was asked by a researcher what I thought of the *Time* cover story on the Freedom Rides, which I had reported on for an intense and at times somewhat scary two weeks. "It was interesting," I said. "Did you get my file?"

Eventually, *Time* did institute what *Newsweek* called "read-backs"—going over the finished version of a story with the principal reporter, as a way of avoiding particularly egregious misunderstandings. One at a time, some of the other pillars of group journalism fell. The introduction of bylines, first at *Newsweek* and then at *Time,* made the authoritative tone more difficult to maintain. (No longer was word handed down from on high; it had been composed by two or three mere mortals.) The lines between sections evaporated. Stories began appearing under the byline of someone who had done both the reporting and the writing. Columnists emerged. Even before the complete Twitterization of the public attention span—even before practically nobody, busy or not, waded through a lot of newspapers—*Time,* which had been invented as a succinct way of keeping busy men informed, found itself using as an advertising motto "Make time for *Time.*" Long before Time Warner tycoons (a word invented by *Time*) thought of dumping the magazine that their corporation had grown out of, the rigid superstructure of the Time Edit I'd known had been dismantled.

I was, of course, gone by then. After floating for six months, I'd been assigned to Nation. That meant that I was stuck in one section for the foreseeable future. It happened to be a section where *Time*'s political views—views that these days would probably be categorized as moderate Republican—were sometimes dropped in somewhere along the group-journalism chain. As it turned out, the senior editor of Nation was someone willing to listen to arguments of why, say, a sneering comment about the Kennedys was not supported by the reporting sent from Washington. I didn't know how long his patience would last, of course, or how long it would be before I'd grow tired of making the arguments. But I didn't storm out of the building because of a political argument. I suppose that, without verbalizing it, I had concluded that reporting and writing are inseparable. Even before an opportunity to join *The New Yorker* came along, I was making plans to return to the South. The civil rights struggle had been covered mostly in terms of organizations and court cases and disruptions, and I thought that, by concentrating on individuals who had been involved in one way or another, I might be able to write a book. All by myself.

Prediction Memo

From *Floater*

1980

Charlie Sayler, a National News writer, was known for the calm with which he assumed that butchery of his copy was taking place. Whenever Sayler was assigned to write a cover story, he began by composing what he called a prediction memo—predicting in detail what would happen day-by-day as the story got written and rewritten and edited and, finally, put to press. Then he would have the prediction memo dated and notarized by the news dealer in the lobby, place it in a sealed envelope, and leave it in the care of Marge Hector, the imposing head researcher of the National News section, who would read it out loud to those assembled for the section's closing party on Friday night. Sayler was particularly proud of a prediction memo he had written when he was assigned to do a cover story on the secretary of state:

"Monday. I arrive at office to find that Loyal Researcher has already put on desk fourteen books on diplomacy, with relevant pages noted by paper clips, plus eight inches of newspaper clippings. I put all of these on floor in the corner so there's room to work on desk. Ace Washington reporter Marvin Rappaport has already started filing main report on Sec. of State. His first take of thirty pages is also on desk. I plan to read that, then get to pile in corner, but first I must read & digest 4,000-word memo from beloved senior editor Martin Baron explaining what should be in the 4,000-word cover story. Baron is worried that if story turns out to be weak Sec. of State will be pushed off cover by Archbishop of Canterbury, who's being heavily promoted by Ed Winstead, wily and beloved senior editor in charge of Religion. There is a rumor that Baron has whispered to Woody Fenton, sanctified managing editor, that British P.M. considers the Archbishop of Canterbury a lightweight. I get time to read the first take from Rappaport late in the afternoon. The pile in the corner remains untouched.

"Tuesday. I arrive to find 2nd Rappaport take of 35 pages on desk. I get halfway through when 3rd take of 40 pages arrives. Does Rappaport never sleep? I ask myself. Also have 20 pages from Chicago on Sec. of State's boyhood and college. 50 pages from Paris and other capitals. 30 from San Francisco on ex-wife's hanging around with kinky crowd. I read that one. Very good stuff. Loyal Researcher comes in with six more inches of clippings. I thank LR profusely and make new pile in another corner of my office.

"Wednesday. I arrive at office. Toss hat on 1st pile in corner. Start writing. 50 more pages arrive from Rappaport. Man has no mercy, no shame, no sense of perspective. I put 50 on 2nd pile. I still feel confident. I've read a lot more of Rappaport's file than Baron, who has files for stories in his other sections to read, also is notoriously slow reader. Baron interrupts my reading often to say he's worried. Winstead has apparently told Woody that Archbishop should be on the cover this week, since he has tricky ticker nobody knows about and could drop dead anytime. Baron is very pissed off at Winstead's dirty pool. Says Archbishop is healthy as a mule, also that smart. I write my heart out. I eat at my desk (multi-ethnic special from Manny's Deli: chopped-liver & bacon on pita). Heartburn awful. 10 P.M. I finish.

"Thursday. Baron says story is great. Also, he wants me to write it over again. I do new version, with more numbers in lede. (Baron likes numbers in lede; once worked for *Wall St. Journal.*) Also, I jiggle paragraphs around a lot. 30 more pages arrive from Rappaport. I put them on 1st pile in the corner, on top of my hat. Baron says the new version is great. Then he rewrites it, including two paragraphs saying Sec. of State not strong enough supporter of international wildlife preservation—anticipating Woody's interest in favorite cause of Big Boss Townsend. Baron's writing is very fluid, since he is not burdened by complicated facts facing anyone who has read large hunks of Rappaport's files. Baron initials the story, sends it on to Woody. I am so grateful I tip him off to San Francisco file on playing around with kinky crowd. 40 more pages arrive from Rappaport.

"Woody says he loves the story. Then he says to write it over again. Wants less of the Sec. of State being soft on destroyers of wildlife. (I figure he wants to please BB Townsend but not piss off Sec. of State so much that Sec. of State will quit inviting him to private briefings.) I take out two of Baron's wildlife paragraphs. Baron puts 1 back in, takes out one of mine. I jiggle paragraphs. He jiggles them back. Sends it to Woody. Woody wants new version. Says it needs spark. I put in spark, also couple of paragraphs I had taken out before. Baron to Woody. Woody writes in 2 paragraphs on world peace he heard at a dinner party from British ambassador when British ambassador was shitfaced drunk & even more pompous than usual. Then he writes in a paragraph about the Third World that somebody stuck in his ear at the Nairobi airport when he took tour of African and Middle East bureaus. Then he says he loves the story. Congratulates me. Tells me I'm a wiz.

"Friday. LR starts checking the story, true to her Researcher's Oath to produce a source for every fact in story and to find some reason why any sentence suspected of being even remotely graceful must be changed in a way that makes it boring or awkward. Checking meeting takes 7 hours and 24 minutes. LR cries twice. I cry once. Sec. of State would cry if he could see what was happening. Names LR calls me: egomaniac (twice), fool, sloppiest writer in section, a person with no regard whatsoever for the truth, dumb shithead. Names I call LR: Queen of the Nitpickers (14 times). LR, tired of arguing with me, tells Most Beloved Head Researcher, Marge Hector, that stuff Woody wrote in is irrelevant and distorts meaning of the story if included. MBHR Marge Hector says, 'Relevant my ass! Does it check or doesn't it?' Finally, story, checked to its teeth, is put on the wire of the Washington bureau as a courtesy to Rappaport—so he'll have advance notice of what his sources are going to hate him for. I brush some papers off my hat & get ready to go out to dinner. Phone call from Rappaport. 'Great story,' he says. 'Did you get my file?'"

Casuals

2020

In the first decades of my time at *The New Yorker* the light pieces that would these days run under the rubric of Shouts & Murmurs or possibly Personal History were referred to around the office as "casuals." Some of the people submitting casuals were, like me, reporters who thought of casual writing as a sideline. Some were fiction writers drawing a small salary that was ostensibly for writing Talk of the Town pieces. Some were people with no connection to the magazine who simply thought they had come up with something funny. Burton Bernstein, a colleague who published a biography of James Thurber, the nonpareil producer of casuals, wrote once that the casual, which sounds like something tossed off, is actually "one of the more difficult and painstaking forms of writing known to humankind." Contemplating casual-writing over the past fifty years or so, I'm reminded of how I began a talk I once gave to people graduating from Columbia with Master of Fine Arts degrees. "When I tried to think of an appropriate subject for people going into the fields you're going into," I said, "the only thing I could come up with was 'Rejection.'" It's not that we didn't sell some casuals. But what stands out in my memory is rejection.

Burt Bernstein, for instance, worked for untold hours on a palindromic casual. It was in the form of a play called "Look, Ma, I Am Kool!," and it had characters delivering lines like "Nail a timid god on rood. Door no dog, dim Italian." *The New Yorker* passed. The alternative market for palindromic casuals was not large. Some months later, Burt showed up at my office to announce that he was compiling and editing a book of casuals written by the generation that followed the legendary era of *New Yorker* writers like Thurber and Benchley and White and Perelman. He asked if I had any pieces that might be included.

"If I may ask," I said, "am I correct in thinking that this is essentially a scheme you've hatched to get 'Look, Ma, I Am Kool!' into print?"

"But of course," Burt said cheerfully.

"In that case," I said, "count me in."

For a time, the magazine had a policy of tacking on a bonus for anyone who sold six casuals in a calendar year. As I recall, the bonus was a higher rate for casuals sold during the remainder of the year, but I always imagined it as something akin to the pinball machine in the movie version of William Saroyan's *The Time of Your Life*: when the machine is finally beaten, lights flash and bells ring and an American flag pops out to wave while "America" is played. Toward the end of one year in what must have been the mid-sixties, Tom Meehan and I had both sold five, and our typewriters were burning up. Tom had written one of the magazine's iconic casuals—"Yma Dream," presented as his dream of hosting a party at which he has to introduce people with names like Yma Sumac and Uta Hagen ("'Ona and Ida,' I say, 'surely you know Yma and Ava? Ida, Ona—Oona, Abba.'"). But he couldn't come up with the sixth casual that year. Neither could I. When I think of that period, the visual metaphor that comes to my mind is Tom and I meeting on the stairs between our floor and the appropriate editor's office, one of us carrying a rejected casual and one of us carrying a casual that is about to be rejected.

In the mid-seventies, Tom, a lovely man, seemed to be strug-
gling. His wife was not well. Writing casuals and freelance pieces
was a chancy occupation for a man with a family to support, and
the project he'd spent years working on otherwise, the book for a
musical, had the marks of a nonpaying long shot. Then, in 1977,
the musical made it to Broadway. It was *Annie*. It won Tom the
first of what turned out to be three Tony Awards, and it seemed
destined to run forever.

Not long after *Annie* opened, my wife and daughters and I had
tea with Tom and some of the kids who appeared in the musical. I
told Tom that everyone at the magazine was delighted about his
reversal of fortune. He said that there had been a time when he
was beginning to feel like that Woody Allen character in *Annie
Hall,* who said life is divided into the terrible and the miserable.

"A Broadway hit can change a lot," I said.

Tom smiled, and said, quietly, "Smash hit."

That same year, Burt Bernstein's anthology was published. It
contained, after an astute foreword by Burt on the state of what he
termed "literate humor," contributions from a wide range of casual
writers. The title of the anthology was *Look, Ma, I Am Kool! And
Other Casuals.*

Show and Tell All

2000

There was a time when I responded to any new memoir about *The New Yorker* the way everyone else on the staff did: I went to a bookstore and, without buying the book, looked in the index for my name. I believe this is called a Washington read, and it may have induced publishers of certain types of books to leave out an index. Finding your name in the index, I should say, was not a cause for joy. Management had neglected to mention in its standard employment agreement that absolutely anything said to anyone connected to the magazine was on the record, so if, in a moment of weakness, you had unburdened yourself to a colleague about an old and completely uncharacteristic shoplifting incident or a marginally kinky sexual predilection or a devastating physical description of the editor who handled your copy, you had to hope that the colleague in question would acquire a crippling case of writer's block before it came time for him to record everything he could recall about life at *The New Yorker*.

Even if your name in the index turned out to be unconnected to an indictable offense, it usually meant that in the author's memory you had said something stupid or embarrassing and he had come back with a wickedly apt rejoinder. When I did read about myself in those books, I usually thought I hadn't said exactly what I'd been quoted as saying, but I could never remember the conversation well enough to be sure. I don't know how all these memoirists held on to such precise memories of casual water-fountain conversations that took place in 1965 or 1973. I'll admit that in those days I never thought of patting them down for wires.

For many years, I didn't give any thought to writing my own book about *The New Yorker.* I couldn't remember many truly mortifying things people had said to me or many clever things I had said back. Whenever my wife read a *New Yorker* memoir, she'd ask if it was possible that I had never uttered a wickedly apt rejoinder.

"I wouldn't say 'never,'" I told her at one point. "When we had that go-around about having a dental plan, someone who thought writers shouldn't concern themselves with such petit bourgeois matters said to me, 'Dostoyevsky didn't have a dental plan,' and I said, 'Yeah, and did you ever get a load of his teeth?'"

"Can you remember any that didn't have to do with the dental plan?" she asked.

"Not offhand," I said. "But it doesn't make any difference, because I don't want to write a book about *The New Yorker* anyway."

Lately, though, I've been getting a little edgy about that policy. It's now clear that I could eventually find myself in the position of being the only person with any connection to the magazine who hasn't discussed his *New Yorker* experience in excruciating detail between hard covers. It has occurred to me that there could come a day, many years from now, when my grandchildren, lacking documentary evidence issued under the imprimatur of a major publisher, refuse to believe that I ever worked for *The New Yorker* at all. I see us all on the porch of our summerhouse in Nova Scotia. My wife and I, ancient but still quite alert in the middle of the day, are rocking to the best of our capacity in our rocking chairs and these so-far-hypothetical grandchildren are sprawled in hammocks and deck chairs and cushions around us. My wife is saying,

"When Gramps was writing those pieces around the country every three weeks for *The New Yorker,* and your mothers were just tiny little. . . ."

"Gidoudahere," little Siobhan says. "Gramps never wrote for *The New Yorker.*"

I start to smile, in a way that I think combines fond forbearance of Siobhan's mistake coupled with appropriate modesty, but then I hear the voice of little Deirdre (in this fantasy, for reasons I can't imagine, all my grandchildren have been given Irish names that I've always had difficulty pronouncing). "My friend Jason's grandfather worked at *The New Yorker,*" little Deirdre says. "He wrote a book all about it." She tells us Jason's grandfather's name, as if intoning the name of some rock star she'd been fortunate to catch a glimpse of in a restaurant.

"In the first place," I say, "to paraphrase what A. J. Liebling once wrote of Hamlin Garland, Jason's grandfather couldn't write for free seeds. In the second place, Jason's grandfather published at the very most a *Talk of the Town* piece or two and maybe. . . ."

"Did you know A. J. Liebling, Gramps?" little Seamus says.

"Not exactly," I reply.

"Because my friend Timmy's nana said in her *New Yorker* book that she knew A. J. Liebling!" little Seamus says.

"In her dreams!" I say, not realizing that I've raised my voice a bit. "In her goddamned dreams!"

My wife shoots me one of those not-in-front-of-the-children looks, and then says, brightly, "Gramps once met J. D. Salinger. Tell about meeting J. D. Salinger."

"So what happened was that I, by pure chance, was walking past the reception desk on the 18th floor," I say. "This would have been maybe 1965. And there was this sort of tweedy-looking guy talking to Donna Jones, the receptionist. It turned out to be J. D. Salinger. Donna introduced us. 'Mr. Salinger,' she said. 'This is one of our writers, Calvin Trillin.' She may have even said 'one of our bright young writers.' I'm not certain. So we shook hands. Salinger and I."

"And what did Salinger say?" my wife asks, trying to help the story along.

"I can't remember exactly," I say, "but it may have been 'Nice to meet you, Calvin.'"

"Was that in a book?" little Siobhan asks.

"Well, no," I say.

Little Siobhan nods, as if her worst suspicions have been confirmed.

Then I hear the voice of little Moira. Until now, we have had no reason to believe that little Moira is paying any attention to the conversation. She is, after all, only three and a half. But she is definitely addressing a question to me.

"Grampy, did you ever have dinner with Mr. Shawn?" little Moira asks sweetly.

"Well, we did have lunch once," I say. "After I'd been at *The New Yorker* only nineteen years. And I have reason to believe that if he hadn't retired before another nineteen years had passed, it would have been quite possible that. . . ."

"My friend Ethan's bubbe used to have dinner with Mr. Shawn all the time," little Moira says. "She wrote a book about it. Do you want to hear some of the things Mr. Shawn said to Ethan's bubbe?"

"No, I do not want to hear some of the things Mr. Shawn said to Ethan's bubbe," I say. "I think I'd rather hear Al Gore's rendering of *Finnegans Wake* than hear some of the things Mr. Shawn said to Ethan's bubbe."

"Granny," little Moira says to my wife, "why is Grampy talking in his angry voice? Is he mad at Ethan's bubbe because she wrote for *The New Yorker* and he didn't?"

"Wrote!" I shout. "Wrote! Is that what you call what Ethan's bubbe was doing, Moira? Wrote!"

"Please don't shout at Moira," my wife says. "At least not until you've learned how to pronounce her name."

Little Moira starts to cry. Little Siobhan is looking at me as if I've just nicked her lunch money. As I look around at my grandchildren, I'm starting to wonder whether I could come up with enough wickedly apt rejoinders for a book about my life at *The New Yorker.*

Part II

REPORTERS AND REPORTING

Covering the Cops

1986

In the newsroom of the *Miami Herald,* there is some disagreement about which of Edna Buchanan's first paragraphs stands as the classic Edna lede. I line up with the fried-chicken faction. The fried-chicken story was about a rowdy ex-con named Gary Robinson, who late one Sunday night lurched drunkenly into a Church's outlet, shoved his way to the front of the line, and ordered a three-piece box of fried chicken. Persuaded to wait his turn, he reached the counter again five or ten minutes later, only to be told that Church's had run out of fried chicken. The young woman at the counter suggested that he might like chicken nuggets instead. Robinson responded to the suggestion by slugging her in the head. That set off a chain of events that ended with Robinson's being shot dead by a security guard. Edna Buchanan covered the homicide for the *Herald*—there are policemen in Miami who say that it wouldn't be a homicide without her—and her story began with what the fried-chicken faction still regards as the classic Edna lede: "Gary Robinson died hungry."

All connoisseurs would agree, I think, that the classic Edna lede would have to include one staple of crime reporting—the simple, matter-of-fact statement that registers with a jolt. The question is where the jolt should be. There's a lot to be said for starting right out with it. I'm rather partial to the Edna lede on a story last year about a woman about to go on trial for a murder conspiracy: "Bad things happen to the husbands of Widow Elkin." On the other hand, I can understand the preference that others have for the device of beginning a crime story with a conventional sentence or two, then snapping the reader back in his chair with an abbreviated sentence that is used like a blunt instrument. One student of the form at the *Herald* refers to that device as the Miller Chop. The reference is to Gene Miller, now a *Herald* editor, who, in a remarkable reporting career that concentrated on the felonious, won the Pulitzer Prize twice for stories that resulted in the release of people in prison for murder. Miller likes short sentences in general—it is sometimes said at the *Herald* that he writes as if he were paid by the period—and he particularly likes to use a short sentence after a couple of rather long ones. Some years ago, Gene Miller and Edna Buchanan did a story together on the murder of a high-living Miami lawyer who was shot to death on a day he had planned to while away on the golf course of La Gorce Country Club, and the lede said, ". . . he had his golf clubs in the trunk of his Cadillac. Wednesday looked like an easy day. He figured he might pick up a game later with Eddie Arcaro, the jockey. He didn't."

These days, Miller sometimes edits the longer pieces that Edna Buchanan does for the *Herald,* and she often uses the Miller Chop—as in a piece about a lovers' spat: "The man she loved slapped her face. Furious, she says she told him never, ever to do that again. 'What are you going to do, kill me?' he asked, and handed her a gun. 'Here, kill me,' he challenged. She did."

Now that I think of it, that may be the classic Edna lede.

There is no dispute about the classic Edna telephone call to a homicide detective or a desk sergeant she knows: "Hi. This is Edna. What's going on over there?" There are those at the *Herald* who like to think that Edna Buchanan knows every policeman and policewoman in the area—even though Dade County has twenty-seven separate police forces, with a total strength of more than forty-five hundred officers. "I asked her if by any chance she happened to know this sergeant," a *Herald* reporter once told me. "And she looked at her watch and said, 'Yeah, but he got off his shift twenty minutes ago.'" She does not in fact know all the police officers in the area, but they know her. If the desk sergeant who picks up the phone is someone Edna has never heard of, she gives her full name and the name of her paper. But even if she said, "This is Edna," there aren't many cops who would say, "Edna who?" In Miami, a few figures are regularly discussed by first name among people they have never actually met. One of them is Fidel. Another is Edna.

It's an old-fashioned name. Whoever picks up the phone at homicide when Edna Buchanan calls probably doesn't know any Ednas he might confuse her with. Edna is, as it happens, a rather old-fashioned person. "She should have been working in the twenties or thirties," a detective who has known her for years told me. "She'd have been happy if she had a little press card in her hat." She sometimes says the same sort of thing about herself. She laments the replacement of typewriters at the *Herald* with word processors. She would like to think of her clips stored in a place called a morgue rather than a place called an editorial reference library. She's nostalgic about old-fashioned criminals. As a girl growing up around Paterson, New Jersey, she used to read the New York tabloids out loud to her grandmother—a Polish grandmother, who didn't read English—and she still likes to roll out the names of the memorable felons in those stories: names like George Metesky, the Mad Bomber, and Willie Sutton, the man who robbed banks because that's where the money was. She even has a period look about her—something that recalls the period around 1961. She is a very thin woman in her forties who tends to dress in slacks and silk shirts and high heels. She wears her hair in a heavy blond

shoulder-length fall. Her eyes are wide, and her brow is often fur-
rowed in concern. She seems almost permanently anxious about
one thing or another. Did she neglect to try the one final approach
that would have persuaded the suspect's mother to open the door
and have a chat? Will a stray cat that she spotted in the neighborhood meet an unpleasant end? Did she forget to put a quarter in
the meter? Despite many years spent among people who often
find themselves resorting to rough language—hookers, cocaine
cowboys, policemen, newspaper reporters—her own conversation
tends to sound like that of a rather demure secretary circa 1952.
Her own cats—she has five of them—have names like Misty Blue
Eyes and Baby Dear. When she is particularly impressed by a bit
of news, she is likely to describe it as "real neat." When she discovers, say, a gruesome turn in a tale that might be pretty gruesome
already, she may say, "That's interesting as heck!"

Among newspaper people, Edna's line of work is considered a
bit old-fashioned. Daily police reporting—what is sometimes
known in the trade as covering the cops—is still associated with
that old-timer who had a desk in the station house and thought of
himself as more or less a member of the department. Covering the
cops is often something a reporter does early in his career—an assignment that can provide him with enough war stories in six
months to last him through years on the business page. Even Gene
Miller, a man with a fondness for illegalities of all kinds, turned
rather quickly from covering the cops to doing longer pieces. The
Herald, which regularly shows up on lists of the country's most
distinguished dailies, does take a certain amount of pride in providing the sort of crime coverage that is not typical of newspapers
on such lists, but it does not have the sort of single-minded interest in juicy felonies that characterized the New York tabloids Edna
used to read to her grandmother. When Edna Buchanan began
covering the cops for the Herald, in 1973, there hadn't been anyone assigned full time to the beat in several years.

In the dozen years since, Edna has herself broken the routine now and then to do a long crime piece or a series. But she invariably returns to the daily beat. She still dresses every morning to the sound of a police scanner. Unless she already has a story to do, she still drops by the Miami Beach department and the Miami municipal department and the Metro-Dade department on the way to work. She still flips through the previous night's crime reports and the log. She still calls police officers and says, "Hi. This is Edna. What's going on over there?"

Like a lot of old-fashioned reporters, Edna Buchanan seems to operate on the assumption that there are always going to be any number of people who, for perverse and inexplicable reasons of their own, will try to impede her in gathering a story that is rightfully hers and delivering it to where God meant it to be—on the front page of the *Miami Herald,* and preferably the front page of the *Miami Herald* on a Sunday, when the circulation is at its highest. There are shy witnesses who insist that they don't want to get involved. There are lawyers who advise their clients to hang up if Edna Buchanan calls to ask whether they really did it. (It could be libelous for a newspaper to call someone a suspect, but the paper can get the same idea across by quoting his denial of guilt.) There are closemouthed policemen. There are television reporters who require equipment that gets in the way and who ask the sort of question that makes Edna impatient. (In her view, television reporters on a murder story are concerned almost exclusively with whether they're going to be able to get a picture of the authorities removing the body from the premises, the only other question that truly engages them being whether they're going to get the picture in time for the six-o'clock news.) There are editors who want to cut a story even though it was virtually ordained to run at least sixteen inches. There are editors—often the same editors— who will try to take an interesting detail out of the story simply because the detail happens to horrify or appall them. "One of them kept saying that people read this paper at *breakfast*," I was told by Edna, whose own idea of a successful lede is one that might cause a reader who is having breakfast with his wife to "spit out his coffee, clutch his chest, and say, 'My God, Martha! Did you read this!'" When Edna went to Fort Lauderdale not long ago to talk about police reporting with some of the young reporters in the *Herald*'s Broward County bureau, she said, "For sanity and survival, there are three cardinal rules in the newsroom: Never trust an editor, never trust an editor, and never trust an editor."

Edna likes and admires a lot of policemen, but listening to her talk about policemen, you can get the impression that they spend most of their energy trying to deny her access to information that she is meant to have. Police officers insist on roping off crime scenes. ("The police department has too much yellow rope—they want to rope off the world.") Entire departments switch over to computerized crime reports, which don't accommodate the sort of detailed narrative that Edna used to comb through in the old written reports. Investigators sometimes decline to talk about the case they're working on. (Edna distinguishes degrees of reticence among policemen with remarks like "He wasn't *quite* as paranoid as the other guy.") Some years ago, the man who was then chief of the Metro-Dade department blocked off the homicide squad with a buzzer-controlled entrance whose function was so apparent that it was commonly referred to as "the Edna Buchanan door." Homicide investigators who arrive at a scene and spot Edna talking intently with someone assume that she has found an eyewitness, and they often snatch him away with cautioning words about the errors of talking to the press rather than to the legally constituted authorities. Edna discusses the prevalence of witnessnapping among police detectives in the tone of voice a member of the Citizens Commission on Crime might reserve for talking about an alarming increase in multiple murders.

Once the police arrive at a crime scene in force, Edna often finds it more effective to return to the *Herald* and work by telephone. The alternative could be simply standing behind the yellow rope—an activity she considers fit for television reporters. She may try calling the snatched witness. With a cross-indexed directory, she can phone neighbors who might have seen what happened and then ducked back into their own house for a bolstering drink. She will try to phone the victim's next of kin. "I thought you'd like to say something," she'll say to someone's bereaved wife or daughter. "People care what he was like." Most reporters would sooner cover thirty weeks of water-commission hearings than call a murder victim's next of kin, but Edna tries to look on the positive side. "For some people, it's like a catharsis," she told me one day. "They want to talk about what kind of person their husband was, or their father. Also, it's probably the only time his name is going to be in the paper. It's their last shot. They want to give him a good sendoff."

There are people, of course, who are willing to forgo the sendoff just to be left alone. Some of them respond to Edna's call by shouting at her for having the gall to trouble them at such a time, and then slamming down the telephone. Edna has a standard procedure for dealing with that. She waits sixty seconds and then phones back. "This is Edna Buchanan at the *Miami Herald*," she says, using her full name and identification for civilians. "I think we were cut off." In sixty seconds, she figures, whoever answered the phone might reconsider. Someone else in the room might say, "You should have talked to that reporter." Someone else in the room might decide to spare the upset party the pain of answering the phone the next time it rings and might be a person who is more willing to talk. A couple of years ago, Edna called the home of a TV-repair-shop operator in his sixties who had been killed in a robbery attempt—a crime she had already managed to separate from the run-of-the-mill armed-robbery murder. ("On New Year's Eve Charles Curzio stayed later than planned at his small TV repair shop to make sure customers would have their sets in time to watch the King Orange Jamboree Parade," Edna's lede began. "His kindness cost his life.") One of Curzio's sons answered, and, upon learning who it was, angrily hung up. "Boy, did I hate dialing the second time," Edna told me. "But if I hadn't, I might have lost them for good." This time, the phone was answered by another of Curzio's sons, and he was willing to talk. He had some eloquent things to say about his father and about capital punishment. ("My father got no trial, no stay of execution, no Supreme Court hearing, nothing. Just some maniac who smashed his brains in with a rifle butt.") If the second call hadn't been productive, Edna told me, she would have given up: "The third call would be harassment."

When Edna is looking for information, slamming down the phone must sometimes seem the only way of ending the conversation. She is not an easy person to say goodbye to. Once she begins asking questions, she may pause occasionally, as if the interrogation were finally over, but then, in the sort of silence that in conventional conversations is ended with someone's saying "Well, OK" or "Well, thanks for your help," she asks another question. The questioning may not even concern a story she's working on. I was once present when Edna began chatting with a Metro-Dade homicide detective about an old murder case that he had never managed to solve—the apparently motiveless shooting of a restaurant proprietor and his wife, both along in years, as they were about to enter their house. Edna would ask a question and the detective would shake his head, explaining that he had checked out that angle without result. Then, after a pause long enough to make me think that they were about to go on to another case, she would ask another question. Could it have been a mistake in the address? Did homicide check out the people who lived in the equivalent house on the next block? Did the restaurant have any connection with the mob? How about an ex-employee? What about a bad son-in-law? Over the years, Edna has come across any number of bad sons-in-law.

Earlier in the day, I had heard her use the same tone to question a young policewoman who was watching over the front desk at Miami Beach headquarters. "What do you think the rest of Bo's secret is?" Edna said as she skimmed log notations about policemen being called to a loud party or to the scene of a robbery or to a vandalized garage. "Is Kimberly going to get an abortion?" At first, I thought the questions were about cases she was reminded of by the log reports. They turned out to be about *Days of Our Lives,* a soap opera that both Edna and the policewoman are devoted to. Fifteen minutes later, long after I thought the subject had been dropped, Edna was saying, "So is this new character going to be a friend of Jennifer's—the one in the car wreck?"

Bob Swift, a *Herald* columnist who was once Edna's editor at a paper called the *Miami Beach Sun,* told me that he arrived at the *Sun*'s office one day fuming about the fact that somebody had stolen his garbage cans. "I was really mad," he said. "I was saying, 'Who would want to steal two garbage cans!' All of a sudden, I heard Edna say, in that breathless voice, 'Were they empty or full?'"

"Nobody loves a police reporter," Edna sometimes says in speeches. She has been vilified and shouted at and threatened. Perhaps because a female police reporter was something of a rarity when she began, some policemen took pleasure in showing her, say, the corpse of someone who had met a particularly nasty end. ("Sometimes they try to gross you out, but when you're really curious you don't get grossed out. I'm always saying, 'What's this? What's that?'") When Edna was asked by David Finkel, who did a story about her for the *St. Petersburg Times,* why she endured the rigors of covering the cops, she replied, "It's better than working in a coat factory in Paterson, New Jersey." Working in the coat factory was one of several part-time jobs that she had as a schoolgirl to help her mother out. Aside from the pleasures Edna associates with reading crime stories to her Polish grandmother, she doesn't have many happy memories of Paterson. Her other grandmother—her mother's mother—was a member of the Daughters of the American Revolution; Edna still has the membership certificate to prove it. That grandmother, in the view of her DAR family, married beneath her—her husband was a Paterson schoolteacher—and her own daughter, Edna's mother, did even worse. She married a Polish factory worker who apparently had some local renown as a drinker and carouser, and he walked out when Edna was seven. As soon as Edna finished high school, an institution she loathed, she joined her mother in wiring switchboards at the Western Electric plant. Eventually, she transferred to an office job at Western Electric—still hardly the career path that normally leads to a reporting job on the *Miami Herald.*

The enormous change in Edna's life came partly because a clotheshorse friend who wanted to take a course in millinery design persuaded her to come along to evening classes at Montclair State Teachers College. Edna, who had been interested in writing as a child, decided to take a course in creative writing. She remembers the instructor as a thin, poetic-looking man who traveled to New Jersey every week from Greenwich Village. He may have had a limp—a war wound, perhaps. She is much clearer about what happened when he handed back the first short stories the students had written. First, he described one he had particularly liked, and it was Edna's—a sort of psychological thriller about a young woman who thought she was being followed. Edna can still recall what the teacher said about the story—about what a rare pleasure it was for a teacher to come across such writing, about how one section reminded him of early Tennessee Williams. It was the one radiant New Jersey moment. The teacher told her about writers she should read. He told her about paragraphing; the first story she turned in was "just one long paragraph." She decided that she could be a writer. Years later, a novelist who had been hanging around with Edna for a while to learn about crime reporting recognized the teacher from Edna's description and provided his telephone number. She phoned him to tell him how much his encouragement had meant to her. He was pleasant enough, Edna told me, but he didn't remember her or her short story.

Not long after the writing course, Edna and her mother decided to take their vacation in Miami Beach, and Edna says that as she walked off the plane, she knew she was not going to spend the rest of her life in Paterson, New Jersey. "The instant I breathed the air, it was like coming home," she told me. "I loved it. I absolutely loved it. I had been wandering around in a daze up there, like a displaced person. I was always a misfit." Edna and her mother tried to get jobs at the Western Electric plant in South Florida; when they couldn't arrange that, they moved anyway. While taking a course in writing, Edna heard that the *Miami Beach Sun* was looking for reporters. The *Sun,* which is now defunct, was the sort of newspaper that hired people without any reporting experience and gave them a lot of it quickly. Edna wrote society news and local political stories and crime stories and celebrity interviews and movie reviews and, on occasion, the letters to the editor.

Now, years later, Edna Buchanan may be the best-known newspaper reporter in Miami, but sometimes she still sounds as if she can't quite believe that she doesn't work in a factory and doesn't live in Paterson, New Jersey. "I've lived here more than twenty years," she said recently. "And every day I see the palm trees and the water and the beach, and I'm thrilled with how beautiful it is. I'm really lucky, coming from a place like Paterson, New Jersey. I live on a waterway. I have a house. I almost feel, My God, it's like I'm an impostor!"

When Edna says such things, she sounds grateful—a state that an old newspaper hand would tell you is about as common among reporters as a prolonged, religiously inspired commitment to the temperance movement. Edna can even sound grateful for the opportunity to work the police beat—although in the next sentence she may be talking about how tired she is of hearing policemen gripe or how irritated she gets at editors who live to pulverize her copy. She seems completely lacking in the black humor or irony that reporters often use to cope with even a short hitch covering the cops. When she says something is interesting as heck, she means that it is interesting as heck.

Some years ago, she almost went over to the enemy. A Miami television station offered her a hundred and thirty-seven dollars more a week than she was making at the *Herald,* and she had just about decided to take it. She had some ideas about how crime could be covered on television in a way that did not lean so heavily on pictures of the body being removed from the premises. At the last moment, though, she decided not to accept the offer. One reason, she now says, is that she faced the fact that crime could never be covered on local television with the details and the subtleties possible in a newspaper story. Also, she couldn't quite bring herself to leave the *Herald.* "If I had been eighteen, maybe I would have done it," she says. "But the *Herald* is the only security I ever had."

Even before the appearance of *Miami Vice,* Miami was the setting of choice for tales of flashy violence. Any number of people, some of them current or former *Herald* reporters, have portrayed Miami crime in mystery novels or television shows or Hollywood movies. Some of the show-business types might have been attracted mainly by the palm trees and the beach and the exotica of the Latin drug industry: the opening shots of each *Miami Vice* episode are so glamorous that some local tourism-development people have been quoted in the *Herald* as saying that the overall impact of the series is positive. But the volume and the variety of real crime in Miami have in fact been of an order to make any police reporter feel the way a stockbroker might feel at a medical convention: opportunities abound. Like most police reporters, Edna specializes in murder, and, as she might express it in a Miller Chop at the end of the first paragraph, so does Miami.

When Edna began as a reporter, a murder in Miami was an occasion. A woman who worked with Edna at the *Miami Beach Sun* in the days when it was sometimes known as "Bob Swift and his all-girl newspaper" has recalled the stir in the *Sun* newsroom when a body washed up on the beach: "I had a camera, because my husband had given it to me for Christmas. The managing editor said, 'Go take a picture of the body.' I said, 'I'm not taking a picture of a washed-up body!' Then I heard a voice from the other end of the room saying, 'I'll do it, I'll do it.' It was Edna."

In the late seventies, Miami, like other American cities, had a steady increase in the sort of murders that occur when, say, an armed man panics while he is robbing a convenience store. It also had some political bombings and some shooting between outfits that were, depending on your point of view, either running drugs to raise money for fighting Fidel or using the fight against Fidel as a cover for running drugs. At the end of the decade, Dade County's murder rate took an astonishing upturn. Around that time, the Colombians who manufactured the drugs being distributed in Miami by Cubans decided to eliminate the middleman, and, given a peculiar viciousness in the way they customarily operated, that sometimes meant eliminating the middleman's wife and whoever else happened to be around. Within a couple of years after the Colombians began their campaign to reduce overhead, Miami was hit with the Mariel boatlift refugees. In 1977, there were two hundred and eleven murders in Dade County. By 1981, the high point of Dade murder, there were six hundred and twenty-one. That meant, according to one homicide detective I spoke to, that Miami experienced the greatest increase in murders per capita than any city had ever recorded. It also meant that Miami had the highest murder rate in the country. It also meant that a police reporter could drive to work in the morning knowing that there would almost certainly be at least one murder to write about.

"A personal question," one of the Broward-bureau reporters said after Edna had finished her talk in Fort Lauderdale. "I hope not to embarrass you, but I've always heard a rumor that you carried a gun. Is that true?"

"I don't carry a gun," Edna said. "I own a gun or two." She keeps one in the house and one in the car—which seems only sensible, she told the reporters, for someone who lives alone and is often driving through unpleasant neighborhoods late at night. It also seems only sensible to spend some time on the shooting range, which she happens to enjoy. ("They let me shoot an Uzi the other day," she once told me. "It was interesting as heck.") A lot of what Edna says about her life seems only sensible, but a lot of it turns out to have something to do with violence or crime, the stuff of an Edna story. Talking about her paternal grandfather, she'll say that he was supposed to have killed or maimed someone in a barroom brawl and that his children were so frightened of his drunken rages that the first sign of an eruption would send some of them leaping out of second-floor windows to escape. As an example of her nearsightedness, she'll mention some revelations in Paterson that seemed to indicate that she had been followed for months by a notorious sex criminal without realizing it. When Edna talks about places where she has lived in Miami, she is likely to identify neighbors with observations like "He lived right across the street from this big dope dealer" or "He was indicted for Medicare fraud, but he beat it."

Edna's first marriage, to someone she met while she was working at the *Miami Beach Sun,* could provide any number of classic Edna ledes. James Buchanan had some dealings with the anti-Castro community, and was close to Frank Sturgis, one of the Watergate burglars. Edna says that for some time she thought her husband was simply a reporter on the Fort Lauderdale *Sun-Sentinel* who seemed to be out of town more than absolutely necessary. The story she sometimes tells of how she discovered otherwise could be written with an Edna lede: "James Buchanan seemed to make a lot of unexplained trips. Yesterday, at the supermarket, his wife found out why. Mrs. Buchanan, accompanied by a bag boy who was carrying a large load of groceries, emerged from the supermarket and opened the trunk of her car. It was full of machine guns. 'Just put the groceries in the back seat,' she said."

Edna tried a cop the next time, but that didn't seem to have much effect on the duration or quality of the marriage. Her second husband, Emmett Miller, was on the Miami Beach force for years, and was eventually appointed chief. By that time, though, he had another wife, his fifth—a wife who, it turned out, was part owner of what the *Herald* described as "an X-rated Biscayne Boulevard motel and a Beach restaurant alleged to be a center of illegal gambling." The appointment was approved by the Miami Beach City Commission anyway, although one commissioner, who stated that the police chief ought to be "above suspicion," did say, "I don't think we're putting our city in an enviable position when we overlook this."

Since the breakup of her marriage to Miller, Edna has almost never been seen at parties or *Herald* hangouts. "I love to be alone," she says. One of the people closest to her is still her mother, who lives not far from Edna and seems to produce ceramic animals even faster than she once turned out fully wired switchboards. Edna's house is a menagerie of ceramic animals. She also has ceramic planters and a ceramic umbrella holder and a ceramic lighthouse—not to speak of a watercolor and a sketch by Jack (Murph the Surf) Murphy, the Miami beachboy who in 1964 helped steal the Star of India sapphire and the DeLong Star Ruby from the American Museum of Natural History—but ceramic animals are the predominant design element. She has penguins and turtles and horses and seagulls and flamingos and swans and fish and a rabbit and a pelican. She has a ceramic dog that is nearly life-size. She has cats in practically every conceivable pose—a cat with nursing kittens, a cat carrying a kitten in its mouth, a curled-up cat. Edna is fond of some of the ceramic animals, but the fact that her mother's productivity seems to be increasing rather than waning with the passing of the years has given her pause.

All of Edna's live animals are strays. Besides the cats, she has a dog whose best trick is to fall to the floor when Edna points an imaginary gun at him and says, "Bang! You're dead!" Some colleagues at the *Herald* think that a stray animal is about the only thing that can distract Edna from her coverage of the cops. It is assumed at the *Herald* that she takes Mondays and Tuesdays off because the weekend is traditionally a high-crime period. (Edna says that the beaches are less crowded during the week, and that working weekends gives her a better chance at the Sunday paper.) Around the *Herald* newsroom, Edna is known for being fiercely proprietary about stories she considers hers—any number of *Herald* reporters, running into her at the scene of some multiple murder or major disaster, have been greeted with an icy "What are *you* doing here?"—and so combative about her copy that a few of the less resilient editors have been reduced almost to the state in which they would fall to the floor if Edna pointed an imaginary gun at them and said, "Bang! You're dead!" Edna's colleagues tend to speak of her not as a pal but as a phenomenon. Their Edna stories are likely to concern her tenacity or her superstitions or the remarkable intensity she maintains after all these years of covering a beat that quickly strikes many reporters as unbearably horrifying or depressing. They often mention the astonishing contrast between her apparent imperviousness to the grisly sights on the police beat and her overwhelming concern for animals. While I was in Miami, two or three *Herald* reporters suggested that I look up some articles in which, as they remembered it, Edna hammered away so intensely at a retired French-Canadian priest who had put to death some stray cats that the poor man was run out of the country. When I later told one of the reporters that I had read the *Herald*'s coverage of the incident and that almost none of it had been done by Edna, he said, "I'm not surprised. Probably didn't trust herself. Too emotionally involved."

Policemen, Edna told the young reporters in Fort Lauderdale, have an instinctive mistrust of outsiders—"an 'us-and-them' attitude." Edna can never be certain which category she's in. Any police reporter these days is likely to have a less comfortable relationship with the police than the one enjoyed by the old-fashioned station-house reporter who could be counted on to be looking the other way if the suspect met with an accident while he was being taken into custody. Since Watergate, reporters all over the country have been under pressure to cast a more suspicious eye on any institution they cover. Partly because of the availability of staggering amounts of drug money, both the Miami and the Metro-Dade departments have had serious scandals in recent years, making them particularly sensitive to inspection by critical outsiders. The *Herald* has covered police misconduct prominently, and it has used Florida's public-records act aggressively in court to gain access to police documents—even documents involved in Internal Affairs investigations. A lot of policemen regard the *Herald* as their adversary and see Edna Buchanan as the embodiment of the *Herald.*

Edna says that she makes every effort to portray cops as human beings—writing about a police officer who has been charged with misconduct, she usually manages to find some past commendations to mention—but it has never occurred to anybody that she might look the other way. Edna broke the story of an attempted coverup involving a black insurance man named Arthur McDuffie, who died as a result of injuries suffered in an encounter with some Metro-Dade policemen—policemen whose acquittal on manslaughter charges some months later touched off three nights of rioting in Miami's black community. There are moments when Edna seems to be "us" and "them" at the same time. Keeping the picture and the press release sent when someone is named Officer of the Month may give Edna one extra positive sentence to write about a policeman the next time she mentions him; also, as it happens, it is difficult to come by a picture of a cop who gets in trouble, and over the years Edna has found that a cop who gets in trouble and a cop who was named Officer of the Month are often the same person.

"There's a love-hate relationship between the police and the press," Mike Gonzalez, one of Edna's best friends on the Miami municipal force, says. A case that Edna covers prominently is likely to get a lot of attention in the department, which means that someone whose name is attached to it might become a hero or might, as one detective I spoke to put it, "end up in the complaint room of the property bureau." Edna says that the way a reporter is received at police headquarters can depend on "what you wrote the day before—or their perception of what you wrote the day before."

Some police officers in Dade County won't talk to Edna Buchanan about the case they're working on. Some of those who do give her tips—not just on their own cases but on cases being handled by other people, or even other departments—won't admit it. (According to Dr. Joseph Davis, the medical examiner of Dade County, "Every police agency thinks she has a direct pipeline into someone else's agency.") Cops who become known as friends and sources of Edna's are likely to be accused by other cops of showboating or of trying to further their careers through the newspaper. When I mentioned Mike Gonzalez to a Metro-Dade lieutenant I was talking to in Miami, he said, "What Howard Cosell did for Cassius Clay, Edna Buchanan did for Mike Gonzalez."

Gonzalez is aware of such talk and doesn't show much sign of caring about it. He thinks most policemen are nervous about the press because they aren't confident that they can reveal precisely what they find it useful to reveal and no more. Edna's admirers among police investigators—people like Gonzalez and Lloyd Hough, a Metro-Dade homicide detective—tend to admire her for her skill and independence as an investigator. "I'd take her any time as a partner," Hough told me. "Let's put it like this: If I had done something, I wouldn't want Edna investigating me. Internal Affairs I don't care about, but Edna. . . ." They also admire her persistence, maddening as it may sometimes be. Hough nearly had her arrested once when she persisted in coming under the yellow rope into a crime scene. "She knows when she's pushed you to the limit, and she'll do that often," Hough told me. "And I say that with the greatest admiration."

A police detective and a police reporter may sound alike as they stand around talking about past cases—recalling the airline pilot who killed the other airline pilot over the stewardess or exchanging anecdotes about the aggrieved bag boy who cleared a Publix supermarket in a hurry by holding a revolver to the head of the manager—but their interests in a murder case are not necessarily the same. If an armed robber kills a convenience-store clerk, the police are interested in catching him; Edna is interested in distinguishing what happened from other killings of other convenience-store clerks. To write about any murder, Edna is likely to need details that wouldn't help an investigator close the case. "I want to know what movie they saw before they got gunned down," she has said. "What were they wearing? What did they have in their pockets? What was cooking on the stove? What song was playing on the jukebox?" Mike Gonzalez just sighs when he talks about Edna's appetite for irrelevant detail. "It infuriates Mike," Edna says. "I always ask what the dog's name is, what the cat's name is." Edna told me that Gonzalez now advises rookie detectives that they might as well gather such details, because otherwise "you're just going to feel stupid when Edna asks you."

．．．

There are times when Edna finds herself longing for simpler times on the police beat. When she began, the murders she covered tended to be conventional love triangles or armed robberies. She was often dealing with "an up-front person who happened to have bludgeoned his wife to death." These days, the murders are likely to be Latin drug murders, and a lot fewer of them produce a suspect. Trying to gather information from Cubans and Central Americans, Edna has a problem that goes beyond the language barrier. "They have a Latin love of intrigue," she says. "I had a Cuban informant, and I found that he would sometimes lie to me just to make it more interesting." It is also true that even for a police reporter there can be too many murders. Edna says that she was "a little shell-shocked" four or five years ago, when Dade murders hit their peak. She found that she barely had time to make her rounds in a thorough way. "I used to like to stop at the jail," she has said. "I used to like to browse in the morgue. To make sure who's there."

Edna found that the sheer number of murders overwhelmed each individual murder as the big story. "Dade's murder rate hit new heights this week as a wave of unrelated violence left 14 people dead and five critically hurt within five days," a story bylined Edna Buchanan began in June of 1980. After a couple of paragraphs comparing the current murder figures with those of previous years, the story went on, "In the latest wave of violence, a teenager's throat was cut, and her body dumped in a canal. A former airline stewardess was garroted and left with a pair of scissors stuck between her shoulder blades. Four innocent bystanders were shot in a barroom gun battle. An eighty-year-old man surprised a burglar who battered him fatally with a hammer. An angry young woman who 'felt used' beat her date to death with the dumbbells he used to keep fit. And an apparent robbery victim was shot dead as he ran away from the robbers." The murder rate has leveled off since 1981, but Edna still sometimes writes what amount to murder-roundup stories. "I feel bad, and even a little guilty, that a murder no longer gets a story, just a paragraph," she says. "It dehumanizes it." A paragraph in a roundup piece is not Edna's idea of a sendoff.

On a day I was making the rounds with Edna, there was a police report saying that two Marielitos had begun arguing on the street and the argument had ended with one shooting the other dead. That sounded like a paragraph at most. But Edna had a tip that the victim and the killer had known each other in Cuba and the shooting was actually the settling of an old prison score. That sounded to me more like a murder that stood out a bit from the crowd. Edna thought so, too, but her enthusiasm was limited. "We've already had a couple of those," she told me. Edna has covered a few thousand murders by now, and she's seen a couple of most things. She has done stories about a man who was stabbed to death because he stepped on somebody's toes on his way to a seat in a movie theater and about a two-year-old somebody tried to frame for the murder of a playmate and about an eighty-nine-year-old man who was arrested for beating his former wife to death and about a little boy killed by a crocodile. She has done stories about a woman who committed suicide because she couldn't get her leaky roof fixed and about a newspaper deliveryman who committed suicide because during a petroleum shortage, he couldn't get enough gasoline. She has done stories about a man who managed to commit suicide by stabbing himself in the heart *twice* and about a man who threw a severed head at a police officer *twice*. She has done a story about two brothers who killed a third brother because he interrupted a checkers game. ("I thought I had the best-raised children in the world," their mother said.) She has done a story about a father being killed at the surprise birthday party given for him by his thirty children. She has done a story about a man who died because fourteen of the eighty-two double-wrapped condom packages of cocaine he tried to carry into the country inside his stomach began to leak. ("His last meal was worth $30,000 and it killed him.") She has done any number of stories about bodies being discovered in the bay by beachcombers or fishermen or University of Miami scientists doing marine research. ("'It's kind of a nuisance when you plan your day to do research on the reef,' fumed Professor Peter Glynn, of the university's Rosenstiel School of Marine and Atmospheric Science.") Talking to Edna one day about murder cases they had worked on, a Metro-Dade homicide detective said, "In Dade County, there are no surprises left."

Edna would agree that surprises are harder to find in Dade County these days. Still, she finds them. Flipping through page after page of routine police logs, talking to her sources on the telephone, chatting with a homicide detective, she'll come across, say, a shopping-mall murder that might have been done against the background of a new kind of high-school gang, or a murderer who seemed to have been imprisoned with his victim for a time by a sophisticated burglar-gate system. Then, a look of concern still on her face, she'll say, "That's interesting as heck."

Shortly after this piece was published in The New Yorker, *Edna Buchanan won the Pulitzer Prize for general news reporting. In 1988, she left the* Herald *to concentrate on writing books, including a series of mysteries featuring a female crime reporter named Britt Montero.*

On the Assumption that Al Gore Will Slim Down if He's Intending to Run for President, a Political Reporter Is Assigned to Watch Gore's Waistline

2007

This job means digging up the dirt
On if a pol has stolen or he's cheating
With some cute waitress from a D.C. bar.
But who knew I'd be tracking what he's eating?

My editor, the clever dog, decided
The way to check that presidential itch is
To follow Gore, especially at meals,
And see if he stays too big for his britches.

Last week I told my desk that Gore might run,
Though he appeared to be at least full-size.

A waiter at a Georgetown place revealed
Gore's order had included "Hold the fries."

But now a source will swear that he was there
When Gore demolished half a cow, then stowed
Away in sixty seconds gobs of pie.
Two pieces. Apple crumble. A la mode.

My major back in school was poli-sci—
Quite valuable, I thought, for this position.
I now know, though, for covering Al Gore,
I should have studied diet and nutrition.

The Case of the Purloined Turkey

1980

A secretly Xeroxed manuscript of Richard Nixon's new book has, as they say in the trade, found its way into my possession. For years, I have been waiting for some carefully guarded document to find its way into my possession. In my mind, the phrase has always conjured up the vision of an important document wandering the streets of lower Manhattan, confused and bewildered, until a kindly policeman on Sixth Avenue provides flawless directions to my house. I figured that a secret document would find its way into my possession if I simply waited around long enough at the same address, looking receptive. That is precisely what happened.

I did not ferret out this document. I might as well admit that I hadn't realized that Mr. Nixon had produced another volume; it seemed only moments since the last one. I had assumed, I suppose, that his literary output would have been slowed up by the bustle of moving from San Clemente and by his previous difficulties with trying to buy an apartment in East Side co-ops that persist in treating him as if he were Jewish or a tap dancer. Despite the interruptions that accompany any move ("The men want to know whether these partially erased tapes in the cellar stay or go, Dick, and what do you want done with the crown jewels of Romania?"), Mr. Nixon managed to turn out a volume for Warner Books called *The Real War.* I know because a Xerox of the manuscript found its way into my possession.

Although it is customary to refuse to divulge the source of any document that has found its way into one's possession, I should say at the start that the person who gave me the document was Victor S. Navasky, the editor of *The Nation.* If anybody feels the need to prosecute or sue, Navasky's your man. I feel no compunction about shifting the blame to Navasky, because he would obviously be the logical target of any investigation anyway, this being his second caper. At this very moment, *The Nation* is being sued by Harper & Row and *Reader's Digest* for $12,500 for running an article based on a smuggled-out manuscript of Gerald Ford's book, which was somehow published under a title other than *The White House Memories of a Lucky Klutz.* In an era when an unfairly dismissed busboy would not think of suing for less than a million, the purpose of suing *The Nation* for the price of a publisher's lunch is obvious: the plaintiffs want to make Navasky out to be not just a thief but a small-time thief.

My involvement in this started innocently when Navasky said to me, "We've got a copy of Nixon's book."

"I hope you didn't pay full price," I said.

"Not that book. The new one. Smuggled out."

Sticky Fingers Navasky had struck again. I was of course, astonished. It's no joke to discover that you've been handing copy in to a recidivist. "If you put it back now, maybe they won't notice that it was missing," I said. I figured that Warner Books wasn't above humiliating Navasky by suing him for something like $18 and car fare.

"Take it," Navasky said, thrusting a bulky bundle into my arms. "Reveal something."

I took it and skulked out the door. The elevator man was reading the sports page of the *Daily News* as we descended. "Just some
laundry," I said to him, gesturing at the bundle I was carrying.
"Shirts. That sort of thing." He kept reading. So far, so good.

When I got home, I went into my office, closed the door, and
began the manuscript. The first sentence said, "As I write this, a
third of a century has passed since I first entered Congress; five
years have passed since I resigned the Presidency." Definitely authentic. I plunged ahead. After what seemed to be about an hour,
I was startled by the jangle of the telephone. It was Navasky.

"Find anything yet?" he said.

I looked down at the manuscript. I was on page 4. "He says, 'The
next two decades represent a time of maximum crisis for America
and for the West, during which the fate of the world for generations to come may well be determined.'"

There was silence on the phone. Then Navasky said, "Skip
ahead."

I skipped ahead to page 105 and started reading. "He says, 'The
final chapters have yet to be written on the war in Vietnam.'"

"Skip some more," Navasky said.

"Well," I said, "on page 287 he said, 'The President has great
power in wartime as Commander in Chief of the armed forces. But
he also has enormous power to prevent war and preserve peace.'"

"Keep skipping."

I read paragraphs on the advantages of summit conferences
and on the difference between totalitarianism and authoritarian-
ism.

Silence. Finally, I said, "Shall I keep skipping?"

There was no answer. Navasky had fallen asleep.

What is the purpose of being willing to reveal the contents of a
purloined manuscript if there is nothing in it that bears revealing?

"Let's give it back," I said to Navasky.

"Our source does not want it back," Navasky said.

"I see his point."

"Maybe we should shred it," Navasky said.

"All I have in that line is a Cuisinart," I said. "I have a better idea. I'll put it back on Sixth Avenue. Maybe it will find its way into someone else's possession."

There was no answer. Navasky had fallen asleep again.

Newshound

2003

There is a consensus in the trade, I am pleased to report, that Johnny Apple—R. W. Apple, Jr., of *The New York Times*—is a lot easier to take now than he once was. Even Apple believes that. When I asked him not long ago about the paragraph in Gay Talese's 1969 book on the *Times*, *The Kingdom and the Power*, which presents him as a brash young eager beaver, he said it was, alas, "quite an accurate portrait," although he doesn't recall boasting in the newsroom that while covering the war in Vietnam he had personally killed a few Vietcong—the remark that, in Talese's account, led an older reporter to say, "Women and children, I presume."

In speaking of those early days, Apple said, "I was desperate to prove myself." You could argue, I suppose, that, in the words of a longtime colleague, "he doesn't have to argue the case anymore." In a forty-year career with the newspaper, he has been a political reporter whose stories at times seemed to set the agenda for a presidential campaign; a war reporter who led the *Times* coverage in Vietnam for two years in the late sixties, and its coverage of the Gulf War a quarter of a century later; a foreign correspondent who has been in a hundred and nine countries (yes, he keeps a tally); the newspaper's premier writer of analytical pieces from Washington; and, these days, a wide-ranging writer on culture and travel and, especially, food. Of course, it's always possible that Apple's accomplishments are not, in fact, the principal source of his mellowing. There are any number of other theories about what might account for descriptions of the mature Apple that actually employ the word "endearing"—theories that include the possibility that we've simply grown used to him. "It's like having a big old Labrador dog," Jim Wooten, of ABC, said recently of Apple. "He knocks over the lamp with his tail. He slobbers on everything. But you still love him."

It is certainly true that Apple, at sixty-eight, could hardly be described as having shyly withdrawn from the spotlight. In a trade whose flamboyant characters are increasingly in short supply, he is still so widely discussed among reporters that Apple stories constitute a subgenre of the journalistic anecdote. Apple stories often portray R. W. Apple, Jr., checking into a hotel so staggeringly expensive that no other reporter would dare mention it on his expense account, or confidently knocking out a complicated lead story at a political convention as the deadline or the dinner hour approaches, or telling a sommelier that the wine won't do (even if the sommelier has brought out the most distinguished bottle in that part of Alabama), or pontificating on architecture or history or opera or soccer or horticulture. He still travels grandly and eats prodigiously. In Apple stories that take place in restaurants or hotels or even newsrooms, the verb used to describe his manner of entry is normally "swept in." Although people often find him charming, he is still capable of reducing a news clerk or a waiter or a campaign travel coordinator to tears now and then—like an ogre past his scariest days who just wants to keep his hand in. All in all, I can imagine that people who meet R. W. Apple, Jr., for the first time in his maturity might assume that some time-travel production of *The Man Who Came to Dinner* had managed to land Sir John Falstaff for the role of Sheridan Whiteside.

Physically, Apple is more noticeable than ever. He has a round face and a pug nose that give him a rather youthful appearance; a former colleague once said that when Apple flashes his characteristic look of triumph he resembles "a very big four-year-old." His form reflects the eating habits of someone who has been called Three Lunches Apple, a nickname he likes. Andrew Rosenthal, now the deputy editorial-page editor of the *Times*, once said that Johnny Apple had the best mind and the worst body in American journalism. Apple famously sees to his early-morning tasks—sending off a flurry of e-mails, perusing his investments, absorbing the newspapers—while encased in one of the brightly striped nightshirts made for him by Harvie & Hudson, of Jermyn Street, the same firm that makes his dress shirts, so that a houseguest not yet fully recovered from a late night at the Apple table can be startled by the impression that a particularly festive party tent has somehow found its way indoors.

Apple's method of locomotion—which he accomplishes in short, almost dainty steps—has some resemblance to a man carefully steering a large stomach down a narrow path that is being cleared at that very moment by native bearers; it is easily mistaken for a swagger. He speaks with as much authority as he ever did, whether the conversation is on Bach or on which three Zinfandels are the Zinfandels worth drinking. To characterize the great man's speaking style, collectors of Apple stories often use the phrase "holding forth," although he is also, truth be told, someone who takes in just about everything everyone else in the conversation says and files it away in what Morley Safer, of CBS, who has been a friend of Apple's since they were in Vietnam together, calls "that PalmPilot of a brain he has." On the whole, what Apple says while holding forth is considered by his friends worth listening to. The way Ben Bradlee, the former editor of *The Washington Post*, puts it is "I'd like to hear Apple on almost any subject, reserving the right to tell him he's full of shit."

.   .   .

Although sometimes years have passed between our meetings, I have kept vague tabs on R. W. Apple, Jr., for long enough to consider my observation of him a sketchy version of what social scientists would call a longitudinal study. I first encountered him in the spring of 1956, my junior year in college. I was then the chairman of the *Yale Daily News,* and Apple walked into my office to introduce himself as the chairman of *The Daily Princetonian.* It turned out to be a position he didn't hold long. A couple of months after he began to spend every waking hour at the *Prince,* he was booted out of Princeton, for the second time. By his standards, I have occasionally acknowledged to him, I failed to throw myself wholeheartedly into the job of running a college newspaper: I graduated.

Looking back, I realize that Apple differed from most of our contemporaries from places like Princeton and Yale who ended up in the trade, in that he'd always known that he wanted to be a newspaper reporter. In the mid-fifties, a trickle of undergraduate journalists moved resolutely from *The Harvard Crimson* toward *The New York Times,* but most people I knew who became reporters in those pre-Watergate days sort of backed in. They couldn't face law school, or the novel just didn't pan out, or they happened to be working for a magazine around the time they realized they were incapable of making a career decision.

Apple had known since he was thirteen, growing up in Akron, Ohio, not simply that he wanted to be a reporter but that he wanted to be a reporter for *The New York Times.* Having found the *Akron Beacon Journal*'s coverage of the 1948 Olympics insufficiently detailed, he'd gone to the library to look up results in the *Times* and decided on the spot that being paid for going to places that weren't Akron and writing about them was precisely the life he'd had in mind. Coincidentally, his skills could well have been designed for the *Times.* Some of his contemporaries who stood out at the paper—Talese, for instance, and David Halberstam and the late J. Anthony Lukas—found newspaper work confining and left fairly early on to write books. For Apple, newspapering was in no way transitional; the *Times* news story seemed to be his natural form. "At an early age, he had a strong idea of what he wanted to be—an outsized romantic idea—and he was able to fulfill it," Tom Brokaw told me. "It isn't just that he found the right trench coat."

Perhaps because his dream came true, Apple had at the start—and still has—an enthusiasm for journalism and for the *Times* that is rare among reporters, most of whom like to grouse about their calling and look upon the organization they work for through narrowed eyes. It's not that he is shy about expressing his opinion of a *Times* editor who has done damage to his copy. But, in the words of the novelist Ward Just, a Vietnam pal who finds his friend's institutional loyalty admirable if somewhat puzzling, "He really is a *Times* man. He believes in the *Times*. You can't separate the two."

Apple's cultural interests also set him apart from most of his contemporaries in the trade. If he's in a European city for a political story or a Midwestern city searching for superior bratwurst, he is unlikely to leave before visiting a museum or inspecting a notable new building—a custom not followed, I'm in a position to say, by most reporters of his era. He is a student of history. Recalling Apple's writings in the *Times,* friends often mention, say, a piece on the Eugene McCarthy campaign which began with a quote from *Henry V* or a piece on Germany after the fall of the Berlin Wall which tossed in an evaluation of Haydn's place in Middle European music. When Apple was Washington bureau chief and thus required to attend by audio hookup the noon and four-thirty meetings held every day by the top editors in New York, he was known to pass the less scintillating moments of the discussion leafing through auction catalogues relevant to the collection of Arts and Crafts vases he has in his weekend house in Pennsylvania. Apple has a wide range of accomplished friends outside the worlds of journalism and politics, and he is up to carrying on, say, a serious discussion of architecture with James Stewart Polshek or a serious discussion of music with William Bolcom. "Johnny is such a flamboyant personality that people sometimes don't get the fact that underneath the occasional oratorical overkill there's a deep, fundamental knowledge," I was told by Howell Raines, who, when he was Washington bureau chief and again when he was executive editor, would have been Apple's boss if Apple went in for that sort of thing.

Apple once told me that his interest in music began in the Lutheran Church, where he heard Bach every Sunday, and some of his interest in art and architecture began while he was at Princeton. ("I didn't do very well by Princeton's lights, but I did very well by my lights.") The writer Jane Kramer, who lived in the same Upper West Side apartment building as Apple in the early sixties, when she was a graduate student and he was working at NBC on the Huntley-Brinkley program, says that he was the only one of her friends in those days whose idea of a good time was dinner at Le Pavillon and whose hobbies included collecting Old Master drawings. A range of interests that includes fine wine and elegant buildings may fit more gracefully on a portly fellow of Apple's years than it did on a hustling cub reporter. Speaking of Apple's air of being a cultivated man of the world, Joseph Lelyveld, a contemporary of Apple's who became the executive editor of the Times, has said, "I used to say that Johnny grew into the person he was pretending to be when we were young. Now I wonder whether he actually *was* that person then and the rest of us didn't know enough to realize it."

During Apple's early days on the paper, he was resented by his colleagues for getting plum assignments without going through the seven levels of purgatory then expected of new boys at the *Times*. To some people in the newsroom, his enthusiasm seemed indistinguishable from buttering up superiors. It didn't help that Apple's contemporaries on the paper were under the impression that he was making more money than they were. "Apple bragged he was being paid fifty dollars more than he actually was, which would have made him the highest-salaried reporter in the city room, except for Homer Bigart," Arthur Gelb, then the deputy metropolitan editor, writes in his memoir, *City Room.* (As Apple remembers it, he did get paid more than the others, the *Times* having matched his salary when he came over from NBC, and word spread through an overheard telephone conversation.) It probably also didn't help that Apple seemed not to notice the effect that all of this was having on his colleagues. "A Cape buffalo is what a Cape buffalo is," Jim Wooten told me, at which point I limited him to two animal images in discussing Apple. "It rambles through the brush. It eats what it wants to eat. It does whatever it wants to do, without knowing how much other animals resent it."

Early on, Apple was jumped over more senior reporters to become the *Times* bureau chief in Albany. "John had developed skills that none of us yet had," I was told by Sydney Schanberg, who was in the bureau, but "he needed training in socialization issues." One of the other reporters in the bureau was Doug Robinson, who became the city editor of *The Philadelphia Inquirer.* Robinson, now retired, would not be thought of as someone who always took a completely respectful view of people he worked for, having got into the habit at one point in his *Times* career of calling the executive editor a "borderline psychotic" and describing the managing editor, the second-in-command, as "a man who couldn't find kitty litter in a cat box." In Albany, Robinson recalls, Johnny Apple was resented partly for an air of superiority that was galling to the other reporters, "particularly when they realized, upon sober reflection, that he *was* superior. That was the part that was the hardest to take—that he was so damn good."

Robinson was the protagonist of what I'm tempted to call the authorized version of the most-often-told Apple story: Statehouse reporters who hung out at a local bar, having decided that their conversation was overly dominated by complaints about Johnny Apple, agreed that anyone who mentioned Apple's name would have to put a quarter in a drink fund—an agreement that made cocktail hour more soothing until, as Robinson recalled recently, "I came in, and I said, 'That son of a bitch! He's done it again!' And I pulled out a whole fistful of quarters, laid them on the table, and excoriated Apple for fifteen minutes."

Apple stories often come in multiple versions, and a lot of tales that may not be true have attached themselves to him, in the way that a lot of quotes have attached themselves to, say, Dorothy Parker or Yogi Berra. Correcting some of them recently, Apple said that it's not true that he conspired on his first honeymoon to book a cabin on a ship to Naples next to the cabin of the then publisher, Arthur (Punch) Sulzberger (Apple insists that the booking was co-incidental). He says he never owned part of a British football team and never chartered a plane to catch up with a political campaign after oversleeping, although he has chartered some planes in his time. It is not true that he once put in for a fur coat on an expense account from Iceland, or maybe Greenland, and, having had that item rejected, filed expenses for the same total again without mentioning the coat and attached a note saying, "Find it." (That's an old chestnut told about any number of foreign correspondents; Apple's coat was down, was bought in Finland, and was paid for by the *Times*.) It is not true that in the most recent political convention in Los Angeles he stayed in a suite at the Bel-Air while just about everyone else from the *Times* was at a charmless commercial hotel; he says that the room he stayed in at the Bel-Air, being decently commodious, may simply have given the impression of being a suite.

Apple now tells Apple stories on himself. In a speech at the Century Club not long ago, he said that when he arrived at Princeton he decided it might be advantageous to claim a hometown with a bit more cachet than Akron ("just till I got my feet on the ground") and chose one he'd seen mentioned in the golf results as the home of the Winged Foot Golf Club. Unfortunately, he had never heard the name of the place pronounced and was thus able to set off great hilarity among a group of Eastern-boarding-school graduates—the sort that some Midwestern high-school boys at Princeton then referred to as Tweedy Shitballs—by saying that he was from "Mamma-RONN-nick."

He knows Apple stories about his girth and Apple stories about his tendency to hold forth—a state that Tom Brokaw has referred to as being "in full Apple." He loves the story about a dinner-table conversation early in his experience as a stepfather. His first marriage had broken up in the seventies, in Washington, when he fell in love with Betsey Brown, a charming woman who speaks in the sort of plummy accent heard among Richmond debutantes discussing cocktail napkins but happens to be a Bryn Mawr graduate who reads more newspapers than Apple does. She was also married, and she had two children. ("Within a limited social circle in Washington," Apple now says, "I think it would be fair to say that it was a brief but fairly vivid scandal.") A trip to Europe had not completely melted the hearts of the children, John and Catherine Brown, who were unaccustomed to being herded through quite that many cathedrals that intently by someone with that much information at his fingertips and that many reference books in his satchel. Then, at dinner one evening, an American Indian design on Betsey's dress inspired the assigning of Indian names, until everyone had one but R. W. Apple, Jr. "That's easy," John Brown, who was then about nine, finally said. "You're Sitting Bullshit." As Catherine tells the story, there was a moment of shocked silence, and then "Johnny gave one of his full-body laughs." After that, the children felt free to name Apple's stomach "Eugene" and, eventually, "Eugene Maximus."

In support of the notion that Apple is something like a lovable old Labrador, it should be said that many Apple stories portray him as enormously generous—generous with his hospitality and generous with the telephone numbers of his sources and generous with his good offices at the *Times* for someone he thinks should work there and generous with his restaurant recommendations ("The only place in Scotland to have Scottish beef is in Linlithgow, and here's the name of the owner . . ."). The political-campaign reporters who rode one bus or another with him—people like Richard Cohen, of *The Washington Post,* and Curtis Wilkie, of *The Boston Globe,* and Jack Germond and Jules Witcover, of *The Baltimore Sun*—liked to play jokes on him and liked to complain about him, but, as Germond said recently, "Most of us had an affection for John, even when he was at his most bumptious."

A *Times* contemporary of Apple's has pointed out that the Apple stories that "make you shudder" tend to date back to the sixties. A number of them were collected in *The Boys on the Bus,* Timothy Crouse's book on the reporters covering the 1972 presidential campaign—a book that served for years as the standard text on R. W. Apple, Jr. "Read one way, the book is immensely flattering to me," Apple told me. "Read another way, it basically says I'm an asshole." The book angered Apple—although one Apple mellowing theory holds that it did him the favor of providing the Cape buffalo a glimpse of how some of the other animals might view him.

What was flattering to Apple in *The Boys on the Bus* was, by and large, its discussion of his competence as a reporter. A McGovern worker was quoted describing his first glimpse of how the national press operates: "Johnny Apple of *The New York Times* sat in a corner and everyone peered over his shoulder to find out what he was writing." Apple's competitors give him mixed reviews on the 1972 campaign—some of them believe he became too attached to the string of endorsements that Edmund Muskie was accumulating—but virtually all of them say, without being asked, that his campaign coverage four years later was worthy of a Pulitzer, a prize he has never won. David Broder, of *The Washington Post*, told me that in 1976 Apple "damn near invented the Iowa caucuses" as a serious element of the presidential campaign—it was Apple who first spotted the potential strength of Jimmy Carter—and after that, as Curtis Wilkie has put it, "he ran rings around everyone."

What Crouse referred to as Apple's "braggadocio, his grandstanding, his mammoth ego" dominated the portrait in *The Boys on the Bus*. An account of Apple's first meeting with David Halberstam is fairly typical of Crouse's Apple stories. It describes Apple sauntering over to Halberstam's desk to inform him, at some length, that at a party the previous evening—a party that included some Sulzberger cousins and a *Times* vice president—Halberstam's name had been mentioned quite favorably. Finally, Crouse wrote, "Halberstam said his first words to Johnny Apple: 'Fuck off, kid!'"

Looking back, Halberstam says of Apple's behavior in those early days, "When it was egregious, which was often, it was never out of malice." Halberstam believes that young reporters at the *Times*—most of them edgy and competitive and still not certain that they deserved to be where they seemed to have fetched up—found Apple hard to take partly because of "a fear that he symbolized your own lesser self." That's not far from the notion that Apple differed from his contemporaries at the *Times* not so much in what he was like as in the fact that he let it show—or, in Crouse's shrewd phrase, that he stuck out "in a business populated largely by *shy* egomaniacs." In Halberstam's view, "It would be interesting to know what went on in Akron to produce this fearful insecurity— the ego, the unfinished quality that made him even worse than the rest of us."

Johnny Apple's father—Raymond Walter Apple, Sr., also known as Johnny—was, the junior Apple finally concluded, a hard case. He was the son of a skilled worker who mixed chemicals for glass.

The family name had been Apfel; it was presumably changed around the time of the First World War, when there was a lot of ill feeling toward people with names reminiscent of the Hun. R. W. Apple, Sr., was a football star at Wittenberg University, a small Lutheran school in Ohio, and, as the family story is told, he fell in love with the homecoming queen, Julia Albrecht, whose equally German but considerably more prosperous family owned a lot of grocery stores that were to make the transition into a substantial Akron supermarket chain called Acme.

According to Johnny, Jr., his father's dream was to be a football coach, but the homecoming queen having said that she didn't want to be married to a football coach, he came into her family's business—eventually helping to run it, apparently with the zeal of the converted. He tried his best to hide his disappointment that his only son was not an athlete, Johnny, Jr., says, but was less successful at accepting that son's decision not to go to work for Acme Markets. Nor did R. W. Apple, Sr., have much respect for the trade his son had chosen over running a successful supermarket chain. "He didn't think it was a legit way to make a living," Johnny, Jr., says. Apparently, R. W. Apple, Sr., never quite got over the notion that R. W. Apple, Jr., was spending his life in something akin to typing.

Earlier this year, I had a talk with Apple about his father. We were speaking in a small Gloucestershire cottage that the Apples bought while he was based in London, where he served as the *Times* bureau chief from 1977 until 1985. Johnny and Betsey Apple had come to rest at the cottage after a trip to the Far East that I had characterized as an attempt to break the world's single-trip expense-account record, now held by R. W. Apple, Jr. His parents, Apple said, had come to see him while he was London bureau chief, a job he reveled in. Like a lot of *Times* bureau chiefs over the years, he acquired some English airs and some English clothing. He was enthralled with British politics and some of the multidimensional people in it. He entertained grand people grandly, and he was once quoted as saying that the *Times* might never transfer him back to the United States, because his bosses at the paper wouldn't want to pay for transporting all of the wine he had in his cellar.

"I was proud of being the London bureau chief of *The New York Times*," he told me, in discussing his parents' visit. "It's not shit. Betsey had made the flat very pretty, and we had some of our most interesting friends to dinner. David and Debbie Owen, among others. I think Margaret Drabble was there. People who had something to say. And I thought, you know, I hope he's proud of me. I hope he finds it nice that I have this job and that I have interesting friends. We had a round table and David Owen asked me a question about something that was happening in the Middle East, and before I could answer, my father said, 'How the hell would *he* know?' And it went downhill from there."

I asked Apple if R. W. Apple, Sr., had ever come to respect what his son had accomplished as a journalist. "When they had their sixtieth-wedding anniversary, I was the MC," he said. "They had the same dinner—lobster Newburg on toast points—that they had in the same place, the Portage Country Club, sixty years before. Many of the same people, because they had stayed put. It was really quite a wonderful evening, and I hope I was modestly funny. And he didn't say anything to me afterward. But after he died, which was a year or two later, my mother said to me, 'You know, when we came home from that party at the club, we were taking off our clothes and he said to me, "Well, maybe I'm wrong. Maybe he *does* amount to something."' I said, 'Mother!' And she said, 'What can I tell you?'"

Unable to match his father's athletic exploits, the younger Apple became a voracious consumer of information about sports and, eventually, the sports editor of the newspaper at Western Reserve Academy—an institution that reminds some people of a small New England boarding school in a small New England town, although the town, Hudson, is about halfway between Akron and Cleveland. By the time he got to Princeton and entered what was then called the "heeling competition" required of those who wanted to work on the *Princetonian,* his writing was already fluid enough to astonish his classmates—a fact he credits partly to the stern efforts of an English teacher at Reserve named Franklyn S. (Jiggs) Reardon, who, in class and on the student newspaper, demanded clear and concise prose. Young Apple had the nearly maniacal energy that eventually resulted in the back-to-back interviews and blizzard of telephone calls that characterized his political reporting. He was also displaying the sort of intense curiosity that can seem to suck all the information out of the room, although the focus of his curiosity was not always on the courses he had signed up to take.

At the time, the *Princetonian* had what amounted to a board of advisory grownups, and the managing editor of *The Wall Street Journal*—Barney Kilgore, who happened to live in Princeton—was among its members. Once Apple was informed that he would not be continuing at the university, Kilgore arranged for him to work at the *Journal,* and he eventually got his degree from the Columbia School of General Studies. The *Journal* employment lasted until there was a lengthy meeting to discuss why other bureaus were getting a certain type of piece in the paper so much more often than the New York bureau, and young Johnny Apple finally said, "Maybe they don't have to spend their time in chickenshit meetings like this."

At least that's Apple's story. I'm not sure I'd take it literally. Not that Apple is one of those reporters, much written about of late, whose copy has often been treated with some suspicion by their colleagues. One foreign correspondent who often covered the same stories as Apple told me, "He's a very good and careful writer, but when he's talking there's some self-aggrandizement—a need to oversell and put the best coloration on his exploits." When Apple is talking about a decision at the *Times,* for instance, his first-person plural sometimes makes the decision sound like, in the words of one colleague, "what Arthur and I worked out." When I asked Apple the precise circumstances of his second expulsion from Princeton, he told me what he had once told Brian Lamb, of C-SPAN, during a television interview—that it came about because he'd criticized the university administration during a campaign the *Princetonian* was waging against anti-Semitism in the eating-club system. Many of his contemporaries on the *Princetonian* remember Apple fondly as a great character among the almost willfully bland undergraduates of the fifties Ivy League, but they're certain that nothing the newspaper wrote about the club system, a perennial target of the *Prince,* had anything whatever to do with his departure. Apple, when pressed, said that the dean, after citing papers unwritten and classes cut and chapel (then compulsory at Princeton) unattended, implied that some of these offenses might have been overlooked if Apple hadn't been such a troublemaker as chairman of the *Princetonian.* Although it's an oversimplification to say so, I think that people who have known Johnny Apple over the years tend to discount a bit whatever he says about himself and to trust whatever he writes in *The New York Times.*

Journalism is sometimes thought of as a field for generalists—a kind word for those contemporaries of mine who couldn't make a career decision—but the needs of a newspaper are often quite specific. So are the skills of most reporters. Apple was never thought of by his editors as an investigative reporter, for instance, but he became known as someone who could be dispatched to cover a story in unfamiliar territory—what is sometimes called in the trade "parachuting in." Given his ability to synthesize information quickly, he also became particularly valued at the *Times* as a writer of the lead-all—a piece on the far-righthand column of the front page which essentially tells readers what has happened in various aspects of an important story since the last time they picked up the paper. A lead-all writer often has to worry about not only knitting together half a dozen disparate developments but also fending off editors in New York who would like all those developments mentioned before the story jumps from the front page to the inside of the paper. Allan Siegal, a longtime assistant managing editor at the *Times* who was widely thought of as the editor in charge of standards even before he was formally given that title, has said that for a lead-all "you need bold synthesis at the top of a story. There are only three people in my time that I can remember doing it consistently: Scotty Reston, Max Frankel, and Apple—people who would write some encompassing statement of what had happened that day and only then go into the procedural details."

One of Apple's other great specialties became the news-analysis piece that is known at the *Times* as a Q-head, a form invented some years ago for James Reston when he was Washington bureau chief. A Q-head, which is supposed to reflect reporting rather than the writer's own views, is the sort of piece that, for instance, outlines the options open to a president facing an important decision, often within the context of how similar presidential decisions played out in the past. Apple's willingness to sound authoritative—some would say Olympian—is an asset in writing Q-heads. So is his historical perspective. So is the fact that he is, as he puts it, "a natural centrist." Writing a balanced analytical piece is much more difficult for a reporter who, consciously or unconsciously, has a political agenda or a deep contempt for one side or the other. Trying to give me some idea of his political beliefs, Apple said during our talk in England that when he was the London bureau chief he found himself somewhat attracted by the policies of the Tory Wets and of the Social Democratic Party. If I had to categorize his politics in American terms, I'd say that he might be a Rockefeller Republican, if there were still such a thing as a Rockefeller Republican—both in the views he holds and in the fact that he does not hold them with great intensity. Like a lot of people who have spent many years reporting politics, he is engaged by the game but not by the ideology.

A Q-head is not necessarily a profound or blindingly original piece of work. Two or three days after it's written, it can look dated or even wrong, particularly in a constantly changing situation like war. When the military campaign against the Taliban in Afghanistan seemed bogged down, for instance, Apple used some Vietnam analogies that were later criticized as not being predictive of how the war went. (John Leo's column in *U.S. News & World Report* was headlined "Quagmire, Schmagmire.") You could argue that some Q-heads, when all is said and done, amount to conventional wisdom, since they reflect the observations of people asked to assess the situation in terms of what happens, conventionally, when such situations occur.

All of that does not mean that there are any number of people on the *Times* who can consistently produce the sort of Q-heads the editors are looking for. According to the current executive editor, Bill Keller, the notion of running a Q-head often doesn't come up until the middle of the afternoon, making it "an intellectual wind sprint." Given the need for a twelve-hundred-word Q-head by six o'clock, someone who can file twelve hundred words of clean copy by six is immeasurably more valuable than someone who, although perhaps equally knowledgeable and equally thoughtful and equally conscientious about doing fresh reporting, is likely to turn in an eighteen-hundred-word piece with some tangled sentences in it sometime around six-thirty. Apple was once asked to give members of the Washington bureau what amounted to a master class in Q-head writing. The difficulty of replicating his touch with the form may be reflected in the fact that, long after he gave up the sort of daily Washington reporting that replenishes sources and stores up information for analytical pieces, the *Times*'s coverage of a momentous event—the attack on the World Trade Center, for instance—tended to include a Q-head by R. W. Apple, Jr.

Andy Rosenthal, one of the people at the *Times* who tell Apple stories with good humor rather than clenched teeth, recalls that in 1999, a couple of years after Apple had turned his attention from government to the table, the Senate, in an unexpected vote, rejected the Comprehensive Test Ban Treaty. Rosenthal, who was then on the foreign desk, called Apple at six in the evening to say that the paper needed what he called a "not since Versailles" Q-head. Apple, pointing out that his stepdaughter's rehearsal dinner was to take place at seven-thirty, berated Rosenthal for making such a request at such a time and, an hour later, filed a Q-head. It was written in clear English. It had historical references to SALT II and the Panama Canal treaties and the tension between Woodrow Wilson and Henry Cabot Lodge during the formation of the League of Nations. It was one thousand one hundred and seventy-one words long. Eleven of those words were, like a tip of the hat to Rosenthal, "Not since the Versailles Treaty was voted down in November 1919. . . ."

In discussions of Apple-mellowing, nobody much goes for my theory that Johnny Apple was saved by gluttony. I'm still attracted by the notion, though, that his outsized supply of energy and drive and competitiveness was drained off at table, in the savoring of a decent Burgundy or the perfect crab cake. (I was present when he found what he described in the *Times* as his "nominee for the single best crab dish in Baltimore, if not the Western Hemisphere"— the jumbo lump crab cake at Faidley Seafood, in the Lexington

Market—and I can testify that his look of triumph did give him some resemblance to a very big four-year-old.) Some of the people who don't go for my theory say that Apple was a glutton to start with, and some, of course, believe that he has not yet been saved. I developed the theory in the mid-seventies, when Apple arrived in London as bureau chief. At the time, I mentioned one piece of evidence in a book, giving Apple the *nom de table* of Charlie Plum, as I have done in print now and then: "In an effort to find the perfect dining spot he had eaten in sixty French restaurants in London within a few months. (When Plum's friends are asked to name his principal charms, they often mention relentlessness.)"

Even before then, Apple had a serious interest in good meals and good wine. When he was in the Washington bureau in the early seventies, before he went to London, colleagues found that a casual "Let's get a bite of lunch" could mean going across the street to what was then one of the fanciest French restaurants in town and having a three-course meal with appropriate wine. Given the fact that most reporters think a bite of lunch has something to do with a BLT, Apple's food and wine standards became an obvious target for pranks: sending a bottle of Lancers rosé over to his table during a political convention in Kansas City; phoning him in the guise of a fawning reader to ask his advice on the proper wine for wild, as opposed to domestic, goose; concocting a scheme in Iran to refill bottles Apple had obtained from the shah's cellar with what Horace Rumpole would call the local plonk.

The pranks had no effect at all on Apple's dining habits. At some point during his long stint in London, he began putting his eating adventures into print, taking advantage of the fact that, as he puts it, "Americans, or at least *New York Times* readers, care about a broader spectrum of British life than they do about French or German or Japanese life." He is not the sort of food writer who makes reservations in the name of Nero Wolfe characters or slips in quietly disguised as the Korean consul general. In restaurants or anywhere else, Apple seems more comfortable once the people he's dealing with are aware of his rank and station. The simplest description I've heard of his customary reception at a restaurant is "Everybody falls to the ground when Johnny walks in."

The Apple-at-table stories that don't involve his three-lunch capacity involve his standards. When his dining companion at the Kansas City restaurant, B. Drummond Ayres, then also of the *Times,* refused to let him send the bottle of Lancers away—after a long day talking to politicians and a long wait for service, Ayres was ready to start in on any tipple available—Apple hid it under the table. On a presidential visit Bill Clinton made to Africa, Apple had dinner one night in Kampala, Uganda, whose restaurant possibilities he had, of course, researched in some depth before leaving Washington. "We go to what Johnny has found out is the best Indian restaurant in the country," Maureen Dowd, who was in Apple's party that evening, told me. "We're the only ones in the restaurant. That would worry some people, but Johnny knows it's the right place because he's there." After tucking in his napkin, she went on, Apple said, in stentorian tones that seemed to be addressed to no one in particular, "No prawns at this altitude!" That remains a phrase that Apple watchers occasionally use to greet each other: "No prawns at this altitude!"

"Oscar Wilde said that a man who could command a London dinner table can rule the world," I was told not long ago by the legal philosopher Ronald Dworkin, who became friendly with Apple when the Apples lived in London, "and Johnny always commanded the dinner table." Dworkin was one of the eight people gathered for Apple's fiftieth-birthday luncheon, held at Gidleigh Park—a Devon country inn and restaurant that had been celebrated by Apple in the *Times* and eventually won what was apparently the first Michelin star ever awarded to an establishment run by Americans. (As a Midwesterner, albeit a Midwesterner with made-to-order English shirts, Apple is particularly proud that Paul and Kay Henderson, who run the place, both graduated from Purdue.) In a private dining room, the celebrants, including the Hendersons, consumed Beluga caviar, sautéed foie gras with quince sauce, salad of red mullet and lettuce with olive-oil-and-coriander dressing, tagliatelle with white truffles, partridge mousse with morels and spinach, roasted saddle of hare, Muenster and single Gloucester cheeses, mango and eau-de-vie-de-poire sorbets, *gateau marjolaine,* coffee, and six wines—all from 1934, the year of Apple's birth. "Around five or five-thirty, I was as close to death by eating as I've ever been," Dworkin told me. "We were about to break up and go up to the bedroom and have a nap. Then Apple was saying, 'We have to have a talk about dinner. Just a quick word. We've eaten rather well. So, something simple. I have an idea. The truffles that came with the tagliatelle came boxed in rice. You could make us a risotto out of the rice the truffles came in. Let's have a Saint-Julien, a late-growth Saint-Julien. A '79 would be all right.'"

Much of this eating and travel is, of course, underwritten by the *Times.* When it comes to what Homer Bigart used to call "feeding at the Sulzberger trough," it is widely acknowledged that R. W. Apple, Jr., is without peer. Joe Lelyveld, who even as executive editor was not known for demanding a prime position at the trough, once stopped in London when he was the foreign editor and took his bureau chief to dinner—a lavish dinner, as it turned out, since his bureau chief was R. W. Apple, Jr. When the check arrived, Apple reached over to scoop it up. "You better let me take this," he said. "They'd never believe it coming from you."

I once suggested to Apple that he bequeath his expense accounts to the Smithsonian Institution. "But the *Times* has them," he said. "I turned them in." He sounded a bit regretful, it seemed to me, that he was not able to give posterity an opportunity to inspect some of his more stunning creations. At the *Times,* the various departments have what is called a cost center—what amounts to a budget line. The foreign desk has a cost center. The editorial board has a cost center. R. W. Apple, Jr., has a cost center. "It's been my fate and privilege over the years to sit next to various people who were approving Apple's expense accounts," Al Siegal says. "There were hoots, and once in a while you'd look up and the person—these were various assistant managing editors—was shaking his head and reading off 'Wine from my cellars. . . .'" Siegal, who is a great admirer of R. W. Apple, Jr., thinks that, all in all, the *Times* has received good value.

Asked about having his own cost center, Apple is suddenly overcome with modesty. "It's because I write for all these different parts of the paper," he told me. Not long ago, Apple was appointed an associate editor of the *Times,* a position that is something of an honorific, and some acquaintances asked what difference the new title would make, since he already seemed to do whatever he wanted. Before being named associate editor, Apple said, there were two hotels he could not stay in on his expense account. Now, as he interprets company policy, he can.

When Apple was in his mid-forties, some friends in the trade decided that he should be the editor of the *International Herald Tribune*—a newspaper based in Paris, where there were more excellent French restaurants than even a relentless Charlie Plum could get to. Apple did not, in fact, become the editor of the *International Herald Tribune*—memories vary on just why—but the conversation reflected a realization by him and his friends, even when he was only forty-five, that R. W. Apple, Jr., was unlikely to rise on the masthead of the *Times.* The London posting had been widely seen as a sort of consolation prize for not being named chief of the Washington bureau, a seventy-reporter operation whose management involves responsibilities that have something in common with those carried by the executive editor. One mellowing theory holds that Apple's own realization that he wasn't going to run the *Times* uncoupled him from one of the engines powering his competitiveness, but Apple himself has always said that he never had any desire to be executive editor of the *Times*. Some of his friends believe that under severe torture he might at least own up to having wanted to be managing editor.

Nearly fifteen years later, the *Times* did make Apple the Washington bureau chief. He held the job for five years, but it did not turn out to be among the high points in his career. Apple says he was conscious of trying not to be what's known in the trade as a big foot, a celebrated reporter who takes over major stories from the person on the beat—he was aware that a previous bureau chief had been presented at his going-away party with a size-18 sneaker—but at the end of the day, I was told by someone who spent years at the *Times*, "Johnny is a performer. You can't be a performer and manage the Washington bureau." Also, Apple was away a lot. People who were there say that Andy Rosenthal, who was what the *Times* calls the Washington editor, actually managed the bureau. "He would introduce me to people as his No. 2," Rosenthal told me cheerfully. "As if he were the lord of the admiralty." Rosenthal was involved in an Apple story treasured by people who worked in the bureau in those years. Apple, infuriated that another reporter's political story from the same region had made the front page while his hadn't, was heard to shout at his No. 2, "I will not be little-footed!"

Apple's tenure as bureau chief ended in 1997. "He could still make calls into the Clinton White House, often at a level or two higher than the beat reporters could," one of his editors told me, but, particularly after the congressional election sweep engineered by Newt Gingrich in 1994, Apple was less in tune with legislators. During our talk in Gloucestershire, he said, "Different sorts of people began to be elected to Congress, and they behaved in different ways. They didn't go to each other's houses. In many cases, they didn't even have houses. Many of them slept in their offices. And this was one of the elements that led to this constant nastiness rather than debate. Furthermore, you began to have fewer and fewer people around who were truly expert in any field, and few left around who are what I always thought of as the mud that holds the straw of the deeply partisan together. As it became much more adversarial and much less substantive, it slipped away from me. I don't mean that I didn't understand it, but I didn't want to live my life in the middle of it."

It was not the first time that Apple had lost his trademark enthusiasm for the task at hand. A decade earlier, just after he'd returned from London to be the *Times*'s chief Washington correspondent, there had been a period when he seemed to have lost interest in pursuing the usual political stories or even in showing up regularly at the bureau. "That was a precursor of finally deciding I just don't want to do this again and again and again," he told me. "I loved doing it when there was a big story running and I could make a contribution. But just to write routine political and foreign stuff, I thought, Oh man!" Newspaper reporting of the sort that regularly results in front-page stories in the *Times*—that is, reporting that has to do with politics or government or foreign policy—is repetitious work. A lot of distinguished reporters eventually get the feeling that they've done what is essentially the same story one too many times. Some of them become columnists, but that was not in store for Apple. The absence of an ideological point of view may be an advantage in a Q-head writer but it is a disadvantage in a columnist. At the *Times,* Apple was regarded as someone with a nearly encyclopedic knowledge of politics, but not as a singular political thinker. Whether or not he ever yearned for a column, as some of his friends maintain, he now says that it wouldn't have been a good fit. "I'm not any good at writing columns in which I say what this country needs or what the world needs is the following," he told me. "I see two sides to too many things."

The path he did take had its origin in his days in the London bureau, when he had begun to write about food and travel. Toward the end of his stint as bureau chief, he'd written a series of travel pieces in Europe—pieces that were eventually collected in a book called *Apple's Europe*. At the time, Apple's increasing interest in writing about bistros and cathedrals was causing some uneasiness among his masters in New York. But, looking back recently on the sort of writing he had done toward the end of his London stay, Apple said, "That was sort of the beginning of my reinventing myself."

Not long after he stepped down as Washington bureau chief, the *Times* made Apple something called chief correspondent—essentially a ticket to write about whatever interested him. Betsey Apple—who, together with her children, can be thought of as another theory of what mellowed R. W. Apple, Jr.—had suggested a travel series about American cities similar to the series Apple had done in Europe. As the trips evolved, she was usually at the wheel while her husband deconstructed the maps with an adroitness that presumably comes from having had to find his way around strange cities in a hundred and nine different countries. She continued in that role in the next series, on food, in which she is routinely mentioned once in each piece, in the way Hitchcock put in a fleeting appearance in each movie. Last fall, at the Southern Foodways Alliance conference on barbecue, in Oxford, Mississippi, Betsey Apple introduced herself to one of the participants by saying, "I'm Betsey. I drive Mister Daisy."

Apple watchers have interpreted Apple's emergence as a food writer in a number of ways. Some of them see it as the *Times* rewarding so many years of extraordinary service by nutting Apple out to a particularly luxuriant pasture. Some see it as Apple's response to having been deprived of the few rewards of the business that have not been bestowed on him—a column or a Pulitzer or an editorship—by following the maxim that living well is the best revenge. Bill Keller and his recent predecessors see it as extending into the so-called special sections of the paper—the sections that increasingly are becoming fundamental to the identity of the *Times* and to its commercial well-being—the work of a reporter who is, in Keller's words, "as much a marquee name in the food section as he is in the political pages." That's the way Apple sees it.

The change in portfolio has made Apple an unusual figure in Washington. He retains all the trappings associated with members of what is sometimes called the permanent government. He has a house in Georgetown. He has known most of the capital's principal players for years. (He met George W. Bush and Al Gore in 1970, when they were serving their fathers as drivers in unsuccessful Senate campaigns; the president, it almost goes without saying, calls him Juanito.) But what he normally writes about day to day is not, say, the future of the North Atlantic alliance but where to find herring that tastes like herring. Apple's friends like to tease him about the switch in subject matter. But they believe that he has emerged triumphant at a time in his career when a lot of reporters who never came in from the field are faced with a choice I used to think of as the Ottawa bureau or the bottle. The byline of R. W. Apple, Jr., still regularly appears in the *Times,* often on stories from places that make his colleagues muse on what the fanciest hotel there is really like. "He's got a second act," Ben Bradlee said of Apple not long ago, "and he probably has others up his sleeve, just in case he eats all the food in the world."

With R. W. Apple, Jr., triumph is a given. He approaches food writing the same way he approached political reporting or war reporting or parachuting in. In preparation for the Baltimore piece that uncovered the blissful crab cake, he told me, he had reread some Mencken and reread some of Russell Baker's memoir of growing up in Baltimore and spent a lot of time on the Internet and on the phone. When he wasn't indulging in one of his three lunches in Baltimore, he was in his room finishing up a piece on the early-twentieth-century East Bay architect Bernard Maybeck ("a precursor of the modern movement like Otto Wagner in Vienna, Charles Rennie Mackintosh in Glasgow, Victor Horta in Brussels, and the brothers Charles and Henry Greene in Pasadena") and a travel piece on Bermuda that began, "When Claudio Vigilante was a waiter at Le Gavroche, the last redoubt of classic French haute cuisine in London. . . ."

At the time I spoke to Apple in Gloucestershire, he had sixteen or seventeen notebooks filled with research from the Far East trip, but it seemed likely he'd be interrupted by war in Iraq before he transformed them all into *Times* stories. The *Times*'s plans for war coverage included calling him from the table for Q-head duty. When the war started, Apple did return to writing Q-heads—which, as it turned out, drew some of the same sort of criticism that had been directed at him during the Afghanistan campaign. Keller believes that, as the *Times* allows more analytical writing in news stories, it is becoming less tied to the notion that "every big news event has to be accompanied by a story about what you were supposed to think about that news event." Still, at the time when war with Iraq seemed imminent, an old *Times* hand told me that it would probably constitute what the management considered "a Johnny Apple moment."

By late spring, Apple was mining the notebooks. The Asia trip had been designed to produce eight pieces for the *Times,* not to speak of a piece on the twenty-fifth anniversary of Gidleigh Park. He had already published a piece on eating dim sum in Hong Kong, but he had before him a piece on Vietnamese pho and a piece on mangosteens in Bangkok and a piece on pepper in Kerala and a piece on Keralan cuisine and a travel piece on Bangkok. A lengthy piece on Singapore street food appeared in the *Times* earlier this month. The reporting, if that's the word, had required eighteen eating stops in a single sixteen-hour day. Cautioned by his guide to taste rather than eat, Apple wrote, "I tried, but I failed. More gourmand than gourmet, I finished much of what was put before me." Presumably, he will now be referred to by some— maybe even by me—as Eighteen Lunches Apple. Relentlessness remains one of Charlie Plum's principal charms.

R. W. Apple, Jr., died in 2006. The memorial service was held at the Kennedy Center and was carried on C-SPAN.

Corrections

1990

January 14

Because of an editing error, an article in Friday's theater section transposed the identifications of two people involved in the production of *Waiting for Bruce,* a farce now in rehearsal at the Rivoli. Ralph W. Murtaugh, Jr., a New York attorney, is one of the play's financial backers. Hilary Murtaugh plays the ingenue. The two Murtaughs are not related. At no time during the rehearsal visited by the reporter did Ralph Murtaugh "sashay across the stage."

March 25

Because of some problems in transmission, there were several errors in yesterday's account of a symposium held by the Women's Civic Forum of Rye on the role played by slovenliness in cases of domestic violence. The moderator of the symposium, Laura Murtaugh, should not have been identified as "an unmarried mother of eight." Mrs. Murtaugh, the president of the board of directors of the Women's Civic Forum, is married to Ralph W. Murtaugh, Jr., an attorney who practices in Manhattan. The phrase "he was raised with the hogs, and he lived like a hog" was read by Mrs. Murtaugh from the trial testimony of an Ohio woman whose defense against a charge of assault was based on her husband's alleged slovenliness. It did not refer to Mrs. Murtaugh's own husband. Mr. Murtaugh was raised in New York.

April 4

An article in yesterday's edition on the growing contention between lawyers and their clients should not have used an anonymous quotation referring to the firm of Newton, Murtaugh & Clayton as "ambulance-chasing jackals" without offering the firm an opportunity to reply. Also, the number of hours customarily billed by Newton, Murtaugh partners was shown incorrectly on a chart accompanying the article. According to a spokesman for the firm, the partner who said he bills clients for "thirty-five or forty hours on a good day" was speaking ironically. There are only twenty-four hours in a day. The same article was in error as to the first name and the background of one of the firm's senior partners. The correct name is Ralph W. Murtaugh, Jr. There is no one named Hilary Murtaugh connected with the firm. Ralph W. Murtaugh, Jr., has at no time played an ingenue on Broadway.

April 29

Because of a computer error, the early editions on Wednesday misidentified the person arrested for a series of armed robberies of kitchen supply stories on the West Side of Manhattan—

the so-called "pesto bandit." The person arrested was Raymond Cullom, twenty-two, of Queens. Ralph W. Murtaugh III, nineteen, of Rye, should have been identified as the runner-up in the annual Squash for Kids charity squash tournament, in Rye, rather than as the alleged robber.

May 18

Because of an error in transmission, a four-bedroom brick colonial house on Weeping Bend Lane, in Rye, owned by Mr. and Mrs. Ralph W. Murtaugh, Jr., was incorrectly listed in Sunday's real-estate section as being on the market for $17,500. The house is not for sale.

June 21

In Sunday's edition, the account of a wedding that took place the previous day at St. John's Church in Rye was incorrect in a number of respects. The cause of the errors was the participation of the reporter in the reception. This is in itself against the policy of this newspaper and should not have occurred. Jane Murtaugh was misidentified in two mentions. She was neither the mother of the bride nor the father of the bride. She was the bride. It was she who was wearing a white silk gown trimmed in tulle. The minister was wearing conventional ministerial robes. Miss Murtaugh should not have been identified on second mention as Mrs. Perkins, since she will retain her name and since Mr. Perkins was not in fact the groom. The number of bridesmaids was incorrectly reported. There were eight bridesmaids, not thirty-eight. Their dresses were blue, not glued. The bridegroom's name is not Franklin Marshall.

His name is Emory Barnswell, and he graduated from Franklin and Marshall College. Mr. Barnswell never attended Emory University, which in any case does not offer a degree in furniture stripping. Mr. Barnswell's ancestor was not a signer of the Declaration of Independence and was not named Hector (Boom-Boom) Bondini. The name of the father of the bride was inadvertently dropped from the article. He is Hilary Murtaugh.

Part III
BIG SHOTS

Invitations

1983

My curiosity about the new *Vanity Fair* has been dominated by one question: Why wasn't I asked to subscribe? Plenty of people were. I happen to know that
one J. E. Corr, Jr., who describes himself as the publisher of *Vanity
Fair*, sent letters to any number of people informing them by name
("Dear Mr. Upscale") that his magazine wasn't meant for everyone
but for "only a handful of bright, literate people." I'm not saying I
look forward to a scene a year or so from now in which some high-
powered ad-agency man asks J. E. Corr, Jr., about his circulation
and Corr, Jr., says, "Oh, well, about a handful." That would be sour
grapes. I will say that it's not a lot of fun being among those for
whom a new magazine "that captures the sparkle and excitement
of our times, our culture" was not meant.

This has happened to me before. A few years ago, a friend of
mine phoned and asked, "What are you doing about Robert L.
Schwartz's letter on subscribing to the *Newsletter of the Tarrytown
Group*?"

"What letter?" I said.

"You know," he said. "The one that says, 'You are cordially invited to join a special, special group of people—the "Creative Mi-

nority," as Toynbee called it—who are stimulated, not threatened, by the changes, upheavals, and discontinuities of modern society. It's a group of people who won't settle for the hollow victory of material success—an idealistic, holistic group that seeks totally new perspectives and concepts to bring about a totally new world for everyone.'"

"Well," I said. "Of course, the way the mails are these days, you can't—"

"Oh," he said. "Oh, sorry."

"Maybe Schwartz knew how I feel about people who refer to anything but holes as holistic," I said. I shouldn't have said that. It sounded like sour grapes. Also, I don't mean to give the impression that I can't rejoice with my friends when they are among the chosen. I was delighted, for instance, when a woman I know named Millicent Osborn—a woman who lives in one of those rather grand old Park Avenue apartment buildings that must strike people like J. E. Corr, Jr., as the sort of place where the elevator chatter is particularly bright and literate—received an exceedingly complimentary letter from John Fairchild, whose company publishes *Women's Wear Daily* and *W.* Fairchild thought Mrs. Osborn might like to subscribe to *W.* "Our compliments, Mrs. Osborn!" he wrote. "For being one of the best-dressed people in New York! For turning 954 Park Avenue into a home that sizzles with decorating excitement! For giving parties that are the talk of the whole state of New York! For getting the fun out of the fashionable living you do!" Fairchild laying it on makes J. E. Corr, Jr., sound practically curt.

I have always liked to think that Fairchild's letter made Millicent Osborn's day. I realize that there are residents of 954 Park Avenue who would not be particularly gratified to hear that their parties are being talked about in places like Buffalo and Elmira, but Millicent Osborn has never suffered from that sort of insularity. I like to think that she picked up Fairchild's letter in the lobby as she was leaving for the supermarket—at a time in her daily routine when she was not feeling her absolutely most stupefyingly glamorous. She opens the letter. John Fairchild is calling her one of the best-dressed people in New York.

"Oh, it's just a simple little shift I've had for years," she says, causing the doorman to tip his hat. "Do you really like it?"

Then she scurries around to make sure that 954 Park Avenue sizzles with decorating excitement. "The grocery delivery boy told me that the Pearces in 12-D still have that dreadful tapestry of a stag at bay," she tells her husband. "Maybe you could have a word with them."

By then, I often imagined a few of the letter writers meeting over martinis and mailing lists to discuss my case. "What about Trillin?" I could imagine J. E. Corr, Jr., of *Vanity Fair* saying.

"Holistically," Schwartz says, "I think he might not interface creatively with your concepts. Also, he's a smart aleck."

"His home doesn't sizzle in the least," John Fairchild says. "I can't imagine who advised him to hang that American Hereford Association poster in the front hall."

"But is he bright and literate?" Corr, Jr., says, consulting his notes. "Does he still make the effort to go to the theater and important films, live concerts, art and photography exhibits?"

The room is silent. "I guess we'll give him a skip," Corr, Jr., finally says. "After all, we're only looking for a handful."

Paper Baron

2001

I t's tempting to see this tale as an illustration of the ancient warning to be careful what you wish for because you might get it. But maybe that's not what it is at all. Maybe it's a confirmation of what mothers are always telling their children about how you have to persevere to achieve your fondest desire, whatever that desire may be. The story begins in the late nineties, at a time when Conrad Black had acquired most of the daily newspapers in Canada, where he was born and raised. What Conrad Black seemed to wish for was not what Canadian mothers have customarily had in mind when they discuss fondest desires. He wanted to be in the British House of Lords.

Americans of a certain age may still think of Canadians as having ties to the United Kingdom and the monarchy strong enough to produce the occasional viscount in places like Saskatoon or Yellowknife. It is true that members of the Canadian Parliament still swear an oath to the Queen, and that the Queen remains Canada's head of state through her representative, the governor general. It wasn't until 1952 that someone who had actually been born in Canada, Vincent Massey, became governor general, and the names of Massey's predecessors from 1952 back to the Great War do not make them sound like people who were completely at home in the New World: Viscount Alexander, the Earl of Athlone, Lord Tweedsmuir, the Earl of Bessborough, Viscount Willingdon, Lord Byng, the Duke of Devonshire, and HRH the Duke of Connaught.

For the past half century, though, Canada's efforts to assume its place in the world as an important and independent nation required that it separate itself from the United Kingdom—at least, until those efforts more urgently required that it separate itself from the United States. There are now laws in Canada, for instance, that make it difficult for a non-Canadian to launch certain types of cultural projects or to own a newspaper. Since Massey's day, the governor general has always been a Canadian. The incumbent, a former television broadcaster named Adrienne Clarkson, was born of Chinese parents in Hong Kong.

Even before Massey, there was a disinclination—particularly among members of the Liberal Party, which has dominated the government for the past hundred years—to accept titles, and in 1919 the Canadian House of Commons passed a resolution asking the British monarch "to refrain hereafter from conferring any title of honor or titular distinction upon any of your subjects domiciled or ordinarily resident in Canada." The author of the resolution, a Conservative MP named William Folger Nickle, said, "I hope we are going to be a democracy in the broad and true sense of that word"—although some saw his motive as having less to do with democracy than with bitterness at having failed to get a knighthood for his father-in-law. There are, of course, people in Canada who still dwell on their ancestors' having been Empire Loyalists or on having fought for King and Country themselves in the Second World War. In general, though, Canada, a country that prides itself on its diversity and its egalitarianism, has gradually lost touch with the sort of life that might tempt a man to take a title like Lord Tweedsmuir and then use it with a straight face.

There are those who would say that the uneasiness Canadians

have with titles reflects something approaching hostility toward anyone who rises too far above the crowd. The great Canadian novelist Robertson Davies used to tell of the response at a reception in British Columbia when the news came that Lester Pearson, later the prime minister of Canada, had been awarded the Nobel Peace Prize. "Well!" somebody said. "Who does he think he is!" Robert Fulford, a Canadian essayist and journalist, notes that this trait has been described as a national characteristic of any number of other countries, including England and Sweden. Australia has a phrase for it: the tall-poppy syndrome. Conrad Black is on record as considering it a particularly Canadian trait. In his autobiography, Black wrote that English-speaking Canadians had "a sadistic desire, corroded by soul-destroying envy, to intimidate all those who might aspire to anything in the slightest exceptional."

Black's observation came in the course of recounting a conversation he'd once had with Pierre Elliott Trudeau, who was discussing his own tall-poppy problems and remarking, according to Black's account, that Canada was difficult to govern partly because French-speaking Canadians boo the loser and English-speaking Canadians boo the winner. Trudeau was a glamorous enough figure to have inspired what was then called Trudeaumania, but glamour has been of limited value in Canadian politics. The only modern prime minister who has formed three consecutive majority governments is the incumbent, Jean Chrétien, who is known as *le petit gars de Shawinigan*—the little guy from Shawinigan, the drab mill town where he was brought up, one of nineteen children born to a paper-mill machinist and his wife. The prime minister is often described as being unable to speak either of Canada's official languages. Still, while leading the Liberal Party to three straight victories he has nearly obliterated what had been the majority party in Parliament, the Progressive Conservatives. A clue to his approach may be that for decades he has managed to be known as "the little guy" even though he is six feet two. Speaking recently of the elements of Chrétien's success, someone who has been close to him said, "The Prime Minister works hard at being humble."

Conrad Black does not. A tall man in his late fifties, he has thickened a bit over the years but is still spoken of as being of theatrical bearing, a man who draws all eyes when he enters a room and is aware of it. "His personality had a staged, directed feel to it," Robert Fulford wrote, after a 1987 lunch with Black to explore the question of whether Fulford would remain as editor of *Saturday Night,* a distinguished old magazine, which Black had just bought. (Fulford, without getting into an un-Canadian snit about it, decided in the negative.) "It was also oddly familiar. Where had I seen it before, a large, handsome man with a supercilious and condescending manner and a baroque vocabulary? Of course: Orson Welles in *Citizen Kane.*"

Black had picked up *Saturday Night* during a period of acquisition, often buying from families that had grown weary of dealing with the business or with each other. (A Toronto newspaper man said recently, "You don't want to be having a fight with your cousin when Conrad's around.") Although he gained a reputation for running a bare-bones operation—one of his partners, David Radler, once joked that his own contribution to journalism was the three-man newsroom, with two of its occupants also selling advertising—he improved some newspapers, particularly in larger cities. Black was never the sort of Canadian mogul who seems vaguely embarrassed about making a lot of money from his enterprises. He rode around in a Rolls-Royce and commissioned a family coat of arms to hang above the door of his Toronto estate, for which he concocted the name Havenwold. As the honorary colonel of the Governor General's Foot Guards during a royal visit to Canada in 1997, Black hovered just behind Queen Elizabeth in a uniform that, in the view of those editors who seemed to take great delight in running the picture at any opportunity, made him look like an overattentive chauffeur.

Black always invited celebrated people he admired—people like Margaret Thatcher and David Brinkley and William F. Buckley, Jr.—to the annual dinner of Hollinger, his media company. In London, where he established his main base of operations after taking control of *The Daily Telegraph* in the middle eighties, he moved among those people who appear to be bound together by believing quite genuinely that there is great cachet in having, say, a British royal or Henry Kissinger around for dinner. At the 1987 lunch, Fulford wrote, Black "dropped the names of Katharine Graham, George Shultz, the Aga Khan, and Henry Kissinger, all in one paragraph. It occurred to me that I might never see this feat equaled in my lifetime."

The historical figures Black was said to admire were even more important than the people he entertained at dinner, and the impression he gave of identifying with them hinted at what one British journalist called "a prodigious sense of his own destiny." Black's wife once told a reporter that he liked to ponder important decisions while sitting in a chair that Napoleon Bonaparte had occupied when signing treaties. His reputation for both acquisitiveness and devotion to great historical figures has been such that his assistant in London once had to state formally, in response to press inquiries, "The proprietor of *The Daily Telegraph* would like to go on the record to say that he does certainly not own Napoleon's penis."

As the nineties came to an end, Conrad Black's empire was a subject of concern to those who write about the Canadian press. They were not particularly interested in his holdings in Great Britain or in Israel (*The Jerusalem Post*) or in the United States (the *Chicago Sun-Times*, among other papers). But they questioned whether it was healthy for one man to control a majority of the daily newspapers in Canada. In three out of the ten provinces, Black owned all the daily newspapers. In a stroke that even his enemies acknowledged as audacious and brave, he had launched, in October of 1998, a multi-section daily in Toronto, called the *National Post*, to compete with *The Globe and Mail* as a national newspaper.

Part of what troubled the people who wrote articles about Conrad Black's having too much power was that he was eager to bring Canadians around to his way of thinking. He clearly considered himself a man of ideas. He had begun as an indifferent and rebellious student. At a Toronto prep school called Upper Canada College, which is sometimes referred to as the Eton of Canada, he was guaranteed outsider status by being a nonathlete who, betraying no concern about how established Wasps were expected to behave in a country that valued the low-key, frequently arrived at school in a limousine and took an interest in how many servants various classmates had. He was ejected for selling copies of final exams. After further academic misadventures, though, Black got degrees in both law and history and eventually turned his master's thesis into a thick biography of Maurice Duplessis, the longtime premier of Quebec. The image many Canadians have of Black was acquired from a scene that a Canadian Broadcasting Corporation crew shot in the home of a fellow tycoon in 1980 as a way of illustrating Black's interest in military history: a man in a baronial room reenacting great battles by moving antique toy soldiers around a baize-covered table. Known for his prodigious memory, Black can recite, say, the armaments and tonnage of all the battleships in the Second World War. It was after listening to a torrent of such information that Margaret Thatcher supposedly responded, "I know, Conrad."

Although Black launched the *National Post* at a time when the truly national political parties in Canada ranged from one usually described as conservative to one sometimes described as socialist (the New Democratic Party), all of them could be included in what Black might categorize as "the odious soft left." The inclinations of the Canadian mainstream are toward the welfare state, which

Black has called an "overgenerous reinsurance policy for an under-achieving people." Members of the Canadian intelligentsia tend to be, if not overtly anti-American, at least resistant to America, a country Black so admires that he has suggested that English-speaking Canada, as an alternative to endless and debilitating haggling with French-speaking Canada in an effort to keep the country together, could do worse than see what kind of deal it could cut with Washington. In speeches and columns and articles, Black made it clear that he—particularly in his role as proprietor of the *National Post*—meant to provide an alternative to the left-of-center policies that he believed were eroding the economy and causing the more enterprising and talented Canadians to flee south in great numbers. At a party he gave for the staff on the first anniversary of the *Post,* he said that the paper's goal was to change Canada from the sort of place in which the government took money away from people who earned it and gave it to people who hadn't.

From the start, the *Post* hammered away at a few of the issues that troubled its proprietor about the Canadian consensus—the brain drain, for instance, and the problems with Canada's national health system and high taxes. It would commission surveys and then massage the results sufficiently so that figures showing that a majority believed the government-run health system worked pretty well could produce the headline "HUGE SUPPORT" FOUND FOR PRIVATE HEALTH CARE. The *National Post* did everything in its power to create a national party that would be an authentic hard-right alternative to the Liberals. Coming up with indications of cronyism by Chrétien concerning a golf-course project near Shawinigan, the *Post* ran what the humorist Larry Zolf estimated to be "more words about Jean Chrétien's home riding in an average day than there are actual voters living and breathing in that economically beleaguered constituency." The relentless coverage eventually so irritated Chrétien that he tracked Black down in Austria in the middle of the night to phone in a complaint.

Some of the columnists Black hired for the *Post* were right-wing, but some of them weren't—and virtually all of them wrote engaging prose. By all accounts, there was a good deal of esprit de corps on the paper. A number of the young journalists agreed with the proprietor's ideas on free-market economics; those who didn't tended to bond with their colleagues partly from being asked again and again by friends and acquaintances how they could work for a monster like Conrad Black. From the start, the layout of the *National Post* was inviting and the selection of stories imaginative. Although the paper continued to lose a lot of money, it was also giving *The Globe and Mail* much more serious competition in circulation than had been anticipated. Many people who didn't agree with the *National Post*'s political views looked forward to picking it up every day.

Given the near extinction of the Progressive Conservatives as a parliamentary party after Chrétien won reelection easily in 1997, the *National Post* was sometimes referred to as the "official opposition." Its personification was Conrad Black, the country's most prominent conservative voice. He seemed to glory in the role. Black has always had a taste for verbal combat. It has been written that he never uses one word when six will do, and among the six there will probably be a couple of words like "puerile" or "febrile," or even "rumbustious." Perhaps the best known of Black's combat quotes is about journalists: "My experience with journalists authorizes me to record that a very large number of them are ignorant, lazy, opinionated, intellectually dishonest and inadequately supervised." And he felt sufficiently experienced to tell that to a committee of the Canadian Senate at the age of twenty-five.

John Fraser, a journalist who is now master of Massey College in the University of Toronto, was one of Black's few friends at Upper Canada College, and their old-school bond was strengthened when they took abrupt leave of UCC the same year. (Fraser was innocent of any participation in the exam-selling scheme but innocent also of the rudiments of physics.) In an essay about what it had been like to work for his school chum—when Fulford left *Saturday Night,* Black installed Fraser as the editor—Fraser wrote, "One of his English editors once said that the proprietor's bark was worse than his bite. While this may be true, it does not give due credit to the bark, for it is a great bark."

Conrad Black once said, in an interview with *The Globe and Mail,* "Every chairman of *The Daily Telegraph* in the history of that paper has been a peer, so I don't think it's that hard to envision achieving that status." Also, the two previous Canadian-born press barons to whom Black was comparable in scale and approach— all made a pile of money in Canada and then became players on Fleet Street—had been transformed into Lord Beaverbrook and Lord Thomson of Fleet. (Beaverbrook's peerage came before the Nickle Resolution; Roy Thomson, a longtime resident of Great Britain, gave up his Canadian citizenship in 1963 to become Lord Thomson.) Margaret Thatcher was Conrad Black's kind of prime minister—self-assured, contemptuous of those in the Party she considered "wet"—and in 1989 Barbara Amiel, a prominent Canadian journalist who was to become Black's second wife a few years later, said to the *Toronto Star,* "There's just no way Mrs. Thatcher can leave office without giving [a peerage] to him." But Mrs. Thatcher did just that, and Black did not have as close a relationship with her successor, John Major. Finally, in 1999, when Tony Blair was prime minister, Black was confidentially informed by William Hague, then the leader of the Conservative Party, that his name would be among those in the Opposition's allocation of new members to be appointed by the Queen to the House of Lords.

Before that information became public, Black made inquiries to satisfy himself that a Canadian could accept the appointment. In the thirty-six years since Lord Thomson had given up his Canadian citizenship in order to accept his title, dozens of Canadians had been given foreign honors of one sort or another, but none had been appointed to the House of Lords, which is, after all, part of the legislature of another country. In 1977, though, the Canadian Parliament had passed a law permitting dual citizenship, and Black's lawyers in Toronto believed that the 1977 law fundamentally changed the equation. Black consulted the Canadian High Commissioner in London and apparently received assurances that the Canadian government would have no reason to object as long as he became a British citizen as well as a Canadian.

Black applied for British citizenship and in a demonstration of bureaucratic alacrity that might have astonished those Bangladeshi kitchen workers who had been waiting some time for the same distinction, received it within a day or two. But there had been a leak. On June 8, 1999, *The Globe and Mail* ran an item saying that Black was "in negotiations with authorities in the British and Canadian governments to allow him to take a seat in the House of Lords," and that the appointment was to be made officially by the Queen in ten days. Chrétien's office, hearing that news for the first time, said the matter required further consideration.

On the day before the list of new appointments to the House of Lords was to be announced, the editor of the *National Post*, Ken Whyte, was awakened by a telephone call from the proprietor, who was terribly upset. "Do you know what that bastard has done?" Black said. The prime minister had informed the British that Canada would not be pleased to have one of its citizens named to the House of Lords. The next day, Black's name was dropped by Tony Blair from the list of nominations.

Black placed an angry phone call to Chrétien demanding that the decision be reversed. Getting no satisfaction, he sued, claiming that he had been caused great public embarrassment by what was essentially an abuse of power by the prime minister. Black was no stranger to litigation. For some years, he had regularly responded to articles he considered defamatory, particularly those that implied questionable business practices, with lawsuits. But the suit against Chrétien, unlike a libel action in a country whose libel laws favor the plaintiff, seemed like a long shot. Also, suing somebody for having caused you "considerable public embarrassment" is sort of a, well, public embarrassment. But Black was not a man who would slink off the field simply because his opponent had managed to get in one good whack.

There was no shortage of people supporting the claim that Black's situation was embarrassing. In expressing mock sympathy for those who worked at the *National Post,* an editorialist wrote in the *Toronto Star,* "it must be hard to convince readers that you work for a serious publication when your boss is making a laughingstock of himself on both sides of the Atlantic." Black was referred to as Lord Almost and Lord Nearly-Nearly and His Lardship. For some time, the political-satire magazine *Frank* had been referring to Black as Tubby and depicting him in cartoon strips in his Foot Guard's uniform. After the peerage was blocked by the prime minister—he is known as Crouton in *Frank*—Black was upgraded to Lord Tubby of Fleet (Pending) or His Tubship. In stories about Black's "peerage interruptus," the picture of him in his Foot Guard's getup was often included—supplanted now and then by a shot of him walking into a costume ball dressed as Cardinal Richelieu.

But Black also had some people on his side, and not just ideological allies. The editor of *Maclean's,* Anthony Wilson-Smith, wrote that the prime minister's "churlishness towards foes" was an unattractive trait and that Conrad Black, a man who was capable of great personal kindnesses as well as public bombast, was "miscast as The Dark Knight." From the start, *The Globe and Mail,* Black's competitor, took the position that he was right and Chrétien was wrong, calling the prime minister's "apparent use of his own high office to settle a score with a powerful critic" a piece of "arrogant despotism." But the judge in Black's case, without hearing testimony, ruled that "any question about the propriety of the

Prime Minister's motivation is for Parliament and the electorate not for the courts." Black appealed.

A few months after that, in August of 2000, the commentators who had been lamenting the concentration of newspapers in the hands of one man were startled to find that they had suddenly lost a topic: Black sold most of his Canadian newspapers, including half of the *National Post*. Black has said that his intention had been to sell only Hollinger's small-town papers—that would have brought in about a billion Canadian dollars to reduce a long-term debt that had apparently become worrisome—but by the time the negotiations were over Black's three-and-a-half-billion-dollar Canadian newspaper empire was just about gone. The buyer was the Asper family of Winnipeg, whose patriarch, Israel Asper, while no left-winger, was a friend of Jean Chrétien's and a former leader of the Manitoba Liberal Party.

However sound the sale was as a business deal—some saw it as a shrewd selloff at the right moment; some saw it as a sign that Hollinger was in trouble—it was widely regarded as a retreat for Conrad Black, who was not at the press conference announcing it. Although Black insisted that the sale had nothing whatever to do with the argument over his peerage, most of the commentators disagreed. In *Maclean's*, Peter C. Newman, a Black biographer, wrote, "His flight from Canadian investment reflects Black's strong feeling that while he is honored elsewhere (i.e., being offered a British title), the one audience whose applause has so far eluded him is from his own country."

Black's retention of a half-interest in the *National Post* was considered by some a way to save face, but he assured both the public and the loyalists on the staff that, under the deal, he would retain complete editorial control for the first five years of the partnership. With constant encouragement from the *Post*, a new conservative party, the Canadian Alliance, had been formed, building on the base of the populist Reform Party, which had been viable only in the western provinces. Although the upset winner of the new party's leadership election, Stockwell Day, wasn't Black's candidate, the *National Post* led the chorus of voices proclaiming that Day—a youthful-looking and energetic born-again Christian—would bring a freshness to Canadian politics that contrasted with the aging and colorless Chrétien.

Stockwell Day turned out to be a disaster—an inspiration for the sly ridicule that may be a concomitant of the tall-poppy syndrome in Canada or may simply be a national gift. He was the sort of candidate who stood at Niagara Falls to say that Liberal policies had caused Canadian talent to flow to the United States like the Niagara River, only to be reminded by just about every paper in the country the next day that the Niagara River flows from the United States to Canada. He was dealt a great blow by Rick Mercer, a television satirist, who, noting that the Canadian Alliance platform favored referenda, used his TV show to suggest a referendum mandating that Stockwell Day change his first name to Doris. Through e-mail, he got hundreds of thousands of signatures overnight.

The Canadian Alliance was swamped in the election, and Day proved to be so inept as the leader of the Opposition that a number of Canadian Alliance MPs left the caucus. Eventually, he became widely known as Stockboy Day, although some people continued to call him Doris. By May of this year, when the appeals-court decision on Conrad Black's case against Jean Chrétien was finally handed down, it had become obvious that the Canadian Alliance was not going to be the vehicle to realize Black's dream of engineering a Thatcherite revolution in Canada. As Rick Salutin, a left-of-center columnist for *The Globe and Mail,* put it recently, Black "built the flagpole and raised the flag and the country didn't salute."

The appeals court upheld the original decision. According to Peter Atkinson, Hollinger's general counsel, he advised Black that an appeal to the Supreme Court could mean years more of litigation, even assuming the Court agreed to hear the case. Black had said more than once that he would not renounce his Canadian citizenship just for a peerage, but Atkinson has said, "if he really wanted the peerage, in this lifetime, there was no alternative." Right after the appeals decision, Conrad Black formally announced that he was giving up his Canadian citizenship. He issued a statement saying, "Having opposed for thirty years precisely the public policies that have caused scores of thousands of educated and talented Canadians to abandon their country every year, it is at least consistent that I should join this dispersal." A *Globe and Mail* piece quoted Black as saying that he would "take back" his citizenship when Canada had a different administration. It also said that, according to citizenship officials, regulations permit former Canadians to reapply for citizenship status after a year of residence in the country.

Three months later, Black sold the rest of the *National Post* to the Asper family. He was widely seen as having abandoned the ruins of a conservative movement that he, more than anyone, had put together. "What finally triggered Mr. Black's departure was the dispute over his bid to be elevated to Britain's House of Lords," Lawrence Martin wrote in *The Globe and Mail*. "He leaves ideological brethren stunned and hurt. They figured that he would have fought the battle longer, that his mission was perhaps as important as the money."

Some people on the *National Post* felt betrayed by Black—"I suggest that they contemplate spending two hundred million dollars founding and launching a paper," he said—but Ken Whyte, the *Post*'s editor, said that many were grateful for "the remarkable ride." Within a few months, the *National Post* had been greatly slimmed down, resulting in the layoff of a hundred and thirty people. There was some sympathy in the Toronto newspaper community for those who had been jettisoned from the *Post,* but it was also said in the provinces of the odious soft left, "They kept preaching that the market should decide everything, and finally the market decided something about them."

"Some of us may have been amused, or baffled, that he would want a peerage so badly he was willing to renounce his Canadian citizenship for it," the *National Post* columnist Christie Blatchford acknowledged in an otherwise adulatory column on Conrad Black published the day after he sold his remaining stake to the Asper family. As Allan Fotheringham, a much less sympathetic columnist, said in *Maclean's*, why would Black "covet a spot in the pastureland of chinless wonders, spavined foxhunters and one lord who was caught selling cocaine in the pristine corridors of Westminster?" Asked that question not long ago, a woman in Toronto who has known Black for many years answered in a very few words: "Pomposity and self-importance." English journalists tend to be equally succinct: "Black wants to be called Lord. It's as simple as that." Some people in Toronto's journalism community see Black as a fundamentally intelligent man who was brought down by a flaw—called pomposity or grandiosity or "his great-man thing"—that made him vulnerable to a wily *gars* like Jean Chrétien. "The most brilliant of men faced the most ordinary of men and he lost," a great admirer of Black's said recently. "And he was made to look like a fool."

"He did want it," Barbara Amiel had written in *Maclean's* not long after her husband's appointment was blocked by Jean Chrétien. "The only parliamentary debates that have any real substance are found in the House of Lords." Black himself has said that for a man who wanted to play a role in politics and didn't want to run for public office—remember what happened when Citizen Kane tried that—the Lords "would be the only opportunity I would ever have to be any kind of legislative person." Beaverbrook stands as an example of how an impressive figure from the Lords might even be asked to join the Cabinet, assuming the Tories someday manage to get rid of Tony Blair. Although no one would claim that the House of Lords is at the center of British politics—its power does not extend much beyond the ability to delay legislation—the Blair reforms that rid it of most of the hereditary lords, a group in which the chinless-wonder and spavined-foxhunter quotient presumably ran pretty high, have made it seem somewhat less antiquated. The House of Lords is also thought of as a good club—convenient, food no more revolting than at most British clubs, a lot of retainers saying "m'Lord" all the time—but the members, particularly now that Blair names the bulk of them, are more likely to be Labour Party donors or trade-union officials than the sort of people Conrad Black has always liked to have to dinner. The name that attracted notice on the list Black was dropped from in 1999 was that of a Southeast London community worker who had been born in Grenada. Contemplating the demographics of the House of Lords these days, John Fraser, who has been watching Black climb in and out of limousines since they were eleven years old, said recently, "It will be Conrad's first opportunity to meet ordinary people."

And why was Jean Chrétien, who had never shown any interest in titles before, so intent on denying Black this opportunity? Simple vindictiveness? The prime minister's office has insisted that the Canadian Honors Policy Committee eventually decided that a Canadian's sitting in the House of Lords would not be "compatible with the ideals of democracy as they have developed in Canada." Chrétien has also hinted at times that he was irritated at what he saw as an effort to sneak the appointment through without his knowledge. A couple of commentators have been tempted by the thought that the prime minister might have been, at least symbolically, moving around toy soldiers of his own—maybe plastic soldiers on the oilcloth of a modest kitchen table. As the game is played in this version, Conrad Black is denied a peerage and, being Conrad Black, counterattacks instead of retreating. He might even go to court. When all political and legal avenues are closed, he, still being Conrad Black, renounces his citizenship in order to advance toward his objective, as Roy Thomson did years before. But the laws of Canada make it difficult for a noncitizen to own a newspaper. Black has to withdraw from the *National Post* and, voila, there goes Chrétien's only significant opposition.

Such a turn of events was apparently one of the many scenarios that had occurred to Chrétien's advisers, but it was not the basis of the prime minister's intervention. On purely political grounds, the decision would not have required an elaborate plot: In a country that suspects people who put on airs, it comes to light that the most prominent conservative is in line for an honor he desperately wants. The man in question is seen by many of his countrymen as a swaggering elitist who has expressed nothing but contempt for them, describing them with phrases like "whining, politically conformist welfare addicts." He has caused the prime minister a lot of grief. The prime minister is able to grant or deny this man the honor, which most voters consider silly at best. In the words of a former Chrétien aide, "What's the downside of saying no?"

Once the renunciation of Canadian citizenship had made Chrétien's *non* irrelevant, Black was quickly back on the peerage track. On October 31, dressed in a red robe with ermine trim, he entered the chamber of the House of Lords to be named Lord Black of Crossharbour, Crossharbour being a part of London near the *Daily Telegraph* offices. It was not completely lost on those who remained Canadians that the ceremony had taken place on Halloween; there were a few jokes on that and other aspects of Black's induction in a meeting of the Liberal caucus. *The Globe and Mail* ran a picture of Lord Black, in his robe, on the front page. The *National Post*'s coverage included two pieces and a formal portrait of the new Lord and Lady Black, posing in one of the House of Lords' paneled rooms. On one side of them was Margaret Thatcher.

On the other side, it almost goes without saying, was Henry Kissinger.

In Hollinger's New York offices, a place with men's-club furnishings and framed autographs of historical figures, a couple of weeks after his induction, Conrad Black was cordial and not the least rumbustious. But he was quite unwilling to accept the generally accepted version of the saga surrounding his peerage. The argument over becoming Lord Black had nothing at all to do with his withdrawal from Canada, he said—not even with his sale of the remaining half of the *National Post,* since the Canadian-ownership law could always be finessed by putting the paper in trust to his children. (His general counsel, Peter Atkinson, has said that, given the level of scrutiny and the presence of a hostile Parliament, restructuring the business to get around the law "would have been very tough.") Black strongly rejected the notion that he had "abandoned the *Post* and fled the land," as one English paper put it. "I was fiercely desirous of throwing a brick in that little central-opinion-formation media pond in Toronto—*The Globe and Mail,* the *Toronto Star,* the CBC, and, to a lesser degree, *Maclean's* magazine—that foists upon the country this false consensus of running things just somewhat to the left of the United States, a fundamentally and radically mistaken policy in my opinion," he said. "So it gave me the utmost pleasure to cause them the level of discomfort that we did. We certainly got an alternate view out there. The problem with that was it's clear that, barring some horrible economic calamity, a majority in Canada are too profoundly seduced by this view of the country as a kinder, gentler, caring, and sharing society and a sort of peacekeeper and social worker to the world."

Black said that he "never took the Alliance all that seriously" and was "never under any great illusion" that his alternative view of Canada would carry the day. It was worth a try, he said, but he was off to greener pastures, having sold his holdings for commercial reasons and put his pet project, the *National Post,* in the hands of the people most likely to assure its survival. He maintains that he can always go back to Canada; in fact, he still carries the special passport he was issued as a member of the Privy Council, whose members, he said, can be non-Canadians—"the Duke of Edinburgh, for instance." The only aspect of the peerage battle that Black would accept as a factor in his withdrawal from his native land was the court decision, in that it reflected "the complete abdication of the judiciary" to the power of what he considers a one-party state.

Actually, he said, the notion that he desperately wanted a seat in the House of Lords was simply not true. "It's all surmise," he said. "It is a conventional wisdom that is not actually based on anything other than . . . people's conception of me being much more preoccupied with that sort of thing than I am." Without having to be reminded that this was conventional wisdom believed by his most loyal employees, his lawyer, and his wife, Black went on, "Of course, I do want it up to a point, but I was not ever prepared to commit indignities to achieve it. There are ways of generating these things, but I never lifted a finger to make it happen."

And the renunciation of his citizenship, which many Canadians find extreme, or even offensive? Black said that even that was not the result of wanting to be Lord Black of Crossharbour. "It was a combination of things," he said. "As the brain drain amplified itself and the currency plunged to new lows, I saw these polls showing that sixty percent of Canadians were pleased with Chrétien as prime minister. And then literally the last straw was the formerly distinguished court just rolling over for the regime. I thought the last act of dissent I could make was to renounce my citizenship, and that it would be inconsistent for me not to do it. Now, with that said, of course it was convenient that that was also the ticket to the House of Lords."

.   .   .

In 2007, Conrad Black was convicted in the United States of fraud and obstruction of justice, charges involving mainly the diverting of funds from non-compete agreements. He served three and a half years in a Florida prison. (He was later pardoned by Donald Trump, a friend about whom he'd written a laudatory biography.) After his release, in 2012, he moved back to Toronto. The speculation is that he resides in Canada through the extension of a temporary resident permit granted at that time, but such information is private.

Presidential Ups and Downs: Washington Pundits Take Their Analytical Skills to the Ranch

2001

C RAWFORD, TEX., AUG. 20—President George W. Bush's failure to catch a fish after he spent two hours on his heavily stocked bass pond this afternoon was considered a defeat for Mr. Bush by most observers here, and one that would weaken his position in swapping fish stories with Democrats and Republican moderates in Congress. A White House spokesman's comment that the President, being a serious conservationist, had "done catch-and-release one better" may have only worsened matters, since most of the press corps dismissed it as a desperate attempt at spin.

CRAWFORD, TEX., AUG. 21—The President scored a solid victory today by working on the clearing of his nature trail for an hour and a half without injuring himself.

CRAWFORD, TEX., AUG. 22—Eating scrambled eggs this morning for breakfast was seen as a victory for the President, who had been having his eggs sunny-side up for more than a week. The President prefers his eggs scrambled. White House officials have been unwilling to discuss the reasoning behind the string of sunny-side-up eggs. However, they are not directly denying a story that the Crawford ranch's cook, Rosa Gonzales, had refused to serve scrambled eggs ever since the President, in an effort to compliment her, tried to pronounce the dish in Spanish—*huevos revueltos*—and came out with something that Ms. Gonzales understood as "very revolting." It is not clear how the situation was resolved in a manner that permitted a return to scrambled eggs this morning, but White House officials did little to hide their jubilation.

CRAWFORD, TEX., AUG. 23—White House spokesmen refused to elaborate on a terse announcement this morning that a two-year-old Hereford steer on the Bush ranch had stepped into a gopher hole and broken its leg—a defeat for the President.

CRAWFORD, TEX., AUG. 24—Even George W. Bush's harshest critics are acknowledging today that the weather has given the President an important victory. "The entire country has been suffering from a heat wave," said a member of the White House staff who has been at the President's ranch for three weeks, "but there can't be any place quite as miserable as this." Daniel Jonas, a Democratic pollster who specializes in issues of empathy, said, "Let's face it: this is a big one for Bush."

CRAWFORD, TEX., AUG. 25—George W. Bush was served *huevos rancheros* for breakfast today—a serious defeat for the President, who does not like highly spiced food.

CRAWFORD, TEX., AUG. 26—Republicans both here and in Washington were glowing today after George W. Bush apparently scored a big victory by losing at golf. "He's just a regular guy with a bad slice," one Party loyalist said. "He knows loss. He understands loss." The low scorer in the foursome, a wealthy oilman from Lubbock, won ten dollars from each of the other players. Late this afternoon, Democrats were saying that the episode might prove to be a defeat for Mr. Bush now that it is known that longtime family friends of the President's parents came forward on the eighteenth green to cover his losses.

CRAWFORD, TEX., AUG. 27—President Bush scored his biggest victory of the week this morning when Rosa Gonzales, his cook, posed, smiling, for a picture with him in the kitchen of the Crawford ranch. Although Ms. Gonzales has not been made available for interviews, the White House has formally denied that she ever referred to the President as "la boquita de un gringo puro"— roughly, "little gringo mouth." In response to reporters' questions at the photo opportunity, the President explained his views on how best to prepare eggs by saying that he is a uniter, not a divider. H. Cole Keegle, an expert on Presidential diet at the Brookings Institution, said, "The President was overdue for a clear-cut victory on this one, and he got it."

Among Friends

1981

Publicly, George Mercer IV was reported missing on February 7, 1980. His picture ran above a small item in both the *Savannah Morning News* and the *Savannah Evening Press.* The item said he had been missing since January 29. It described him as being twenty-two years old, five feet eight inches tall, about a hundred and fifty-five pounds. It asked anyone having information about him to telephone the Savannah Police Department. The picture showed a young man with the sort of thick mustache and blow-dried hair that make a lot of twenty-two-year-olds seen at racquetball clubs or singles bars or pleasure-boat marinas look pretty much alike to the unpracticed eye. The item in the two papers said little about George Mercer IV beyond giving his physical description, but not many people in Savannah needed to be told who he was. The Mercers have long been a prominent family in Savannah—a city particularly conscious of prominent families. In Atlanta, a successful businessman who wants to upgrade his background beyond simply awarding posthumous commissions to a few Civil War ancestors may allow his neighbors to infer that his family was originally from Savannah, Georgia's first settlement.

The Mercers are the sort of family he would be trying to suggest—the sort of family whose discussions of military forebears tend to focus not on the Civil War but on the American Revolution. The Mercers are among the families that people in Savannah sometimes allow themselves to refer to as "the bluebloods"—a phrase that would be difficult to utter without a smile in Atlanta, one of the Southern cities where the most powerful citizens in town used to be known as "the big mules." In Savannah, the bluebloods still have the sort of power that big mules might have in another city—partly because Savannah has been the sort of place that respects their credentials, partly because Savannah has not been the kind of place that attracts a lot of ambitious newcomers who might shoulder them aside. Until their family company, which manufactured Great Dane truck trailers, was bought up by a conglomerate several years ago, the Mercers were one of Savannah's major industrial employers. George Mercer III, who did not remain with Great Dane after the purchase, is the chairman of the board of Savannah's Memorial Hospital and a former member of the Chatham County Commission. Although no one named Mercer is a force in the business life of Savannah these days, the Mercers remain the Mercers—stalwarts of the Oglethorpe Club, the kind of family that can ordinarily sort out any difficulty with a telephone call. It could be assumed by readers of the *Savannah Morning News* and the *Savannah Evening Press* that the police would spare no effort in trying to find George Mercer IV. As it happened, there was another agency interested in the search for George Mercer IV—the Federal Bureau of Investigation. The FBI had reason to believe that he had been kidnapped.

On River Street, where bars and restaurants have opened in restored warehouses in the past several years, FBI agents were already showing bartenders a photograph of George Mercer IV. The people George Mercer IV went around with often ended up on River Street late in the evening—sometimes early in the evening.

Some of Mercer's friends were from his childhood—people who had gone to the same private schools and the same debutante parties—and some were just the people a single young man might meet over a pitcher of beer on River Street or at a party after a rugby match or during the quiet exchange of marijuana that such young men think of as routine these days. The time they put in on River Street—or in similar bars near Armstrong State College, on the south side of Savannah—was not a matter of respite from working their way up in their chosen fields. Most of them had not got around to choosing a field. They tended to be young men who had put in a semester of college here and a semester of college there, but not enough semesters to have reached the point of selecting a major. Even those who still had recourse to the family's refrigerator or its speedboats needed spending money, but the jobs they took to get it tended to be temporary or seasonal or part-time. Their ambitions for the future often seemed to settle on schemes for getting rich quickly, perhaps through being on the ground floor of some technological breakthrough in communications. For a while, George Mercer IV and a childhood friend talked of opening a video-disc outlet in Atlanta. They also talked about obtaining the Southeast regional franchise for a new electronic method of producing advertising spots.

George Mercer IV had a lot of enthusiasm for the schemes. His friends thought of him as rather gullible. He had been slow in school, with learning problems that included dyslexia. Once, when he was putting in a semester or so at LaGrange College, someone matched up the information that he liked to compose songs on the guitar with the information that his great-uncle was the songwriter Johnny Mercer, and the publicity resulted in the scheduling of a couple of public appearances. At the last minute, though, Mercer withdrew. He had decided he wasn't ready. His father diagnosed the problem as the sort of preperformance nervousness he calls "buck fever." After LaGrange, Mercer tended to play the guitar in public only when there were just four or five people left at the party. He spent some time at Armstrong State and at the night school of the University of Georgia, in Athens. Toward the end of 1979, while back in Savannah living with his parents, he got a job selling vacuum cleaners. It may not have appeared to be an appropriate job for a Mercer, but, as it happened, George Mercer IV seemed to enjoy selling vacuum cleaners. Some of his friends thought that the job had done a lot for George's self-confidence. His father agreed. He was hoping that sooner or later George Mercer IV might move from selling vacuum cleaners to selling Great Dane trailers. Then George Mercer IV disappeared.

Demands for ransom came almost immediately. There were notes. There were telephone calls. The instructions tended to be complicated, even bizarre. George Mercer III was instructed to draw a circle in orange spray paint at a certain intersection to indicate his cooperation. There were instructions to take the ransom—forty-two thousand dollars—in a small motorboat down the Ogeechee River, flying a flag with a yellow triangle sewn onto a field of green. At one point, the ransom was actually left in a wooded area, but nobody picked it up. When the item reporting George Mercer IV missing appeared in the *Savannah Morning News* and the *Savannah Evening Press,* FBI agents hadn't even known whether he was dead or alive—but they did have a pretty good hunch about who might have written the extortion notes. When they walked up and down River Street showing George Mercer's picture, they also carried with them a picture of Michael Harper.

Nobody has ever described Michael Harper as slow or gullible. "He could put anything over on anybody he wanted to," someone who knew him told the investigators. A slim, bearded young man about the age of George Mercer IV, Harper had grown up in a suburb of Savannah, the son of a certified public accountant. He didn't have as many semesters of college as Mercer had, but people he came in contact with regularly described him as brilliant and accomplished—a wizard with electronics and math and computers, an expert at scuba diving and flying airplanes, a talker so glib that he had worked as a disc jockey when barely out of high school. They also described him as somewhat mysterious. No one seemed to know precisely where he lived. The jobs he mentioned holding ran from assistant manager of a fast-food chicken outlet to operator of what he described as a hush-hush project at Hunter Army Air Field called Quest Laboratories. The get-rich-quick schemes he discussed with friends were more complicated than opening a video-disc outlet—shadowy mail-order deals, for instance, and a plan to use a Savannah Police Department badge to hoodwink a couple of dope dealers out of some marijuana. One of Harper's schemes landed him in jail. In 1974, when he was only seventeen, he had been sentenced to fourteen months for trying to extort forty-five hundred dollars from a former neighbor by threatening to kill the man and his entire family. Later, in Augusta, he was convicted of theft by deception and given a probated sentence. Roger McLaughlin, one of the FBI agents assigned to the Mercer kidnapping, had worked on the 1974 extortion case, and he thought he recognized Harper's style. Within a couple of days, the FBI had ascertained that Harper had moved back to Savannah from Augusta and that he knew George Mercer IV. They had met at a rugby match.

One of the people who happened to be sitting at the bar of Spanky's, on River Street, when the FBI showed the bartender pictures of George Mercer IV and Michael Harper was Richard Sommers, an ebullient young man who constitutes the photography staff of a weekly Savannah newspaper called the *Georgia Gazette*. The *Gazette* was founded two and a half years ago by a young man named Albert Scardino and his wife, Marjorie, a lawyer who serves as publisher and occasional typesetter. Albert Scardino, who has a graduate degree in journalism from the University of California, had tried freelancing for a while, and had worked for the Associated Press in West Virginia, and had produced a film on the coastal islands of Georgia which was shown on the Public Broadcasting System. For a while, he had tried to raise money—from George Mercer III, among others—for a series of films on wilderness areas around the world. Aside from the journalistic experience he had picked up, Scardino had another qualification for being the founding editor of a weekly newspaper in Savannah—serious Savannah credentials. His father—a urologist named Peter Scardino, who came to Savannah soon after the Second World War—is not merely a prominent doctor but someone widely respected as a leading force in improving the medical standards of the community. Dr. Scardino is not interested in colonial genealogy—he is quick to say that the only revolution his ancestors might have fought in was the one led by Garibaldi—and he is not the sort of man who would spend much time at any club not organized around the subject of urology. Still, his badges of acceptance in Savannah include membership in the Oglethorpe Club. For years, he and his wife have served on some of the same committees the Mercers serve on and have attended some of the same parties the Mercers attended. One of Albert Scardino's younger brothers grew up with George Mercer IV.

Although a lot of the weekly newspapers that have sprung up in the past decade seem designed specifically for the editors' contemporaries—or for some mythical twenty-nine-year-old purchaser of stereo equipment—the *Georgia Gazette* was founded to appeal to a general readership basically defined by its dissatisfaction with the commonly owned *Savannah Morning News* and the *Savannah Evening Press*. In Savannah, the *News-Press* is widely described as innocuous or undistinguished; a contemporary of Albert Scardino is more likely to refer to it as "a Mickey Mouse operation." Albert and Marjorie Scardino hoped that after a few years of weekly publication the *Gazette* might gradually increase its frequency until it became a daily alternative to the *News-Press*.

From the start, the *Gazette* did not grow at the pace the Scardinos had envisioned. Capital was a problem. They did manage one business coup, though, which promised to buy them some time for building advertising and circulation: in January 1979 the *Gazette* replaced the *Evening Press* as what is known in Georgia as the sheriff's gazette—the newspaper designated to carry the advertisements that lawyers in the county place to satisfy requirements of public notice. The sheriff, one of the three county officials empowered to decide which paper is designated, had persuaded a probate judge to go along with a switch to the *Gazette*—either because the sheriff was impressed by Albert Scardino's arguments about the benefits of encouraging competition or because, as people around the courthouse say, he was irritated at the *Evening Press*. The designation meant thousands of dollars a year in automatic advertising, and the advertising meant a subscription from every lawyer in the county, and the readership of lawyers meant one more sales point to potential advertisers. The *Georgia Gazette* is not the sort of alternative weekly in which official advertisements seem incongruous. It carries conventional business and social news, as well as some pieces that might offend potential advertisers and investors. It has never been known for sensationalism or scatology. Albert Scardino comes to work in a coat and tie. The *Gazette* had obviously taken some care to recognize the value that Savannah places on being respectable—which is why people in Savannah were astounded when Albert Scardino, against the wishes of the Mercer family, published a front-page story on February 11 revealing that George Mercer IV was not merely missing but presumed kidnapped, and that Michael Harper was the chief suspect.

Although the FBI agent at Spanky's had not said why he wanted to know if anybody had seen George Mercer IV or Michael Harper, Richard Sommers could think of only two reasons for the FBI to be involved—a large drug bust or a kidnapping. Sommers had started questioning some of Mercer's friends, and Scardino had bluffed a lot of the rest of the story out of a local police official. Although George Mercer III would not admit that his son had been kidnapped, it was clear that he did not want a story printed. "In the tried-and-true Savannah tradition, he called one of our stockholders," Scardino said later. It was argued, by the stockholder and others, that a story might endanger George Mercer IV if he really had been kidnapped. Albert Scardino was not persuaded. Mercer had been missing for ten days. The FBI was openly looking for him. When Scardino pressed an agent at the Savannah FBI office to say whether a story might be harmful, the agent would only repeat FBI policy about not commenting on a case in progress. Scardino says he could not see the sort of clear and present danger that would have caused him to go along with, say, the embargo on stories about the American Embassy employees hiding in the Canadian Embassy in Tehran. He telephoned George Mercer III to inform him that the story would be printed and to suggest that the Mercers make some preparation for the press interest that would follow—preparations such as designating a spokesman. The man Albert Scardino was dealing with, after all, was practically a friend of the family. George Mercer III said, as Scardino recalls it, "You'd better quit worrying about a couple of little birds and streams and start worrying about the value of human life."

A lot of people in Savannah thought that Albert Scardino made a mistake in printing the story. They thought that whatever he had learned in journalism school about the people's right to know simply did not apply. Some people thought that Scardino was just trying to make a splash. Some people thought the story might endanger young George Mercer's life. Some people were certain it would endanger Albert Scardino's newspaper. They were amazed that Scardino, whose background had obviously enabled him to understand how the city worked, could have suddenly chosen a course that was so patently self-destructive. The Mercers and those close to them were furious. The Trust Company of Georgia, where people like the Mercers have always done their banking, canceled a large advertising campaign that was about to begin in the *Gazette*. Twenty people wrote angry letters to the editor canceling their subscriptions. Some people pointedly snubbed Albert Scardino on the street. One aunt of George Mercer IV ended an angry telephone conversation with Marjorie Scardino late one night by saying that she hoped the Scardino children would be kidnapped. Albert Scardino heard that a regular subject of conversation at one luncheon table at the Oglethorpe Club was how to put the *Georgia Gazette* out of business.

Some people claimed that the *Gazette* story, aside from any danger it might pose for George Mercer IV, would warn Michael Harper to get out of town, and they may have been right: on the day the story was published, Harper left Savannah. He had the bad luck, though, to hitch a ride with a van that was stopped for speeding. Within a day, he was back in jail—held for a probation violation—and the FBI started amassing enough evidence to charge him with trying to extort forty-two thousand dollars from George Mercer III. Harper admitted nothing. He did say that if the police would let him out of jail he would help look for Mercer—probably in Greenville, South Carolina. Finally, toward the end of April, the police found Mercer themselves—buried in a shallow grave in the woods on the grounds of Armstrong State. He had been shot twice. Michael Harper was charged with murder.

The coroner said that George Mercer IV had probably been killed the first day he was missing. The implication that the *Gazette* story had appeared well after Mercer's death did not do much to reduce animosity toward Albert Scardino. "The real improper thing," Scardino has said, "was not that we endangered his life but that an upstanding, powerful, rich member of the community asked us to do something, and we ignored his request." A lot of people in Savannah would probably agree that there was something in the Mercers' anger beyond the genuine concern that any family would have for the safety of a son. Albert Scardino believes that people close to the Mercers were furious not simply because they had been defied but because they had been defied by someone whose family had been accepted into the group of people in Savannah accustomed to sorting out any difficulty with a telephone call. "That was the special betrayal that caused the special animosity," he says. Richard Sommers, who did not grow up with the Mercers and the Scardinos, has a different way of explaining the special animosity. "They didn't consider the crime a crime against society but a crime against them," he said recently. "They wanted it handled their way. We treated it as a crime against society. We made them common."

In July, Albert Scardino learned that at the end of 1980 the legal advertising that had been given to the *Gazette* a year and a half before would revert to the *Evening Press*—cutting the *Gazette*'s annual income by some thirty percent. The official who pushed for the reversion was the same sheriff who had been the *Gazette*'s champion. For a year and a half, of course, the *Evening Press* had been trying to win back the advertising, using every form of pressure at its disposal; the officials in charge of the designation were even lobbied by *News-Press* reporters assigned to cover their activities. Last spring, though, the officials began to receive telephone calls from what one of them has called "surprisingly high places." George Mercer III says he had no part in a campaign to deprive the *Gazette* of legal advertising, but he also acknowledges that he had heard about the telephone calls—made, perhaps, by people he describes as "misguidedly thinking they were representing me." There are, as Mercer suggests, a number of other ways that the reversion can be explained. For a while, Scardino himself had an ornate theory involving the Georgia senatorial election. It may even be, of course, that the sheriff simply changed his mind for sound reasons of public policy—although that interpretation is not bolstered by his refusal to discuss the matter. Albert Scardino now believes that the change was brought about by a combination of factors, but he has become convinced that one of them was a decision made over lunch at the Oglethorpe Club.

This winter, Michael Harper finally went on trial. Just before the trial started, he pleaded guilty to extortion, but he still contended that George Mercer IV had been alive the last time he saw him. According to his defense on the murder charge—revealed by the *Georgia Gazette* just before the trial got under way—everything had flowed from an attempt that he and George Mercer IV made to raise capital for a business they wanted to launch: a custom-stereo-speaker concern called Quest Labs. Harper said that he and Mercer and two other people, whom he refused to name, had tried to raise the capital by buying more than forty thousand dollars' worth of marijuana for resale. They had bought the marijuana on credit, Harper said, but it had been stolen before they could resell it. Under threat of death from the people who wanted their forty-two thousand, the four partners had decided to extort the money from George Mercer's father—with young George himself as a full participant. When the extortion scheme fell apart, Harper said, the four had fled in different directions. Harper calmly, sometimes brilliantly, defended his story on the witness stand. The jury took four hours to convict him of murder. He was sentenced to life imprisonment. Maintaining his innocence to the end, Harper said he could only offer his condolences to the Mercer family on George's death. "He was a friend of mine," Harper said.

Not many people in Savannah believed Harper's story. It sounded like a knockoff of the defense in the Bronfman kidnapping. Still, there are a lot of people who don't believe that, as the prosecution maintained, Michael Harper simply kidnapped George Mercer IV and shot him in cold blood to avoid having a prisoner to guard while negotiating the ransom. The *Gazette* coverage has constantly pointed out loose ends in that version of what happened. There are other stories floating around Savannah to explain what might have happened between George Mercer IV, the gullible son of a rich family, and the brilliant but twisted Michael Harper. A lot of them, like a lot of stories that try to explain mysteries these days, have to do with drugs. What makes some people in Savannah feel vulnerable is that George Mercer IV and Michael Harper knew each other at all. George Mercer III still finds it astonishing that the young people Michael Harper encountered didn't know or didn't care about his criminal record. Thinking about it recently, a resident of Savannah in his sixties said, "What this business with drugs and the new lifestyle and all that has changed is this: we didn't use to have to worry about our kids' mingling with someone like that."

After a short period of coolness, people close to the Mercers began to treat Dr. Peter Scardino and his wife the way they had treated them before George Mercer IV disappeared. George Mercer III is quick to express his respect for Dr. Scardino. The Scardinos were quick to express their sympathy to the Mercers. Whatever might have been done by relatives of the Mercers, Dr. Scardino has never thought of the Mercers themselves as the sort of people who could tell a mother that they hoped her children would be kidnapped. A few days after the trial, George Mercer III said, "I'm too drained spiritually and mentally and physically to have any animosity toward anybody," but he couldn't speak of Albert Scardino without the animosity's coming to the surface. The family's bitterness toward Scardino had been increased, in fact, by the *Gazette*'s coverage of the trial, which Mercer considered a matter of "gross callousness and insensitivity." Despite prosecution testimony to the contrary, the *Gazette* wrote, investigators had been told that

George Mercer IV did some minor dealing in marijuana and perhaps cocaine. Even the *News-Press*, whose coverage of the case had been dominated by politesse (a February feature about George Mercer IV and his friends had been headlined MERCER CALLED "TYPICAL" YOUNG MAN), had been forced to bring up the subject of drugs in covering Michael Harper's defense. A day after the sentencing, the Mercers, who had been dealing with the press through a family spokesman, asked a local television reporter they knew to come to their house with a film crew. Mrs. Mercer read a statement saying that their son had not been involved in drugs and could not have been involved in any schemes with Michael Harper. After she had read the statement, Mrs. Mercer added, "I would like to say that George was not a friend of this man."

In 1984, Albert Scardino won the Pulitzer Prize for a series of editorials on "various local and state matters." The Pulitzer had little effect on his newspaper's financial situation. In 1985, the Georgia Gazette *shut down.*

Don Rumsfeld Meets the Press

With condescending smile so tight,
He seems to take a great delight
Explaining to the press this fight,
As if they're kids who aren't too bright.
When wrong he needn't be contrite:
Don't might and arrogance make right?

The Years with Navasky

1982

When I was approached about writing a column for *The Nation,* I asked for only one guarantee: Would I be allowed to make fun of the editor? When it comes to civil liberties, we all have our own priorities.

The editor, one Victor S. Navasky, responded to this question with what I believe the novelists call a nervous chuckle.

Why would I consider involving myself in such an unpromising enterprise? My first mistake, many years ago, was an involvement with *Monocle: A Magazine of Political Satire* and its editor, the same Victor S. Navasky. In those days, when we were all young and optimistic, I used to assure Navasky that the lack of a sense of humor was probably not an insurmountable handicap for the editor of a satirical magazine. (He always responded with a nervous chuckle.) As an editor, after all, he was exacting. During the New York newspaper strike of 1963, *Monocle* published a parody edition of the *New York Post,* then predictably liberal, and I suggested as the front-page headline "Cold Snap Hits Our Town; Jews, Negroes Suffer Most." Navasky refused to use the headline merely because there was no story inside the paper to go with it—a situation that a less precise thinker might have considered part of the parody. Even then, I must say, Navasky's hiring policies seemed erratic—particularly his appointing as advertising manager a high-minded young man who found advertising so loathsome and disgusting that, as a matter of principle, he refused to discuss the subject with anyone.

What was most memorable about Victor S. Navasky at *Monocle,* though, was his system of payment to contributors. The largest check I received from *Monocle*—it was for organizing, chairing, and editing a panel on being a Yankee reporter in the South—was for three dollars. The panelists got two.

In the late sixties, *Monocle* folded. I wasn't surprised. My assurances to Navasky about his not needing a sense of humor had been quite insincere. Also, I had once observed the advertising manager's reaction to being phoned at the *Monocle* office by a prospective advertiser: "Take a message," he hissed at the secretary, as he bolted toward the door. "Tell him I'm in the bathroom. Get rid of him."

Then, only about ten years later, Navasky fetched up as the new editor of *The Nation.* Historians tell us that *The Nation* was founded in 1865 to give a long succession of left-wing entrepreneurs the opportunity to lose money every week in a good cause. I thought about Navasky's stewardship of *Monocle* for a while and then sat down to write him a letter of congratulations on his new job. It said, in its entirety, "Does money owed writers from *Monocle* carry over?" I received no reply.

I realize that this history with Navasky is one reason for some speculation by scholars in the field about the sort of negotiations that could have led to my agreeing to do a column for *The Nation.* ("If he got caught by Navasky twice, he must be soft in the head.") The entire tale can now be told. The negotiations took place over lunch in the Village. I picked up the check. I was prepared to remind Navasky that I was no longer the carefree young bachelor who barely complained about being stiffed regularly by the *Mono-*

cle bookkeepers but a responsible married man with two daughters and an automatic washer-dryer combination (stack model).

Once we had our food, Navasky made his first wily move. He suggested two very specific ideas for regular columns I might be interested in writing for *The Nation*—both of such surpassing dumbness that I long ago forgot precisely what they were. One of them, it seems to me, was on the practical side—a weekly gardening column, maybe, or a column of auto repair hints.

"Those are the silliest ideas I ever heard," I said, with relief. "The only column I might like to do is so far from Wobbly horticulture, or whatever you have in mind, that I don't mind mentioning it because you obviously wouldn't be interested—a thousand words every three weeks for saying whatever's on my mind, particularly if what's on my mind is marginally ignoble." If I was safe from an agreement, I thought I might as well take advantage of one of those rare opportunities to say "ignoble" out loud.

"It's a deal," the crafty Navasky said, putting down the hamburger I was destined to pay for and holding out his hand to shake on the agreement. Caught again.

"I hate to bring up a subject that may cause you to break out in hives," I said, "but what were you thinking of paying me for each of these columns?" I reminded him of the responsibilities of fatherhood and the number of service calls necessary to keep a stack-model washer-dryer in working order.

"We were thinking of something in the high two figures," Navasky said.

I tried to remain calm. When I phoned my high-powered literary agent, Robert (Slowly) Lescher, I said, "Play hardball, Slowly."

Slowly got him up to a hundred.

In an early column I asked why *The Nation* published only every other week in the summer even though the downtrodden are oppressed every day of the year. The question reflected the sort of attitude that caused one portion of *The Nation*'s readership to suspect that I was someone who had let the agony of the Scotts-boro Boys fade from his memory. I got a furious letter from one of those readers after I was asked by a television interviewer to describe *The Nation*. I had contemplated the question for a while and then said "Pinko." (When the interviewer said I surely had more to say about it than that, I said, "Yes, it's a pinko magazine printed on cheap paper, so if you make a Xerox copy of an article the Xerox is a lot better than the original.") As a stand-in for that portion of the readership, I included a character in my column called Harold the Committed, who was always asking me whether I'd like to see the world as we know it destroyed in a nuclear holocaust ("No, not really, Harold"). He once suggested that one of my daughters go to the Greenwich Village Halloween Parade as "the dangers posed to our society by the military industrial complex."

"Harold," I said, "We don't have anybody at home who can sew that well."

She went instead as a chocolate chocolate-chip ice cream cone with chocolate sprinkles.

The 401st

1982

The minute I saw *Forbes* magazine's list of the four hundred richest people in the United States, my heart went out to the person who was four hundred and first.

"He's nothing but some rich creep," Alice said.

"Creeps have feelings, too," I said. The phrase she had used suddenly conjured up a picture of the poor soul I was worrying about: Rich Creep, the Manhattan megadeal cutter and man about town. He lives in the Carlyle. He dates models. He eats breakfast at the Regency, where deals are made so quickly that a careless conglomerateur could find himself swallowing a middle-sized corporation while under the impression that he was just mopping up his egg yolk with the end of a croissant. He dines every night at places like La Caravelle and Le Cirque. "Bonsoir, Monsieur Cripp," the head-waiter says when Creep walks in with an icily beautiful fashion model who weighs eighty-eight pounds, twelve of which are cheekbones. "If I may make a suggestion, the overpriced veal is excellent tonight."

On the way to breakfast one morning, Creep happens to see the cover of *Forbes* at the Carlyle newsstand. THE RICHEST PEOPLE IN AMERICA, the headline says, THE *FORBES* FOUR HUNDRED. He snatches the magazine from the rack and, standing right in the lobby, he starts going through the list—at first methodically and then desperately. Finally, he turns and slinks back to his room. He can't face the crowd at the Regency. They'd pretend nothing has changed, but then they'd start trying to find some smaller corporation for him to swallow up—the way a nanny might sort through the picnic basket to find the smallest piece of white meat for the least adventurous child. He cancels his dinner date for the evening. He's afraid he might be given a cramped table near the kitchen, where the draft from the swinging doors could blow the fashion model into the dessert cart. He's afraid that the same French waiters who once hovered over him attentively while he ate ("Is your squab done expensively enough, Monsieur Cripp?") will glance in his direction and whisper to each other, "*Les petites pommes de terre*"—small potatoes.

So who says I have no sympathy for rich people? And this is nothing new. When *Fortune* first published its list of the five hundred largest corporations in America, my heart went out immediately to the corporation that was five hundred and first. Of course, I had no way of knowing its name—that tragic anonymity was the basis for my sympathy—but I always thought of it as Humboldt Bolt & Tube. I felt for the folks at Humboldt Bolt & Tube. I could see them giving their all to build their corporation into one of the largest corporations in America—busting unions, cutting corners on safety specifications, bribing foreign heads of state, slithering out of expensive pollution-control regulations—only to remain unrecognized year after year.

As the Fortune 500 became an institution in American life, I often pictured the scene at the Humboldt Country Club in Humboldt, Nebraska, when an important visitor from Wall Street asks casually over drinks, "Do you have any Fortune 500 companies in Humboldt?"

For a while, no one speaks. The "old man," as everyone in Humboldt calls Harrison H. Humboldt II, the son of Bolt & Tube's founder, looks out at the eighteenth green, the hint of a tear in his eye. His son, Harrison Humboldt III, tries to decide whether he should mention the second largest granite pit west of the Mississippi. He decides against it.

Part IV
R.I.P.

Russell Baker

2019

When Russell Baker was asked how he happened to become a *New York Times* columnist, he sometimes said that when he was a reporter covering Congress for the *Times,* he spent a lot of time sitting on the marble floor outside an executive session of some congressional committee, waiting for congressmen to come out and lie to him.

Russell would know that the congressmen were lying, and the congressmen would know that Russell knew they were lying, and Russell would know that the congressmen knew Russell knew they were lying. Furthermore, Russell said, having grown up partly in Baltimore, where neighbors were accustomed to sitting on those iconic Baltimore marble stoops while passing the time of day, he knew that too much sitting on marble could give you piles. So, Russell decided he'd rather be a columnist than a reporter.

Having heard Russell tell that story, I would not advise taking it literally; it was more in the spirit of a column he once wrote that began "When Francisco Franco died, he went to the New York Department of Motor Vehicles." Whatever tale he spun about how his role at the *Times* came about, it was inevitable that Russell Baker would become a newspaper columnist.

It's not that he didn't excel in aspects of the trade other than column writing. His memoir of a Depression-era childhood, *Growing Up*, won the Pulitzer Prize for biography, adding to the Pulitzer he had already won for commentary. By the time he freed himself from that dangerous marble floor, he'd forged a highly successful career as a reporter. In the nineties, he became known to millions as the host of *Masterpiece Theatre*, and after his retirement from the *Times* he wrote insightful *New York Review of Books* essays that were not subject to those 800-word space constraints he'd faced in column-writing—a calling he sometimes compared to doing ballet in a telephone booth.

He did that ballet for thirty-six years. Russell's obituary in the *Times* said that "he could be tongue-in-cheek one day and melancholy the next, then folksy, anguished, lyrical or acid." A *Times* reader who turned to the column entitled "Observer" might read a fanciful tale about a man who woke up to find himself with someone else's feet, and he might read this dead serious description of Richard Nixon: "There were darknesses in his soul that seemed to leave his life bereft of joy. He was a private, lonely man who never seemed comfortable with anyone, including himself, a man of monumental insecurities for whom public life, I thought, must be a constant ordeal."

Whatever mode Russell was in, he preferred the unadorned to the gussied-up. That was reflected in his own prose and in his comments on the tendency of Americans to write and speak the sort of English that turned "use" into "utilize" and "do" into "implement." He called it fat English. "Show them a lean, plain word that cuts to the bone," he wrote, "and watch them lard it with thick greasy syllables front and back until it wheezes and gasps for breath as it comes lumbering down upon some poor threadbare sentence like a sack of iron on a swayback horse."

Russell was an enemy of pretention and pomposity. A genuinely modest man himself, he made light of politicians who go around the country boasting of their humility, and he resisted the tendency to remove the president from the lives of ordinary Americans. "You never see a President waiting in the rain at a bus stop," he wrote. "After a while Presidents quite naturally forget that there are such things as bus stops, and if they stay in office long enough, they even forget that it rains."

After Russell and his wife, Mimi, moved from Washington to New York in 1974, he wrote somewhat less about politicians and somewhat more about the pleasures and perils—mostly perils—of the city. Once, while taking a walk near his apartment, he was barely missed by a raw potato that had apparently fallen from a tall building. "But what if the potato had scored a direct hit with fatal consequences?" he wrote. "After a certain age, most people probably speculate occasionally on the manner of their ultimate departure, but the possibility of becoming a potato victim was one that had never occurred to me. And I did not like it. . . . Even friends would find it hard to suppress private little smiles as they passed the news. Coming through a raw-potato near miss intact has one advantage. It is such a rare event that the odds against being involved in two during one lifetime are overwhelming. Hence, it is as close to statistical certainty as a thing can be that falling potato will not be the instrument of my farewell."

After a dozen years in New York, Russell and Mimi moved to Loudon County, Virginia, the county where he had spent his impoverished early years. Mimi died in 2015; she and Russell had been married for sixty-five years. Russell died in January of 2019, at age ninety-three. His son Alan said there'd been complications after a fall. Apparently, there was no potato involvement.

Molly Ivins

2007

n her columns Molly could, of course, make you laugh out loud, but that gift for humor may have masked some of her other talents. Occasionally—for instance, in her column about a visit to the Vietnam War memorial that brought back memories of a young man whose name is etched on that wall—she could make you cry. She could see through phoniness at long distances. The week after she died, Paul Krugman of *The New York Times* searched through the columns she'd done from Austin at a time when most of the Washington press corps was swallowing the administration's case for a war that would leave us triumphant in the Middle East. In January of 2003, she wrote, "I assume we can defeat Hussein without great cost to our side (God forgive me if that is hubris). The problem is what happens after we win. The country is 20 percent Kurd, 20 percent Sunni and 60 percent Shiite. Can you say, 'Horrible three-way civil war'?" Here's what she wrote that October: "I've got an even-money bet out that says more Americans will be killed in the peace than in the war and more Iraqis will be killed by Americans in the peace than in the war. Not the first time I've had a bet out that I hoped I'd lose."

Whatever talents she had in other areas, though, Texas politics provided her best hunting ground. She had a spectacular command of the vernacular, and she took an infectious joy in the show. It was Molly who wrote that if a certain congressman's IQ dropped any further he'd have to be watered twice a day. It was Molly, in search of that telling detail, who reported that a Texas gubernatorial candidate was so afraid of getting AIDS while visiting San Francisco that when he was in the shower he wore shower caps on his feet. The picture of Molly that lingers in the mind is her finishing a discourse on some particularly bizarre activities of a legislator and then saying, after a great laugh, "Ain't he a caution!"

Those of us who adored her adored her not for her formidable talents but for the sort of person she was. Her interest in helping the powerless was as genuine as her contempt for the public officials who concentrated on helping the powerful. Her loyalty had no bounds; no matter which journalistic organization actually paid her salary, I believe she was always, in her heart, Molly Ivins of *The Texas Observer*. Reporters visiting Texas on a political story got from Molly not resentment about intrusion on her turf but a jolly welcome to pull up a chair and watch what she referred to as "the finest form of free entertainment ever invented."

She was fantastic company. When you caught sight of her at a political convention, you realized that you were going to have some fun regardless of how long the speeches went on. When the *Nation* cruise stopped in St. Thomas, the thought of spending the day in what is essentially a shopping mall with sun could be brightened by Molly organizing an expedition looking for what she called, as I remember, slutty shoes.

She responded to having cancer the way you would have expected her to. If there's anything a Texas liberal knows about, it's fighting on even when the odds are stacked against you. When she was given an award in New York not long ago, she used her acceptance speech to tell the story of trying to find a prosthetic breast in Paris, hers having been lost in some misdirected luggage. As I remember Molly's description of her efforts to communicate, the French phrase she used for prosthetic breast was something like "that from which the baby sucks, except a false one of that from which the baby sucks," and the items offered by puzzled clerks included a baby bottle and a glass eye. In other words, she cussed cancer and she analyzed cancer and, being Molly, she even made fun of cancer. Weren't she a caution!

John Murphy

1988

When those who are familiar with the history of *The New Yorker* meet someone associated with the magazine, they often want to know if *The New Yorker* still harbors people who are—personally, spontaneously, without the polishing of the fourth draft—funny, in the way the people associated with the Algonquin Round Table were said to be funny. Over the years, some of the questioners were given an answer that surprised them. It began, "There's this guy in the makeup department. . . ." The guy was Johnny Murphy. There's no telling how Murphy would have fared at the Algonquin—his circle frequented O'Lunney's, an Irish bar across the street—but in these halls he was the wit most quoted.

It didn't seem to strike him as ironic that someone who was considered the funniest man at a magazine did no writing. He was from an oral tradition. Where Johnny Murphy's people came from, one definition of a writer is "a failed talker." People who are funny out loud usually have either a gift for the story or the ability to drop a telling remark into the appropriate lull. Murphy had both. He was a master of the instant deflating answer and of the straight-faced hilarious question. He was also a master at telling the sort of joke associated with salesmen and bartenders. The people at the Algonquin Round Table probably weren't much good at those.

He often transformed that sort of joke into an anecdote. He would wave the victim over and draw him close, as if about to divulge some juicy bit of office gossip. Then he would begin to confide what happened to him on the commuter train just the other day, or what he had seen on the way from Grand Central. Somehow, people who had been suckered weekly for twenty years, people who knew very well that nobody could see that many things on the way from Grand Central, would hear half the story before realizing that they were being nudged toward the punch line of a joke—maybe even a joke that had drawn groans at the Knights of Columbus when told by someone without the gift.

Murphy came to *The New Yorker* at seventeen and went to work on the switchboard. After a couple of years of combat duty with the Marines in the South Pacific, he began working in the makeup department—the small band of people who put the magazine together each week. At *The New Yorker,* the task of the people who lay out the magazine is not to make a weekly design statement but to accommodate the words and the drawings. When it's done gracefully, which is the way John Murphy did it, it's a form of sleight-of-hand—an art that succeeds by being invisible. Eventually, Murphy became head of the department. On some magazines, the person who has the responsibilities he had is called the art director—a title that would have struck him as riotously funny. He was nobody's art director. He considered himself a working man who did his job and took pleasure in his family (he and his wife, Helen, raised seven children) and didn't bellyache about whatever the good Lord sent his way. When a doctor told him that he had six months to live, he said, "Well, that's sixty cases of beer."

He lived longer than six months, but last week John Murphy died, at sixty-two. Except for the two years he spent in the Marines, he worked at this magazine, without interruption, for forty-five years. He was a joyful presence the whole way.

Richard Harris

1987

Richard Harris was what one editor at *The New Yorker* used to call a hard case. His judgments often seemed harsh. He did not give the benefit of the doubt. He tended to find almost any situation worse than it had first appeared. When he came across a sunny scene, his eye invariably fell on what was in shadow—the unworthy motive, the cowardly evasion, the failure to measure up. He viewed the world with an unfiltered gaze. Applying that gaze as a reporter for this magazine, he was able to turn out penetrating and prodigious articles on the American legislative and judicial process. The work exhausted him, but it never mellowed him. When he died last month, at the age of sixty-one, he was still a hard case.

He struggled to hit his stride as a writer, and then, when he had, he struggled with every piece he wrote. During his first several years at *The New Yorker*—when he tried his hand at a variety of subjects, mostly around the city—he had such difficulty getting pieces into the magazine that he often said he was considering publishing a book entitled "The Rejected Works of Richard Harris." Then, in 1964, nine years after his first piece ran in *The New Yorker,* he published an article called "The Real Voice"—a long, meticulously reported account of the efforts led by Senator Estes

Kefauver to pass a bill regulating the drug industry. He had found his calling. When "The Real Voice" was published as a book, one reviewer said it should "enter literature as a classic of muckraking, alongside the works of Ida Tarbell and Lincoln Steffens."

Thereafter, Harris concentrated on government and politics and the judicial process. He wrote about the forty-five-year effort of the American Medical Association to prevent government-subsidized medical care. He wrote a series on where the rights guaranteed in the first ten amendments to the Constitution stood in modern America. He wrote articles on the FBI and on a delegate to the Republican National Convention and on a senatorial campaign in Tennessee. He wrote a number of pieces on the Watergate crisis. Whatever the subject, the pieces had Harris's imprint. They were exhaustively researched. They were written in strong, uncluttered prose. They were unsparing. They tended to find the situation worse than it had first appeared. The book that came out of his series on the Bill of Rights was subtitled "Tales of Tyranny in America." In a piece about the Justice Department's transition from the Johnson administration to the Nixon administration he warned, three years before Watergate, that the policies of Nixon's Justice Department amounted to a step toward "abandonment of the rule of law." Near the end of that piece he wrote, "Most people no longer seem to care—if, indeed, they know—what is happening to their country."

He cared a lot. Like many deeply skeptical reporters, he was a closet idealist, accustomed to almost constant disappointment. He was, someone close to him once said, "a gloomy optimist." Unlike Diogenes the Cynic, who walked around in broad daylight with a lantern "in search of an honest man," Harris actually hoped to find one. Occasionally, he did. In a couple of cases, the honest man turned out to be, of all things, a United States senator.

Although he spent years at war with people in this country who called themselves conservatives—a war mainly over his constant warnings that they were doing their best to abridge individual liberties—he was himself a man of conservative instincts. He set great store by old-fashioned, idealistic values. His idealism was reflected in some of the titles he used, even though he would have pointed out, somewhat testily, that they were used ironically: "A Sacred Trust" and "Honor Bound" and, most of all, "Justice." In an essay on the Watergate prosecutions, he wrote about justice this way: "The decency of a society, it is said, can be measured by its criminal laws. In a crude society, the purpose of those laws is to secure order. In a civilized society, the purpose is to secure order and freedom. And in a good society, the purpose is to secure order and freedom fairly."

There are intense reporters who can turn off the unfiltered gaze, but Harris was not among them. An acquaintance could disappoint as easily as a congressman could. Harris looked at, say, a publishing house he was dealing with the same way he might look at the Department of Health and Human Services. He often found himself having to cross people off his list. He was a man of great charm—his comments were often witty, his manners bordered on the courtly—but he did not consider the spreading of good cheer to be among his responsibilities. He was often angry. In 1978, he got angry enough at *The New Yorker* to walk out. The next time he submitted anything was this summer, when, in the space of a few weeks, he handed in two pieces—both departures in form from his previous work. When the first piece came in, a friend at the magazine said, "Considering it's Harris, I suppose you could say that if he stayed away only nine years he wasn't really mad."

The people who knew him well—people who hadn't been crossed off the list, people who had somehow found their way back on, even some people who believed they were probably off for good—thought of him as a splendid companion and a fiercely loyal friend. His friendships were intense. His friends were sometimes exhilarated by contemplating the possibility that they were living up to his expectations. For his part, he seemed to relish his friends the way he relished those occasional honest men he came across in his work—valuing them all the more, perhaps, because discovering them had been a pleasant surprise. If they were in need, he showed up as if under contract—honor bound. But the gaze never softened. The conversation was provocative. The jury remained out. "He made it difficult," the person closest to him at his death said last week, "but he was worth the trouble."

John Gregory Dunne

2003

A novel I once wrote about working at a newsmagazine had a claimer rather than a disclaimer, and the claimer said, "The character of Andy Wolferman is based on John Gregory Dunne, though it tends to flatter." Andy Wolferman was a brilliantly resourceful gossip who came into the office of the protagonist most mornings and said, "This you will not believe." John seemed unfazed by being cast in that role. He always assumed that keeping people informed was part of his duties. After the book came out, he did say, "Just as a matter of curiosity, why was my character Jewish?" And I said, "That's the 'tends to flatter' part, John. You don't want to be lace-curtain Irish all your life, do you?" And he said, "Boarding school Irish, Calvin, boarding school Irish."

He would have corrected me just as quickly if I had placed the Dunnes too high rather than too low on the Irish totem pole. He enjoyed recalling that at the reception his mother gave to introduce her new daughter-in-law to the swells of West Hartford, after John and Joan Didion married in California, there were only two Protestants in attendance—Joan and the society reporter for the *Hartford Courant*. On any subject, including the life of John Gregory Dunne, he prided himself on peeling away one more layer of the onion to get at the plain truth. Sometimes, what John found at the core was discomfiting. Sometimes it was funny. In John's hands, remarkably, it was often discomfiting and funny.

He got a great kick out of being the Irishman who was revealed after the boarding school layer was peeled away. We sometimes talked about what we called his Irish drawer—the imaginary file drawer he devoted totally to grudges. Crossing John wasn't the only way to get into the Irish drawer. A less-than-respectful review of one of Joan's books could put the reviewer in there before the ink was dry. Anybody who chose to mention his daughter, Quintana, in print was skating on thin ice, with the freezing depths of the Irish drawer beneath him. A slight to one of John's friends could land you in the Irish drawer, even if John, who took some pride in having what used to be called an Irish temper, had been in a ferocious argument with that same friend just a week before.

Some of his friends got regular phone calls from John first thing in the morning, sort of to bring us up to speed. The text for the day's lesson might be an essay in *The New York Review of Books* or half a dozen histories of World War II he'd just read or some intelligence from someone he'd had dinner with the night before or an item in the tabloids. John was devoted to the tabloids. He didn't bother to identify himself. Who else would be starting a conversation in New York at 9 A.M. by saying, "Did you happen to see the op-ed page of the *Los Angeles Times* this morning?"

So for some of us, there's a particular time of day when memories of John are especially sharp, and when we're most likely to look back at the great good fortune of having been recipients of those phone calls—of having heard what John had gleaned from his astonishing range of reading and socializing, and had managed to polish to a fine sheen before breakfast. It's at around 9 A.M., with the phone not ringing, that I'm most likely to think back on those particularly treasured occasions when I picked up the phone and actually heard the unmistakable voice of John Gregory Dunne saying, "This you will not believe."

Morley Safer

2016

M orley Safer once told me that Don Hewitt, the founding producer of *60 Minutes,* hated ambiguity. That may be one reason that Morley fit right in. Both on and off the job, he could be exquisitely explicit. Interviewed on Larry King's program not many years ago, he was asked what he thought of reality TV. He said that reality TV was sleazy and manipulative. King had used the show *Survivor* as an example. "But it's on your own network," King said. "Sleazy and manipulative," Morley repeated.

On *60 Minutes* in 1993, he famously compressed his opinion of a lot of modern art into two words: "worthless junk." His own art did not trigger an intense search for meaning. It was unambiguous. In 1980, when he had a show in a SoHo gallery of his renditions of hotel rooms—a show that prompted *Time* magazine to call him "the Matisse of the Marriott"—he summed up his paintings in a phrase: "they show exactly what's there." He was, in his art as well as in life, a realist. On the occasion of that SoHo show, he explained to a reporter what he was after, using the Morley combination of flat fact and sly wit. Here's what he said: "Capturing the unique colors—the burnt oranges, the vivid turquoises—that are frequently encountered in American hostelries poses an extraordinary challenge to the artist. You realize that the bedspreads and rugs in Holiday Inns were designed for one purpose—so that people can get sick on them and it won't show."

As a traveling man myself in those days, I had a critique of the show that I thought met Morley on his own terms. I told him that, as much as I'd liked it, I had to point out that in his painting of one room—as I remember, it was at the Dallas–Fort Worth Airport Hilton—he had the night table on the wrong side of the bed. He told me that I was mistaken. The painting showed exactly what was there.

Morley's approach to his painting was one of the many ways in which he was conservative, in the sense that he resisted change. A campaign lawn sign I saw this summer carried the slogan "Change is Progress." Morley, with that information alone, would have voted for the other guy. He stuck to his style of painting. He was reluctant to give up his old Royal typewriter for a computer. He clung to his cigarettes. And he never quit being a Canadian. In fact, there was a time when he and several other Canadian expatriates formed what they called the Canadian Government in Exile. Morley was the prime minister.

From his stories of the Canadian Government in Exile, I could imagine him presiding over a cabinet meeting in the manner I'd seen him preside over a Passover Seder—that is, with some seriousness in dealing with the parts he considered important and a willingness to make an executive decision about which boring parts could be dispensed with. According to Morley, the Government in Exile didn't operate quite like the government in Ottawa. He told me, for instance, that one cabinet minister was elevated to that post for the suggestion that Canada name as its national bird the black fly. The government in exile was in favor of Canadian bilingualism, although it thought the two languages should be English and Yiddish.

When Morley was interviewed on the *Today* program about

that 1980 show of his art, Tom Brokaw asked him why he spent those evenings while out on a story doing paintings of hotel rooms. Morley said, "It beats drinking with the crew." I suspect the crew missed Morley when he was engaged with his paintbrushes. He was terrific company. At his retirement, he'd done nine hundred nineteen *60 Minutes* stories, meaning he was conversant with at least nine hundred nineteen subjects. And I suspect he had an anecdote or two stored up for each one of those. We're going to miss the stories. We're going to miss the anecdotes.

My favorite anecdote—partly because it reflected what Morley thought about a reporter being a celebrity—was from a story he'd done on Kwajelein Atoll in the Marshall Islands, a remote speck of land that the United States has sometimes used for missile tests. One night Morley was, in fact, drinking with the crew at the local gathering spot, called the Kwaj Lodge. There was some entertainment, and at some point the MC said, "I understand we have an American television personality in the audience tonight, Morley Safer." Morley waved, and then, after the applause had died down, the MC said, "Will you give us a song, Morley?" So Morley did.

Andrew Kopkind

1994

W e were, God forgive us all, Ivy League newspaper editors who had gathered to discuss launching a magazine called *Ivy*. This was 1956. The word "elitism" was not yet abroad in the land. Andrew D. Kopkind, the editor of the Cornell paper, was the one person at the table to bring up the possibility that a magazine aimed exclusively at the Ivy League might seem rather, well, snooty. Andy Kopkind and I were friends for the next thirty-eight years, and the impression that he knew some things the rest of us hadn't yet figured out never left me.

He was a large, expansive, playful, kindhearted man with a slight stammer and a generous laugh and an exquisitely developed sense of the ridiculous. When he died, a London newspaper that called him "the most important radical journalist of his generation" added that he was "easily the most entertaining." I would have described him as the most entertaining person of his generation. If the extraordinary array of people who felt close to him—old comrades from the sixties, interns at *The Nation* who met him last year, even some doctors who hadn't expected someone so ill to be such good company—had been polled on the question of the perfect companion for a long car ride, he would have won in a breeze.

I started taking long car rides with Andy in Europe, in the late fifties. From the start he believed that a good one-liner rose above politics. In the seventies, when he was living in Vermont, I happened to ask him what Goddard, the famously avant-garde college there, was like. He paused, giving the subject some consideration, and then said, "Cockamamie is the word that leaps to mind." He could talk about anything, and he had a memory that, years after the fact, permitted him to summon up a brilliantly textured word-picture of the International Control Commission plane's arrival in Hanoi or to give a verbatim rendition of Danny Kaye's first album.

For a few years, in the early seventies, my wife, Alice, and I hardly saw Andy. I think he needed to separate himself from old friends for a while as he sorted out his life. In those years we felt that without him, our family had contracted. Occasionally, one of us would turn to the other and say, "God, I miss Andy!"

When he reappeared, the rhythm of his life had changed. He was disentangled from what he called "careerism." He had come to terms with being gay and had begun a relationship with the film maker John Scagliotti that endured for the rest of his life. No matter where he lived from then on, his headquarters were in southern Vermont.

His political beliefs remained undiluted. In the sixties, he had come to believe that what seemed like two sides in the great American political debate actually amounted to one side, and not a side he wanted to be on; he never joined up. And his interests were broader than ever. Personally and professionally, he gloried in being what he described as a "Zeitgeist sniffer." I was again asking him to explain, say, the dynamics of gentrification or the origin of grunge dress.

In the last year of Andy's life, I spent more time in his company than I had since those early car rides. He was just as funny, just as unwilling to let a plate be cleared away when a dumpling was still on it. He could still do Danny Kaye. Nearly five hundred people showed up at his memorial service. I think all of them felt part of an expanded family while he was alive. I think all of them will find themselves saying, "God, I miss Andy!"

Murray Kempton

1997

Yes, it would be surprising if the Last Gentleman turned out to be a newspaper reporter. But Murray Kempton, who may have been the Last Gentleman, definitely identified himself as "newspaper reporter" on his tax forms. "And even now, when my entitlement to make that quiet affirmation seems to diminish year by year," he said in a speech in 1995, at a time when his entitlement had not diminished at all, "a newspaper reporter is as fervently all I want to be as it ever was."

Many brand-name journalists could call themselves reporters only at the risk of drawing sneers from the working stiffs in the newsroom. But Murray Kempton, a palpably erudite columnist who wrote sentences so ornate that they could inspire attempts at team parsing, was accepted as a peer by the working stiffs, even as they recognized that he was, column by column, peerless. Hundreds of them had covered stories with him—looking forward to a courtroom recess or a news-conference delay as a time when Murray might trot out a few of the sentences he was auditioning for his lead or might muse on some human characteristic that somehow linked, say, Montaigne and Bessie Smith and Frank Costello.

Like any true gentleman, he had manners that were unaffected by the station of his listener. Whether bidding farewell to a senator or a taxi driver, he'd often use a phrase that sounded as natural coming from Murray as it must have sounded coming from his great-grandfather the Episcopal bishop: "God bless you." When we first met, during the 1961 Freedom Rides, my seven or eight months in the South constituted virtually the entirety of my experience in the trade, but Murray, who had covered the Emmett Till case, discussed the civil rights movement with me in a tone he might have been expected to reserve for addressing Thurgood Marshall.

However many Southern race stories or Washington hearings or national political conventions Murray Kempton covered, he was essentially a local New York columnist, someone who treated the Associated Press daybook as his menu and then headed for the entrée—traveling, even well into his seventies, on his bicycle, dressed in a three-piece suit and the silver leg clips presented to him by his *Newsday* colleagues on one of his birthdays.

Three renowned local columnists died in 1997, a year when the Grim Reaper seemed to have it in for people who had gone through hell already trying to make four or five deadlines a week. All of them specialized in the observed rather than in the deskbound meditations on the news that are sometimes known in the trade as thumb-suckers. Mike Royko, in the Chicago tradition, was a tough guy from the neighborhoods; Herb Caen, in the San Francisco tradition, was a boulevardier who sang the praises of what he called Baghdad by the Bay. Murray Kempton, an awesomely insightful man working in a city known for its cynicism, was, somehow, a moralist.

When a public figure seemed to have acted dishonorably, Kempton's disdain could be profound; the damning judgment was usually presented elegantly, often in the tone of someone who had reached it reluctantly. But he could also find honorable behavior in unexpected places. I always thought he operated on the assumption that a variety of uncontrollable factors, from being presented with an employment opportunity at a moment of financial distress to having an uncle in the rackets, might lead people into lines of work that someone of Murray Kempton's politics and sensibility would ordinarily be expected to deplore—contract killer, for instance, or Republican senator. Murray was interested in how people played the hand they'd been dealt.

He had the true reporter's eye for facts that had to be faced. In one of our first conversations, he paused after discussing the bravery of a CORE Freedom Rider whom he had known from dangerous demonstrations through the years and then said, "Of course, the man would walk a mile to get beaten up." But in judging human frailty, he was someone who knew, as his great-grandfather had known, that we are all but poor sinners—the mighty, the commentator himself, and those he often referred to in columns as his betters.

Knowing the possibility of grace and redemption in every poor sinner, Murray was uncanny in his ability to find some way in which almost anyone who had been smitten was morally superior to those who had done the smiting—although if he ever discovered admirable qualities in a fallen newspaper publisher, it escaped my notice. For years, there was, in effect, a sort of office pool in the city's newsrooms on whether anyone was beyond Murray's capacity for sympathizing with the beleaguered or disgraced. Whoever had Richard M. Nixon in the pool lost. So did whoever had Carmine (the Snake) Persico.

Part V

CONTROVERSIES

Out of Style

1994

The Stamps, Coins and Camera columns
have been discontinued.
  —Notice in the *Times,* Sunday, January 2, 1994

J ust like that. Gone. Vaporized. It was as if they had never been there. A reader who had returned from a few weeks out of town might have assumed, as he leafed through the trendy new Styles section looking for tips on how to acquire the mannerisms of an in-the-know teenager, that the authors of three columns—"Stamps," "Coins," "Camera"—had fallen ill at once, struck down by some odd virus that affects only obsessive hobbyists.

According to an accompanying notice, "Chess" and "Bridge" will continue to appear on certain weekdays but are no longer part of the Sunday paper. Apparently, the back pages of the Styles section will now be given over completely to weddings. It's as if those hip kids who run the weekly Friday-night sock hop had persuaded the principal that permitting the wonks of the Chess Team and the Stamp Club to hang around for meetings on the same evening just ruins everybody's fun.

As it happens, I have no interest in stamps, coins, cameras, chess, or bridge. My only hobby is reading the wedding announcements in the Sunday *Times*. Over the years, I've developed the same sort of skill in making small distinctions in the backgrounds of the bride and groom that stamp collectors make in various Luxembourg commemoratives. I know the pecking orders of schools and suburbs; I know which debutante balls can be bought into and which are authentically snooty, I know where the fissures run between and within ethnic groups. I long ago acknowledged the source of my interest: I enjoy contemplating the sort of tensions that are likely to come out at the reception. You think that's a mean-spirited basis for a hobby? There are coin collectors whose motives are not so pure, either.

Given my own interests, you might think the *Times* announcement would cause me to celebrate—to treat myself to some champagne and the kind of hors d'oeuvres you'd expect to find at the wedding of a Greek-American Columbia Law School graduate from Ozone Park to an intern whose B.A. is from Yeshiva. That might have been my response, in fact, if it hadn't been for my childhood friend Herbert.

For many years, Herbert has read the Sunday *Times* almost exclusively for its coverage of coins, stamps, and cameras. I say almost because if he had a little extra time on his hands it was his custom to peruse the chess and bridge columns as well. "Chess is still going to be in on Tuesdays," I said to Herbert shortly after reading the announcement. "You'll be able to catch the bridge column five days a week—just not on Sunday."

"Thanks," Herbert said, without enthusiasm. "It's nice of you to say so."

"Herbert," I said, "you can't take this personally. It's not as if the editors of the *Times* got together and decided that there's a certain sort of reader they don't want to have around on Sundays."

I felt I had to say that, because, frankly, Herbert has always had a little problem in the self-esteem department. Some of his friends think it dates back to the time when the principal asked the Chess Team and the Stamp Club to move their meetings to Thursday nights for some trumped-up reason that everybody knew was a cover for the distaste of the Friday sock hop crowd. Herbert was recording secretary of the Stamp Club that year.

"I guess there's no chance of my letter getting in now," Herbert said, referring to a letter he'd written to the stamps column about a Nicaraguan air-mail stamp he felt was underappreciated.

"Maybe the chess column would run it on a slow Tuesday," I said.

"No, it's gone," Herbert said.

He's right, of course. On Sunday mornings now, I can picture Herbert in his favorite armchair. The Styles section, featuring a front-page piece on whether the fashion of wearing navel rings has played itself out, lies unread at his feet. He's staring into space. With that picture in my mind, it's difficult for me to conjure up wedding receptions. I still read the announcements—actually, I've been looking for something that might pique Herbert's interest, such as the son of a noted coin collector hitching up with the associate editor of a stamp magazine—but often on Sunday mornings now I stare into space myself.

Dirty Words

2011

n 1993, when *The New Yorker* for the first time ran a photograph of a bare-breasted actress, a subscriber wrote me to express outrage at what had happened to a magazine once known for its elegant, understated prose. The only defense I could think of was that they were small breasts, so you could say that the tradition of understatement was still alive. But then I started wondering, "Why did she write *me*?" Was she implying that it was because of people like me that a once high-minded magazine had come to this?

I should explain.

My father and William Shawn, the second editor of *The New Yorker*, were born within six months of each other, in the first decade of the twentieth century, and they had an identical abhorrence of language that was obscene or off-color or crude. At his most exasperated, my father would say, "For cryin' out loud." When I was a child, in Kansas City, I thought "for cryin' out loud" was the oath grownups reserved for particularly dire circumstances. Even after I learned some more offensive phrases, I would have never used them in my father's presence, and I suppose I assumed, when I joined *The New Yorker* in 1963, that I wouldn't use them in Mr. Shawn's magazine, which was thought of as straitlaced even by the standards of the period.

I think the first time it occurred to me that Mr. Shawn and I might have some problems about language was in 1965. I had done a piece on the research in dreaming sleep, and it included the fact that cats deprived of dreams seemed intent on mounting other cats. As we were closing the piece, my editor said that Mr. Shawn, without insisting, was wondering if we might use a euphemism for "mount." I said, "What did he have in mind?" And the editor said, "Made a sexual advance toward."

"But it's a cat!" I said. "We're talking about a cat!" We stuck with "mount."

A couple of years later, I did a piece about Lester Maddox, then the governor of Georgia, and his campaign to bring virtue of the no-drinking, no-blasphemy, no-miniskirt variety to the statehouse. I'd written that, apparently forgetting about his campaign, Maddox had said the federal government could take its education money and "ram it." Mr. Shawn said no to "ram it." I went in to see him. I said I had no burning desire to get dirty words into *The New Yorker*. What he was telling me, though, was that I had to stop listening when the other reporters were allowed to keep listening, and I didn't know if I could do that. Finally, he said he'd think about it overnight.

I went home and poured myself a large scotch and told my wife that I didn't know what I would do if the answer the next morning was no. I had enormous respect for William Shawn. I even respected his resistance to unseemly language. My argument about other magazines having carried the Maddox quote had not cut any ice, because he didn't care what other magazines did. But how could I justify withholding something that was relevant—even something silly that was relevant—from the readers? Was it really conceivable that *The New Yorker* and I would come to a parting of the ways over "ram it"—a relatively inoffensive phrase uttered by a man who was, to use a word Mr. Shawn probably wouldn't have allowed in the magazine either, a pissant. The next morning, Mr. Shawn phoned me and said that "ram it" could be in the magazine.

I know what you analytically inclined Easterners are thinking. I did have a burning desire to get unseemly language into *The New Yorker* because I was acting out against my father, whom I deeply resented for sleeping with my mother. People from Kansas City don't hold with that sort of thinking, and, in defense of our way of seeing things, I just might mention that Mr. Shawn and I didn't have another confrontation over language for seventeen years.

When we did, it was around the time *The New Yorker* was, as the Wall Street people say, in play, and rumors that it might be sold by the Fleischmann family were causing great nervousness in the halls. A farmer in Nebraska had pulled a gun on a couple of deputies who had come to repossess some of his farm equipment, and he eventually found himself inside his house surrounded by the Nebraska State Police SWAT team. Talking on the phone with the SWAT team negotiator, the farmer suddenly shouted, "It's the goddamned fucking Jews." As my story went on to explain, he had fallen into the hands of some prairie fascists who were then preying on farmers with economic problems. When my editor read that quote, he said something like "You've got to be kidding!" or "Lotsa luck on that one."

I said I felt I had to talk to Mr. Shawn about the quote, which was vital to my story, although I knew he had a lot on his plate, and I wasn't going to get on my high horse if he said no. Mr. Shawn asked about the possibility of a euphemism. I told him that the quote was from a state police transcript. We talked about other options for a while, and finally he said, "Just go ahead and use it." I mumbled something and backed slowly out of the office, thinking that if I made an abrupt move, he might change his mind. The quote appeared in *The New Yorker* the next week, and I'm happy to say nobody seemed to notice.

These days, of course, such words do not draw attention, and, as a reporter, I'm grateful for having no restrictions on what I can listen to or look at. In a recent piece I did about a shooting in southwestern Kansas, one of the people involved had among his tattoos not only a life-size hangman's noose that encircled his neck and ran down his chest but also a word on the inside of each bicep that, when he assumed a strongman's pose, combined to say, "Fuck You." It was a detail I couldn't have left out, particularly because he struck the strongman's pose for the final time a few seconds before he was shot to death. In a piece about someone being driven off Grand Manan Island amidst allegations of drug dealing, I was able to use a quote from a local I would have hated to leave out: "He had asshole issues that were much larger than just being a drug dealer."

Still, when I'm in my own voice rather than, say, quoting somebody or somebody's tattoos, I would never use offensive language in *The New Yorker*. I've always known that my father and Mr. Shawn would disapprove.

The Life and Times of
Joe Bob Briggs, So Far

1986

The problem was how to deal with trashy movies. It's a common problem among movie reviewers. What, exactly, does the film critic of a main-line American daily newspaper do about movies like *The Night Evelyn Came Out of the Grave* and *Malibu Hot Summer* and *Bloodsucking Freaks*? Does he pick one out, on a slow week, and subject it to the sort of withering sarcasm that sometimes, in his braver daydreams, he sees himself using on the executive editor? Does he simply ignore such movies, preferring to pretend that a person of his sensibilities could not share an artistic universe with such efforts as *Mother Riley Meets the Vampire* and *Driller Killer* and *Gas Pump Girls*?

The Dallas Times Herald had that problem, and in late 1981 it seemed to have stumbled onto a solution. The assistant managing editor for features, Ron Smith, had asked the movie reviewer, a young man named John Bloom, to look into the question of why drive-in movie theaters, which were folding in most places, still thrived in patches of the country that included the area around Dallas. Bloom came back with a proposal: He could review the sort of movies that play in Texas drive-ins—they are sometimes called exploitation movies—through the persona of a fictional drive-in customer who was able to distinguish between a successful zombie-surfing movie and a zombie-surfing movie that didn't quite work. "I had been thinking about doing a column from someone with a personality that is completely opposite of what we think is tasteful," Bloom recalled not long ago. "I had been saying to Ron, 'What would happen if a movie critic loved *I Spit on Your Grave* and hated *Dumbo*? What if this guy suddenly had an aesthetic revelation and started looking at Charles Bronson as an *auteur*?'"

Bloom first suggested a reviewer named Bobo Rodriguez. He envisioned Bobo as a "kind of all-purpose ethnic, like Andy Kaufman's foreigner: you don't know what nationality he is but he's quintessentially foreign." Smith rejected Bobo Rodriguez as a character Dallas minorities were bound to find offensive no matter how many times they were assured that the real target was pretentious film criticism or respectable Anglo moviegoers. The character Bloom came up with instead was a young redneck he called Joe Bob Briggs. Smith liked that idea. He decided to give Joe Bob some space in the back pages of *Weekend,* the paper's Friday entertainment tabloid—a low-priority operation that was generally avoided by reporters and was probably best known to readers as the part of the *Times Herald* most likely to come off on your hands. In January of 1982, the *Times Herald* ran Joe Bob Briggs's first movie review, under the heading "Joe Bob Goes to the Drive-In." The movie being considered was *The Grim Reaper,* in which the title character "likes to kill people and then chew on them for a while." Joe Bob liked it.

In an accompanying piece introducing his new colleague to the readers of the *Times Herald,* John Bloom said he had met Joe Bob at the snack bar of the Century Drive-In, in Grand Prairie, Texas, during an all-night Bela Lugosi marathon. According to Bloom, Joe

Bob was, at nineteen, a drive-in authority of enormous experience: he had seen sixty-eight hundred drive-in movies and had still found time for at least three marriages. Experience had not brought a strong sense of responsibility. Only a month or so after the column began—a month during which John Bloom found a Brazilian film called *Pixote* to be "powerful" and "unsettling," and Joe Bob praised not only *Mad Monkey Kung Fu* ("We're talking serious chopsocky here") but a snakebite horror movie that his girlfriend of the moment, May Ellen Masters, refused to watch with her eyes open—the new columnist disappeared. (Bloom had taken some vacation time.) Bloom finally reported that he had found Joe Bob—in jail, in Bossier City, Louisiana. Joe Bob had been arrested for beating up an auto mechanic named Gus Simpson, who not only had sold Joe Bob's baby-blue Dodge Dart for parts to Junior Stebbens, of Mineral Wells, but also had been discovered by Joe Bob with the perfidious May Ellen Masters in a room at the Have-A-Ball Tourist Courts. By that time, it was clear from the volume of inquiries about Joe Bob's whereabouts that "Joe Bob Goes to the Drive-In," which Smith had envisioned as an occasional feature, or maybe even a onetime event, had become a Friday staple of the *Times Herald.*

Eventually, Bloom's authorship became a sort of open secret in the Dallas newspaper world, but for the better part of a year it was a real secret even from the people who worked in the *Times Herald* newsroom. A lot of readers believed that the Joe Bob Briggs column was in fact written by a nineteen-year-old redneck who had seen sixty-eight hundred drive-in movies. "They bought that," Ron Smith said recently, sounding amazed as he recalled it. "There were people on this staff—serious newspaper people—who bought that." Many of those who finally became suspicious, of course, settled their suspicions on John Bloom. He was, after all, the only person on the paper who claimed to have met Joe Bob. He was the movie reviewer. His initials were similar to Joe Bob's initials. Close readers might have even noticed that when Bloom wrote about Joe Bob in those first weeks of shepherding the column into the paper he fell into rather Joe Bobbian phrasing himself—as when he wrote that Joe Bob's adventures around Bossier City had left his head looking like "the inside of a Big Mac after it's been left on the dashboard three or four days," or when he wrote that Joe Bob's previous car had been ruined at the Ark-La-Tex Twin "when a dough-head in a Barracuda crunched his rear door and scared Dede Wilks half out of her halter top." Bloom's basic defense against the accusations of authorship was that he could hardly have been less like Joe Bob. A soft-spoken, reserved, almost withdrawn young man who had graduated with honors from Vanderbilt, Bloom drove a Toyota instead of a baby-blue 1968 Dodge Dart. He spoke with a trace of Southwestern accent, but it would have been difficult to imagine him using Joe Bobbisms like "He don't give a diddly" or expressing his admiration for an actress by saying, "Bootsie is not just another humongous set of garbanzas." An admirer of foreign films, Bloom wrote essays on the *nouvelle vague* while Joe Bob was rating movies according to the amount of innards displayed ("We're talking Glopola City") and the number of severed body parts that can be seen rolling away and the number of breasts exposed ("the garbanza department").

Bloom wanted Joe Bob to "talk about movies the way most people talk about movies: they give the plot, with emphasis on their favorite scenes, then they sum up what they think of it." Joe Bob tended to tell the plot ("So this flick starts off with a bimbo getting chained up and killed by a bunch of Meskins dressed up like Roman soldiers in their bathrobes"), and his summaries eventually developed into his best-known trademark: "Sixty-four dead bodies. Bimbos in cages. Bimbos in chains. Arms roll. Thirty-nine breasts. Two beasts (giant lizard, octopus). Leprosy. Kung fu. Bimbo fu. Sword fu. Lizard fu. Knife fu. Seven battles. Three quarts blood. A 39 on the vomit meter. . . . Joe Bob says check it out."

What some readers wondered about such material was not who

was writing it but how it got into the newspaper. The short answer was that it was sneaked in. Ron Smith and Bloom, playing around with ways to handle a section of the paper that even the editors didn't read very closely, hadn't taken the Joe Bob gimmick seriously enough as a long-term proposition to consult any of the sort of editors Joe Bob began referring to in print as high sheriffs. If a gathering of top editors had been presented with a formal plan to run a truly tasteless weekly column by a fictional trash-movie fanatic, Joe Bob Briggs would presumably have gone the way of Bobo Rodriguez. *The Dallas Times Herald* was a lively newspaper, but even lively newspapers are cautious institutions. As it was, the Joe Bob column impressed itself on the consciousness of the paper's principal editors after it had begun gaining a foothold with the readers. Not long after that, it became apparent that "Joe Bob Goes to the Drive-In" was on its way to becoming the most talked-about feature in the paper. "You can't imagine what incredible appeal it had in those early months," someone who was at the *Times Herald* at the time said recently. "When the Friday paper came out, everyone in the newsroom stopped whatever he was doing to turn to *Weekend* and find out what outrage Joe Bob was perpetrating now." The same thing was happening all over town. Friday was Joe Bob Day among young professional people who worked in the shiny new office buildings of downtown Dallas. Friday was also Joe Bob Day among folks who, in the words of one *Times Herald* reporter, "were grateful that there was finally someone in the paper who wrote normal."

The top editors of the *Times Herald* were constantly being reassured that the perpetration of outrages was all right. It was satire, they were told; it was not really written by some crazed redneck, after all, but by the thoughtful and enlightened John Bloom. But they were still uneasy about running Joe Bob's column. Daily newspapers have never been comfortable with satire. Daily newspapers have never been comfortable with columnists who perpetrate outrages. Then, in November of 1982, *The Wall Street Journal* ran a long front-page story by G. Christian Hill headlined AFICIONADO OF TRASH AT THE TIMES HERALD IS A BIG HIT IN DALLAS. The *Journal* piece conferred an almost instant legitimacy on "Joe Bob Goes to the Drive-In." The high sheriffs at the *Times Herald* breathed easier. The Los Angeles Times Syndicate—whose parent company, the Times Mirror Company, owned *The Dallas Times Herald*—offered Joe Bob a syndication contract. A young woman who had met Bloom through handling the advertising for some Dallas exploitation-movie distributors became a literary agent on the spot and sent a Joe Bob Briggs book proposal to fifty editors whose names she got out of a guide to the publishing industry. Joe Bob wrote the proposal's covering letter himself. Since it was important correspondence, he used his special stationery— the stuff decorated with reproductions of movie posters for drive-in classics like *Doctor Butcher, M.D.* and *The Slumber Party Massacre* and *Vampire Playgirls.*

The letter began, "Dear Big Shot Publisher: Cherry Dilday is typing this sucker up for me, so if we got technical problems, I'm telling you right now, I'm not responsible. Cherry claims she got a typing diploma from the Industrial Trades Institute on Harry Hines Boulevard, but I know for a fact that she left school after two weeks to go to the dog track in West Memphis with Dexter Crook. She'd probably amount to something today if she'd stayed for the full three. Correct me if I'm wrong, but I've been told you're interested in getting filthy rich off my book." Several of them were. Joe Bob signed a contract with Dell.

Among large American cities, Dallas has had a reputation for being run, rather smoothly, by an oligarchy. While other cities of the Old Confederacy were battling over the demands of the civil rights movement, for instance, whatever desegregation could not be avoided in Dallas was arranged quietly from above by a group of conservative white businessmen called the Dallas Citizens Council—a fact often mentioned to explain why Dallas's black community has been slow to develop aggressive and independent leaders of its own. The Citizens Council also installed slates of city councilmen. Jim Schutze, who does an urban-affairs column for the *Times Herald,* has written that until 1978, when city councilmen began being elected in single-member districts instead of at large, Dallas was, in effect, a "well-run predemocratic city state." The oligarchy's newspaper was *The Dallas Morning News*—an appropriately sober, locally owned, journalistically conservative paper, whose editorial page is even now described occasionally as Dixiecrat. Until a dozen years ago, the *Morning News* dominated the Dallas newspaper market. Its competition, *The Dallas Times Herald,* was an afternoon paper that had a smaller circulation and carried advertising that ran more toward Kmart than toward Neiman-Marcus. Like a lot of afternoon papers, the *Times Herald* concentrated on local coverage—particularly the juicier murders. The joke names for the two papers in Dallas were the *Morning Snooze* and the *Crimes Herald.*

In the middle seventies, all that changed. The Times Mirror Company—a huge, expansionist communications corporation whose empire includes the *Los Angeles Times* and *Newsday*—had bought the *Times Herald* in 1969, in a deal that included five-year contracts for the management that was in place. As the contracts expired, the *Times Herald* launched an ambitious campaign to overtake the *Morning News* and become the preeminent newspaper of Dallas—a prize of considerable value, since the Dallas market was expanding daily in the Texas boom that had been touched off by the Arab oil embargo and fed by Sun Belt migration. The *Times Herald* gradually transformed itself into an all-day paper. New editors were hired from papers like *The Washington Post* and *The Philadelphia Inquirer,* and the new editors brought in eager young reporters from all over the country. The news coverage was aggressive, and the editors made it clear that they were unconcerned about which powerful citizen or potential advertiser might be in the line of fire. A sign on the newsroom wall said, "The Only Sacred Cow Here Is Hamburger." The newsroom took on the sort of élan that in the early sixties was associated with the *New York Herald Tribune.* Reporters were encouraged to come up with stories that had what the new managing editor, Will Jarrett, called "pop" or "sizzle." The editorial page found a moderate niche in that vast area of opinion that lay to the left of *The Dallas Morning News,* and it put forward late-twentieth-century views on racial and social issues. The *Times Herald* solidified its position as the newspaper that concerned itself with the problems of Dallas's minorities, but, in a way, the new version of the paper seemed to be directed toward a new Dallas audience—the people who had moved to the Sun Belt from the North, the younger Dallas natives who had turned away a bit from the economic and cultural conservatism of their parents. It worked. In 1980—at the height of the boom—the *Times Herald,* which had started many laps behind, almost pulled even with the *Morning News* in circulation.

John Bloom was among the brightest of the *Times Herald*'s new crop of bright young reporters. Will Jarrett had remembered him from a summer Bloom spent as a college intern at *The Philadelphia Inquirer.* Jarrett found Bloom in Nashville, where he was editing a country-club magazine, and hired him, even though two other editors who met him thought he was too shy to be a reporter. Bloom says he was the paper's "fluff specialist" for a while—the reporter papers depend on to write their way out of a story on the first day of spring or a story on the new baby giraffe at the zoo—but he also worked on stories about mistreatment of Mexican-Americans taken into police custody and about a resurgence of the Klan. After only two years on the paper, he was chosen to be what the *Times Herald* called its Texas Ranger—a reporter who roams across the state looking for stories. In 1978, he left to join *Texas Monthly,* a magazine whose young nonfiction writers were bringing it a national reputation, and then, toward the end of 1981, he returned to the *Times Herald* as the movie reviewer. Only a couple of months later, he went to the Century Drive-In in Grand Prairie and discovered Joe Bob Briggs.

There are any number of people on newspapers around the country who could easily be imagined sliding into the character of Joe Bob Briggs—people who wrap themselves in the blue-denim cloak of childhoods in places like west Texas or south Georgia— but John Bloom was not among them. Nothing about him suggested that he might harbor within him a wild nineteen-year-old redneck. Bloom was the son of schoolteachers—Southern Baptists from Texas who, early in his childhood, settled in Little Rock. It was not a childhood spent beating up auto mechanics or watching trashy movies at drive-ins with the likes of May Ellen Masters and Cherry Dilday and the other girls Joe Bob was always describing as "dumb as a box of rocks." As an infant, Bloom had contracted polio, and he spent part of junior high school with a withered right leg in a brace. He grew into a tall, exceedingly thin, almost theatrically handsome young man with pale skin and a thatch of black hair and an almost imperceptible limp. In person, John Bloom would have fulfilled the expectations of a reader who had a strong vision of what a sensitive commentator on the *nouvelle vague* should look like, but he would have been a surprise to readers who had followed the ragged adventures of Joe Bob Briggs. When he is asked why he didn't acknowledge authorship of "Joe Bob Goes to the Drive-In," he sometimes says, "I was almost afraid people would feel disappointed if they met me."

Although Bloom obviously didn't turn out to be too shy to be a reporter, he never really became part of the newsroom crowd. At both the *Times Herald* and *Texas Monthly,* his colleagues thought of him as a sort of outsider, who was likely to have odd hours and odd friends. Editors considered him enormously talented and quietly intent on having his own way. Partly because Bloom had written long, thoughtful pieces for *Texas Monthly* on an articulate fundamentalist minister and on the Wycliffe Bible Translators, he was sometimes called John the Baptist. People who knew him on *Texas Monthly* tend to use the same phrases when they talk about him, which might suggest a unanimity of opinion except that one of the phrases is "You never really feel you know him." They sometimes spoke of him as Good John and Bad John—the Good John seen as sensitive and intelligent, the Bad John as cold and manipulative—and not many of them felt close enough to him to know which was the actual John Bloom. Neither Good John nor Bad John seemed to presage Joe Bob Briggs. During Bloom's time at *Texas Monthly,* some of his colleagues felt him to be edging toward the right politically but certainly not to the sort of right represented by Joe Bob Briggs, who once wrote that he wasn't terribly happy about being syndicated in San Francisco because "it goes against my principles to write a column for communist-speaking cities." Looking back recently at Bloom's days on *Texas Monthly,* the magazine's editor, Gregory Curtis, said, "I wasn't surprised he could become someone else, but I thought he might have turned into a Baptist preacher."

However unlikely it was, though, John Bloom could, when it came time to write Friday's column, transform himself with great ease into Joe Bob Briggs. Bloom seemed to be among those writers who find the use of an alter ego or a pseudonym liberating: He has said that producing a Joe Bob column took him about three hours, counting the time spent watching the movie. Almost from the beginning, Joe Bob wrote about his own life as well as about such matters as the transvestite wrestling scene in *Chained Heat.* Joe Bob might start talking about how he'd asked Junior Stebbens to do a complete overhaul on the Toronado he bought after the demise of the Dodge Dart or about how the young woman he always referred to as Ugly on a Stick "went down to Tex Pawn and tried to get a 30-year breast improvement loan," and almost forget to get around to the movie he had just seen. He always printed letters from readers—preference given to hate mail—and he always showed no respect in his replies. ("We're talking jerkola at the minimum. We're probably talking wimp.") Jim Schutze believes that in those early months Bloom, through local references and an ear for local language, created not just a generic redneck but some- one representative of the people who had been left out of the new Dallas—"the people on the fringe of Dallas, this Yankee island, who were country, who had to drive in for work in their pickups."

Bloom saw Joe Bob not simply as a redneck but as a particularly smart, diabolical, anarchistic redneck who was "full of latent sex- ual and violent energies"—someone who wasn't afraid to say any- thing. What a country storyteller named Gamble Rogers once said of the ornery and fearlessly outspoken cracker was a central fea- ture of Joe Bob's character: "He don't care. He flat do not care." In fact, Joe Bob took pleasure in saying whatever seemed likely to offend someone, and his response to finding out that what he said had indeed given offense was to say it again. (Writing in *Patriotic Gore* about a Tennessee cracker who was an alter ego of a mid- nineteenth-century journalist named George Washington Harris, Edmund Wilson said, "One of the most striking things about *Sut Lovingood* is that it is all as offensive as possible.") It was a charac- teristic that made people turn to Joe Bob first thing on Friday morning—wondering what he might have gone and said now and wondering how long he was going to get away with it.

It was also, of course, the characteristic that made the high sher- iffs at the *Times Herald* edgy. Early in Joe Bob's career, they estab- lished a special system under which each Joe Bob column was read by two copy editors, both of whom had instructions to summon an assistant managing editor at any sign of trouble. It isn't un- usual for Texas writers to use a plainspoken character like Joe Bob.

Molly Ivins, a popular *Times Herald* columnist who's based in Austin, tends to find her best material in the true adventures of Texas politicians—the gubernatorial candidate, for instance, whose fear of AIDS was so strong that on a trip to San Francisco last spring he wore shower caps on his feet while standing in the hotel bathtub—but she also refers often to a sort of all-purpose Texas ol' boy she calls Bubba. Having such a character write the column himself, though, presented some special problems. One of them was what some people called the Archie Bunker factor—the problem of whether the column is making fun of Joe Bob or of the people Joe Bob makes fun of. Also, part of Joe Bob's impact was based on saying something the readers would not have expected him to say. Although Bloom has always denied any strategy beyond trying to make jokes, there was a feeling at the *Times Herald* that Joe Bob had to "up the dosage" every Friday. "John's the sort of guy who wants to push and push," one of the high sheriffs said recently. "Kind of like a college editor trying to get a bad word in the paper." At times, he was precisely like a college editor trying to get a bad word in the paper—the only difference being that the word's excision would provide Joe Bob with a joke about being muzzled by the high sheriffs or by "the jerkola French-fry head communist censors in Washington."

A couple of years after the column began, an editor's note in *Weekend* said that Joe Bob, mentioning such irritations as "too many high sheriffs" and "too many guys named Todd living in Dallas," had left what appeared to be a letter of resignation written on a page torn from a Big Chief spiral notebook. "Life is a fern bar and I'm out of here," Joe Bob wrote. "I'm history." But Joe Bob was back the next week, praising a movie called *The Being* for an "excellent slime glopola monster with moving mouth." By that time, there were people on the *Times Herald* who thought that the steady increase in dosage would inevitably make Job Bob history sooner or later, and one editor had offered the opinion that the high sheriffs might consider the advantages of simply picking an opportune moment to have Joe Bob's Toronado spin out on the interstate.

It would obviously be unusual under any circumstances for a newspaper to kill its most popular feature. It would have been particularly difficult in the circumstances the *Times Herald* found itself in. By the time the Joe Bob Briggs column had become established, it was clear that the race with the *Morning News* was being lost. There were any number of theories to explain what had happened. The *Morning News*, partly because of the competition and partly from the infusion of some new blood in management, had greatly improved, making up in thoroughness what it might have lacked in sizzle. Its editorial page still might not have given great offense to those who drafted the Dixiecrat platform in 1948, but its news department had, in Will Jarrett's grudging words, "kind of started practicing modern journalism." ("Newspaper competition is usually like high-low poker," Molly Ivins has said. "But in this case both players went high.") Meanwhile, the *Times Herald* was having some problems. For a variety of reasons, it was without strong editorial leadership for a while. There was a newsroom power struggle that sapped a lot of the paper's energy. Some observers outside the paper thought that the management had never learned the prescribed Dallas method of getting along with the business leaders—people who have assumed the synonymy of their interests and the city's interests for so long that they routinely describe any story not respectful to business as "anti-Dallas"—and some reporters inside the paper grumbled that management was beginning to get along with the business leaders too well. Some people thought that the *Times Herald* had, in covering all those extra laps necessary to catch up with the *Morning News*, simply run out of wind. Among the shrinking bright spots was "Joe Bob Goes to the Drive-In," which might have been the best-read feature in either paper. The *Times Herald* didn't simply tolerate Joe Bob. It put his name on billboards. It sold baseball caps that said, "Joe Bob Briggs Sez Check It Out" and T-shirts that said, "Joe Bob Briggs Is a Close Personal Friend of Mine."

The Baptists had been the first to complain. When it comes to objecting to offenses against public order and morality in Texas, they are rarely beaten to the punch. Southern Baptists are well represented in Dallas—the First Baptist Church, led by the Reverend W. A. Criswell, is the largest Baptist congregation in the entire country—but the first serious complaint from Baptists about Joe Bob Briggs came from a minister in Tyler, who said that Joe Bob's preoccupation with sex and violence revealed a sick mind. The Baptists were not alone. Joe Bob offended gays with some of his San Francisco jokes, and he offended feminists with his Miss Custom Body Contest. Joe Bob offended so many different people that the sheer variety of those he had outraged became part of the standard defense of his column: Joe Bob's admirers said that he was "an equal-opportunity offender." Joe Bob's response to complaints or criticism can be judged from an opinion survey he conducted after a San Francisco film critic named Peter Stack differed with him on whether a movie called *Basket Case* was an inept and disgusting splatter flick or the single best movie of 1982. Inviting the readers to settle the question democratically, Joe Bob provided a ballot that said, "Question: In your opinion, is the french-fry-head San Francisco writer named Peter Stack a wimp or not?" Stack did not come out well in the balloting.

Despite Joe Bob's habit of referring to all females as bimbos and his ubiquitous breast count and his celebration of movies that featured the dismemberment of women ("I'm telling you these bimbos get hacked up until it's chop suey city") and his sponsorship of the Miss Custom Body Contest ("All contestants must be able to count to the number seven, and may not sue such a demonstration as their 'talent'"), the first strong attack from feminists didn't come until Joe Bob had been appearing for two years. A lot of women who read the *Times Herald*—including a lot of women who considered themselves feminists—thought Joe Bob was funny. A number of them thought that he served to demonstrate just how ludicrous Texas he-men were. In fact, before it became general knowledge that Joe Bob was a creature of John Bloom, Molly Ivins, who is widely known as a strong feminist, was regularly accused of being the author of "Joe Bob Goes to the Drive-In."

When the attack came, it was led by Charlotte Taft, who runs an abortion clinic called the Routh Street Women's Clinic. At the time, she had been feeling vaguely guilty about not organizing a protest against the local showing of *Pieces,* a movie that had been picketed by feminists elsewhere because of its concentration on hideous violence against women. Someone who runs an abortion clinic in Dallas—where right-to-lifers seem to attack in endless waves, like Chinese regulars pouring over the 38th Parallel—can't always get around to the side issues. Then she came across a capsule review of the movie in the *Times Herald. The Weekend* section had got into the habit of running capsules by both of its movie reviewers, distinguishing them only by the initials at the end. Between reviews by JB of *The Osterman Weekend* (one star) and *The Right Stuff* (a star and a half), JBB's capsule review of *Pieces* said, "Best chainsaw flick since the original *Saw,* about a gonzo geek pervert who goes around a college campus cutting up coeds into itty bitty pieces. Two heads roll. Arms roll. Legs roll. Something else rolls. Nine living breasts, two dead breasts. No motor vehicle chases. Gratuitous kung fu. Eight corpses. One beast with a chainsaw. Four gallons of blood. Not much talking. Splatter City. Joe Bob says check it out." The review included Joe Bob's rating: four stars.

Casting around for allies, Charlotte Taft found support from an old adversary—William Murchison, a conservative columnist on the *Morning News.* Murchison wrote that the celebration of a movie like *Pieces* was not simply a feminist issue but a humanity issue—a reminder that people who make movies seem to take no notice of someone like Mother Teresa but think nothing of turning out a movie that "devalues the human species." The reply in Joe Bob's column was headlined JOE BOB ATTACKED BY COMMUNIST FRIEND OF MOTHER TERESA. In it Joe Bob said, "Last week this royal jerkola with a bad haircut named William Murchison wrote a column called 'Chain-Sawing Our Culture.' He wrote it on the editorial page of the Dallas Morning Snooze. . . . It has this itty-bitty picture of Willie Murchison with his lips mashed together like the zombie-monster in *Dr. Tarr's Torture Garden,* and his eyes look exactly like the guy in *I Drink Your Blood.* He also has a little resemblance to the woman-carver in *I Dismember Mama,* but I'm sure that's just a coincidence." A couple of weeks later, Joe Bob finally got down to the issues at hand: "*Numero uno:* I have enormous respect for women. Especially when they have garbanzas the size of Cleveland. *Numero two-o:* I am violently opposed to the use of chainsaws, power drills, tire tools, rubber hoses, brass knuckles, bob wire, hypodermics, embalming needles or poleaxes against women, unless it is *necessary* to the plot. *Numero three-o:* I don't believe in slapping women around, unless they want it. *Numero four-o:* I would like to settle this matter in the easiest way possible, so I hereby challenge Charlotte Taft to a nude mud-wrestling match. . . ."

Charlotte Taft decided that a better way to settle it was to organize a letter-writing campaign to the *Times Herald.* It was based on the same argument she had made in her letter to the editor—that men in Dallas still seemed to think it was all right to make jokes about violence against women, decades after a supposedly responsible newspaper would dare find anything funny about, say, ridiculing black people. Eventually, though, the feminists decided that their efforts were going nowhere. The editors of the *Times Herald* seemed uninterested. The feminists themselves were by no means unanimous in condemning Joe Bob. Molly Ivins, for one, said that the complaints were "displaced anger." Interviewed for a feature on Joe Bob by KERA, the local public-television station, she said that what should be protested was "the vicious and degrading pornography" of exploitation movies, not someone who was "making brilliant fun of the kind of people who go to watch those movies." Charlotte Taft was never won over to that point of view. "John Bloom wanted to have it both ways—some readers taking it at face value and some taking it as satire," she said not long ago. "But part of satire is to instruct, not to wallow in the fun of saying what's not supposed to be said. If there's an Archie Bunker, there has to be a Meathead. What I saw in it was self-indulgence—the self-indulgence of someone who wants to tell a racist joke and pretends to be making fun of someone telling a racist joke. It was indulging in an adult the humor of a seventh grader—a seventh-grade boy." She had decided, though, that all she was doing in her protest was providing material for Joe Bob, who wrote a lot about the high sheriffs' being pressured by what he always referred to as the National Organization for Bimbos.

John Bloom agreed that protest was just playing into Joe Bob's hands. On the KERA program, he was interviewed as Joe Bob's closest friend, and he said of the attacks by feminists, "One thing Joe Bob's critics should learn is that you should never attack an anarchist. He has nothing to lose." Using criticism as material for making fun of the critic was among the characteristics that, after two years, had been established firmly enough to be an unvarying part of Joe Bob's character. He could be counted on to reoffend the offended, just as he could be counted on to refer to women as bimbos, and to persist in trying to sneak in words that the high sheriffs considered inappropriate. John Bloom and Ron Smith and the other people at the *Times Herald* who dealt with Joe Bob, all of whom spoke of him in the third person even among themselves, still had the power to arrange for his Toronado to spin out on the interstate, of course. But as long as Joe Bob existed, he was, in certain ways, on his own.

.   .   .

"He's *gone* to all these movies," Charlotte Taft has said. "I find that kind of scary." Even those who didn't find it eerie that an honors graduate of Vanderbilt could thrive on a steady diet of splatter flicks might have wondered just how many chainsaw dismemberments and kung-fu battles anyone could sit through without becoming too bored even to maintain an accurate body count. As it turned out, though, John Bloom got tired of movie reviewing before Joe Bob did. In 1984, Bloom gave up reviewing to become the paper's Metro columnist—someone responsible for three columns a week. Writing the Metro column was considered a full-time job, but once a week Bloom continued to turn into Joe Bob Briggs. In January of 1985, that became twice a week. Blackie Sherrod, one of the most popular sportswriters in Dallas, had jumped to the *Morning News*, and the *Times Herald* countered with a new sportswriter of its own—Joe Bob Briggs. Bloom had started out in newspapers writing sports for the *Arkansas Democrat* while he was still in high school; he went through Vanderbilt on a Grantland Rice Scholarship, awarded by the Thoroughbred Racing Associations. Will Jarrett has said that he saw the sports column, "Jock Talk with Joe Bob," as more than simply a counter to Sherrod. "I thought of it as Phase Two," he said not long ago. "The bimbo thing was kind of played out. He was depending a lot on ethnic humor. There was a lot of material in sports. John knew the field. It was a way to ride his popularity and get rid of some of the problem areas." Even writing about sports, of course, Joe Bob did not avoid the problem areas completely. In one of the first "Jock Talk" columns, he managed to make up a Boston Celtics theme song called "Attack of the Stupid White People" and to refer to Tony Nathan, of the Miami Dolphins, as "the only slow Negro in the NFL."

Will Jarrett had been off editing *The Denver Post* during most of the time Joe Bob was steadily dismantling many of the barriers against tastelessness the high sheriffs had erected, and he says that when he returned to Dallas, in 1984, he was surprised to see what Joe Bob was getting away with. There were occasional flare-ups from offended readers—there were complaints from members of Mothers Against Drunk Driving (MADD), for instance, when Joe Bob organized a group called Drunks Against Mad Mothers (DAMM)—but Jarrett got the impression that a lot of readers had been following Joe Bob Briggs long enough to shrug off most of what he said as just the sort of thing Joe Bob would say. *Times Herald* editors had never truly lost their nervousness about running the column, though, and some people around the newsroom were, in fact, troubled by what they saw as an increasing reliance on ethnic cracks. Reviewing a movie called *Breakin'*, for instance, Joe Bob managed to mention not simply "Negro Dancing" but also "Meskins," the perils he saw in Vietnamese immigration ("Pretty soon you can't go in 7-Eleven without wondering whether those guys are putting dog meat in the frozen burritos"), and a character "whose idea of a good time is to go sit on the beach with guys from the chorus line and talk about their Liberace record collections, if you know what I mean and I think you do"—all in the course of saying that he had been shown the path from racism by his friend Bobo Rodriguez: "I never did ask Bobo what race he was, but I'm pretty sure he was a Negro. His skin was the color of Taster's Choice Decaffeinated, which means he could go either way, but one time he tried to change his name to Bobo al-Salaam, and when he did that everybody started calling him 'Al' because they thought he was saying 'Al Sloan.'"

Although some of Joe Bob's fans around the *Times Herald* may have fallen away, he was publicly more popular than ever. His column was being syndicated to fifty papers or so, making him a figure of renown even in San Francisco—a place he normally referred to as "Wimp Capital of the World" or "Geek City, U.S.A." He was so popular in Cleveland that when the editors of the *Plain Dealer* decided to drop his column for tastelessness an avalanche of reader mail persuaded them to put it back. In some film circles, he was a

sort of cult figure—someone who could attract Stephen King to
the Third Annual World Drive-In Movie Festival and Custom Car
Rally. There were those, though, who thought that Joe Bob's national popularity was his undoing. They thought that "the golden
age of Joe Bob" had been in the early months of the column, when
Joe Bob could be understood in a local context and could spice up
his column with local stunts, like organizing a letter-writing campaign to the public official he held responsible for the removal of
the drive-in-movie screens at Texas Stadium ("Dear French-fry
Head Mayor of Irving . . ."). There were those who thought Joe
Bob's undoing was that Bloom was spreading himself too thin by
writing five columns a week. Theories about Joe Bob's undoing
were widely discussed and closely analyzed in the spring of 1985,
because on one April Friday the worst fears that *Times Herald* high
sheriffs had entertained about the Joe Bob Briggs column finally
materialized.

The offending column, published a couple of months after rock
stars gathered in California to record a song for African famine
relief, was headlined JOE BOB, DRIVE-IN ARTISTS JOIN FORCES FOR
MINORITIES WITH "WE ARE THE WEIRD." Joe Bob said that the
best-known drive-in artists in the world had gathered together to
sing the song: "They all stood there, swaying from side to side,
arms linked (except for The Mutant, who don't have arms) and
singing their little hearts out." Although Joe Bob's song does not
lend itself to summary—it's never precisely clear who's singing
about exactly what—the first chorus was representative of its
tone:

> We are the weird.
> We are the starvin,
> We are the scum of the filthy earth,
> So let's start scarfin . . .

There's a goat-head bakin
We're calling it their food,
If the Meskins can eat it,
They can eat it, too.

The drive-in stars' recording was, Joe Bob wrote, "for the benefit of minority groups in Africa and the United Negro College Fund in the United States, cause I think we should be sending as many Negroes to college as we can, specially the stupid Negroes."

It wasn't immediately clear how such a column found its way into the *Times Herald* and the distribution network of the Los Angeles Times Syndicate. The copy editors apparently had not flagged an assistant managing editor. According to one rather ornate theory, Joe Bob had for months been trying to sneak the word "twat" past the two copy editors, and they were concentrating so hard on spotting it—examining each syllable in the name of any town Joe Bob invented, searching any new organization for contraband acronyms—that they weren't paying enough attention to the content of the column. According to another theory, the copy editors, after a few years of reading Joe Bobbian copy, had grown desensitized, as some people are said to get after prolonged exposure to pornography. Bloom has always insisted that a managing editor who happened to walk by his desk and glance at the column on his computer monitor read the entire song, laughed, and said, "Great stuff!"

There were plenty of readers around Dallas who were as accustomed to Joe Bob's ways as the copy editors were, but not many of these readers were black. Even though the black community regarded the *Times Herald* as the newspaper sympathetic to its interests, "Joe Bob Goes to the Drive-In" had never attracted a wide black readership. The first Joe Bob column that a lot of black people in Dallas read was the column that included a famine-relief song with verses like:

Send em a heart so they'll know that someone cares
And a lung, and an elbow, and three big toes.
As the Big Guy told us, we should always clean our plate,
Cause then all the Africans' stomachs won't look gross.

"After a while, you get sort of used to Joe Bob," Ron Smith has said. "But if you read that thing flat cold it'll send chills up your spine. And that's the way a lot of black people read it."

Willis Johnson, who runs a morning talk show on KKDA, Dallas's leading black radio station, was not in the habit of reading Joe Bob's column, but he got a call from a listener—a reporter for the *Morning News,* as it happened—who told him he would do well to make an exception in this case. Johnson, who was outraged by the column, read it over the air, and the mounting anger soon monopolized his program. The *Times Herald* was also having serious trouble within its own building. Black *Times Herald* employees were furious about the column, and a meeting at which Bloom tried to explain himself only made things worse. By then, it was obvious that the outrage over the "We Are the Weird" column was of another order than the customary Joe Bob controversies that always blew over after some angry letters and a few Joe Bobbian jokes at the complainants' expense. One of Willis Johnson's callers had been John Wiley Price, a black county commissioner. Price is among a small group of militant black officeholders in Dallas who have tried to ease aside the black ministers whose style of leadership flowed from the old accommodation with the white business community. On the air, Price and Johnson agreed to go downtown on Tuesday afternoon, right after a weekly black-leadership lunch, and demand to know why the *Times Herald,* the newspaper that supposedly represented fair treatment for minorities in Dallas, had on its staff someone who used phrases like "stupid Negroes" and found it humorous to ridicule starving people in Africa. When they arrived that Tuesday afternoon, they found that they had been joined by several hundred other people. In a city that had basically skipped the public confrontations of the civil rights struggle, the presence of a large crowd of black people marching into a white institution in an angry mood was virtually unprecedented.

Jarrett and two other editors met with as many of the protesters as could be jammed into a small auditorium. The room was hot and got even hotter when television lights were turned on. The people in the audience were fanning themselves with whatever was at hand. The three editors, surrounded by protesters, were sweating. That morning's edition had already printed an apology of a completeness that Will Jarrett called unique in his years of newspaper experience: "Joe Bob Briggs' column that appeared in Friday's *Times Herald* offended many readers. The *Times Herald* deeply regrets that the column was published. It was a misdirected attempt at satire. A great deal of insensitivity was reflected in the column. We apologize." But the crowd did not seem satisfied with an apology, however abject. "One apology in one postage-stamp-size corner of the front page is not enough," a black attorney said. "This column needs to be gone." Jarrett started out by saying that the question of whether "Joe Bob Goes to the Drive-In" would be run in the next Friday's paper was still being considered, but after a number of angry speeches he finally said, "I'm deeply concerned about it. I'm deeply concerned about the reaction. I'm deeply concerned about the staff reaction to it. So the Joe Bob Briggs column, the *Weekend* column, the drive-in-movie column, is dead." In a much smaller, more conventional meeting a few days later, the *Times Herald* pledged that twelve of the next twenty-two editorial positions filled would be filled by members of a minority. But for most of the black people of Dallas nothing could quite match the exhilaration of that public capitulation in the steamy auditorium, right there in front of the television cameras. Above the cheers that followed Jarrett's announcement the voice of a woman in the first few rows could be heard shouting, in triumph and amaze-ment, "We did it! We did it!"

John Bloom was a hundred and fifty miles away from Dallas that afternoon, delivering a speech at Texas A & M. Will Jarrett drove out to Dallas–Fort Worth Airport to meet Bloom's return flight, but the plane had arrived early; Bloom was already on his way back to the city. It was days before they finally met again. Bloom wouldn't talk to Jarrett on the telephone. He was hurt and angry. He saw the front-page apology as a writer being "publicly disavowed by his own newspaper, not for any factual error or mis-representation, but purely because his opinion is unpopular." He considered the way that Jarrett had canceled the column—publicly, without telling the columnist—basically unforgivable. Jarrett, who had brought Bloom to Dallas and remained close to him in the years that followed, was astonished that Bloom wouldn't come to the phone. "What I was worried about was John Bloom," he has said. "I realized that Joe Bob was more important to him than John Bloom was. John Bloom wouldn't talk to his editor for three days, even though Joe Bob had done the damage. I didn't fire John Bloom. I fired a mythical character John Bloom had always said he didn't agree with. Why was he mad at me?"

Jarrett had hoped that Bloom would continue writing his own column, and maybe even the "Jock Talk with Joe Bob" column. But John Bloom decided to resign from the *Times Herald.* In a final Metro column, which Jarrett declined to print, Bloom wrote that the real issue was not racism but the fact that some subjects, like African famine relief, had been put off-limits for satire because "they are too close to our subconscious fears and guilts," and he reminded Jarrett of the newsroom sign that had said, "The Only Sacred Cow Here Is Hamburger." He didn't discuss the offending column except to say that on the question of who the "we" was in lines like "we are the scum of the filthy earth"—the question that some *Times Herald* people referred to as Joe Bob's pronoun problem—"I realize I'm the person who should know the answer to this question, but I'm afraid I was too busy laughing to worry about Joe Bob's illogic." By the time Bloom resigned, there couldn't have been many people left in Dallas who were still unaware of the true authorship of the "Joe Bob Goes to the Drive-In" column—all pretense had been dropped in the barrage of news coverage of the controversy—but Bloom said he was resigning in sympathy with Joe Bob.

No one else at the *Times Herald* showed much sympathy. A lot of *Times Herald* reporters—and a lot of other Dallas reporters—were indeed horrified at what seemed to be a capitulation under pressure in the *Times Herald* auditorium. "It created a precedent that's dangerous," Molly Ivins has said. "I know that Reverend Criswell could have five thousand people there about me at the drop of a hat." But that didn't translate into newsroom support for Joe Bob. In fact, most of the people in the newsroom had, in the first days of the controversy, signed a bulletin-board statement demanding that Joe Bob's column be more closely edited in the future. *Times Herald* reporters did not see what had happened as a case of one of their own being crushed by management. They didn't consider John Bloom one of their own. Not many of them actually knew him, and some of them may have resented him with the special resentment reporters reserve for someone who seems to be getting away with the sort of writing that would be routinely edited out of their own copy. Some of them, particularly the younger ones, had long felt that it was dishonest for a newspaper to keep up the pretense that a fictional columnist actually existed. Also, as Jim Schutze put it recently, "they were the ones who answered the phone when people started calling in and saying, 'The trouble is these colored people don't know good say-tire when they see it.'"

Even more important, a lot of the reporters simply hated the "We Are the Weird" column. They didn't know who the "we" in the song was, either—figuring out how the humor worked in the column required an almost scholarly knowledge of Joe Bobbian context—but, unlike Bloom, they weren't too busy laughing to care. Satire is obviously most offensive when the reader's first response isn't laughter; it lies there, waiting to be analyzed. Those in the newsroom who thought Joe Bob's problem was more in his delivery than in his subject matter pointed out that the rock stars' African-relief effort was not, in fact, a sacred cow; a number of political cartoonists and columnists had already taken a crack at it. But the column's subject matter was at the heart of the opposition. "Satire is a weapon you use against the powerful," Molly Ivins, who was not on Joe Bob's side this time, has said. "You don't use satire against the weak." Bloom's position seemed to be that a truly liberal society wouldn't recognize any subject as off-limits: now that black people are equal partners in modern, post-segregationist America, it would be patronizing not to subject them equally to the occasional satiric knock. What people like Molly Ivins found wrong with that was the assumption that black people are now equal partners in modern America. Presumably, most people at the *Times Herald* would have agreed with Bloom that these days a newspaper columnist is a lot less likely to get away with a joke about starving Africans or "stupid Negroes" than with a joke about the president, but not many of them seemed to think it followed that such jokes had to be made.

"For forty-eight hours, I thought, Well, it's over. It's gone up in flames. And it's kind of an ignominious end," Bloom said not long ago. "Then I started getting these letters. A large number of responsible editors and reporters had been saying, 'The guy got what he deserved,' but the readers were saying, 'You can't let them do this.' Joe Bob was always responsive to readers." The column had been dropped by the Los Angeles Times Syndicate as well as by the *Times Herald,* but, without missing a week, Joe Bob signed with the Universal Press Syndicate, which has some experience with controversy as the distributors of Garry Trudeau's *Doonesbury*. The first Universal column dealt, of course, with the *Times Herald* decision to kill the column—or with the assassination of Joe Bob in Dallas, as Bloom saw it.

"November 22, 1963. April 16, 1985," the column began. "They said it couldn't happen again.

"I guess I'll always remember where I was when they killed me on national TV, right after the Maybelline commercial. I guess we all will. Who couldn't remember the look on the High Sheriff's face when he said, 'Joe Bob's dead!' . . . Even though the High Sheriff was arrested at the scene by TV reporters with bad hair, there were immediate rumors of an international communist conspiracy, the 'three-gun theory,' the 'act of God theory,' the bizarre 'one-garbanza theory,' and the 'What would happen if you dropped Joe Bob Briggs off a seven-story building and watched him splatter all over the pavement?' theory." After some Joe Bobbian talk about the protest and a list of astonishing coincidences ("Lincoln and Kennedy were both assassinated on a Friday. Joe Bob was assassinated on a Tuesday. Makes you think."), Joe Bob found space for a quick summary of a movie called *Lust in the Dust*: "Four breasts. Fifteen dead bodies. One riot. One brawl. One gang rape, with midget. Two quarts blood. One beast (Divine). Thigh crushing. Bullwhip fu. Nekkid bimbo-wrestling. . . ." It would have been uncharacteristic, of course, for Joe Bob to acknowledge any regrets about the "We Are the Weird" column or apologize to those it might have offended, and Bloom, when asked about an apology, tends to say something like "Apologize for what? There's not a single fact in the column. They say it's insensitive and in poor taste. Well, Joe Bob is insensitive and in poor taste. I'll admit that."

The decision of the *Times Herald* to kill the Joe Bob drive-in column, which John Bloom seems to have heard as a decision to kill

Joe Bob, served to make Joe Bob a much larger part of John Bloom's life. Bloom continued to write under his own name—eventually, he began doing a monthly piece for Dallas's city magazine, *D*, and he started a book on Route 66—but in the freelance market Joe Bob Briggs was likely to get more assignments than John Bloom. For one thing, he was much better known, particularly after the "We Are the Weird" controversy. John Bloom is one of a number of talented young Texas writers. Joe Bob Briggs is a writer who can provide a unique way for *Film Comment* to deal with exploitation movies or for *Rolling Stone* to deal with the end of the Texas boom. Writing under his own name, Bloom had difficulty finding a publisher for a serious nonfiction book he and another *Texas Monthly* writer, Jim Atkinson, wrote about a Texas murder; it was finally published by the Texas Monthly Press. As Joe Bob Briggs, he had assumed, correctly, that there were big-shot publishers in New York interested in getting filthy rich off his books. The change was more than Joe Bob's simply easing out of the three-hour-a-week compartment Bloom had kept him in. A couple of months after Bloom left the *Times Herald,* his agent got a call from someone in Cleveland who offered to set up a speaking engagement for Joe Bob Briggs. Bloom, who had not even officially admitted writing the Joe Bob column until the "We Are the Weird" controversy erupted, decided to accept the date as Joe Bob. In a high school just outside Cleveland, he did a sort of one-man show, costumed in a cowboy hat and a more pronounced drawl. After that, those who phoned Bloom's agent with lecture inquiries were asked whether they were interested in John Bloom or Joe Bob Briggs. Joe Bob's rates were higher.

Bloom has said that in those first months of being on his own he was intent on keeping Joe Bob alive, partly because he was convinced that the high sheriffs' intentions toward Joe Bob continued to be murderous. Their weapon was a copyright. Although no objection had been raised to the Universal Press Syndicate's distribution of "Joe Bob Goes to the Drive-In," the *Times Herald* warned Dell, which was about to publish a collection of Joe Bobbiana, that John Bloom owned neither the name Joe Bob Briggs nor the rights to the material that had appeared in the *Times Herald.* The argument over rights exacerbated a hostility that already carried the special bitterness of a disagreement between people who had once been close. In his stage appearances as Joe Bob, Bloom had taken to referring to his old employer as the *Slimes Herald* and singing a song about how he'd like to make "editor fondue" out of the high sheriff who fired him—a high sheriff who happened to be John Bloom's old friend and mentor, Will Jarrett. ("A heart attack would do it, or trampled by a mob, or eaten by a giant bumblebee.")

Bloom claimed that the paper wanted to prevent the publication of Joe Bob's books out of spite. The high sheriffs of the *Times Herald* and the Times Mirror Company were indeed furious about the "We Are the Weird" incident—some of them saw it as one horrifying column destroying a position with the minority community that had taken years to establish—and they were apparently wounded by Joe Bob's insults. At one point, the paper offered to release the material under conditions that included a promise not to ridicule the *Times Herald* or its executives. The proposed agreement would also have given the paper control over which columns appeared in a book. Jarrett has said that the main issue was whether the *Times Herald* could acquiesce in the republication of the "We Are the Weird" column: "We'd be in the position of saying, 'Right, this is awful, it should never have been printed, we're going to kill the column,' and then turning around and saying, 'Sure, go ahead and publish it in a book, make a lot of money.' The black people would have said we were hypocrites." Bloom rejected the proposed agreement, and after months of meetings and lawyers' letters and phone calls he filed legal papers against the *Times Herald* in an attempt to liberate Joe Bob Briggs.

. . .

Last summer, a little more than a year after the cancellation of the column, Bloom's lawyer won a declaratory judgment on one of the two questions at issue—the question of who had a right to use the name Joe Bob Briggs—and a date was set to hear arguments on whether Bloom had the right to reprint the columns that had appeared in the *Times Herald.* Outside the courtroom, the blood-feud aspect of the disagreement had begun to dissipate. Will Jarrett had already left the paper, in a purge that also claimed some executives on the business side. Not long after the declaratory judgment, the Times Mirror Company, in what *The New York Times* story called "an apparent acknowledgment that it was unable to win the heated Dallas newspaper war," announced that it was selling the *Times Herald.* The buyer was a young, Texas-born newspaper magnate who said he was moving the headquarters of his enterprises from New Jersey to Dallas and intended to become active in "the Dallas leadership community." The Joe Bob suit was specifically excluded from the assets and liabilities passed on to the new owner, and it was assumed that the sale had completed the transformation of the Joe Bob controversy from a serious altercation into the sort of loose end that a large corporation likes to have tied up before it leaves town. Times Mirror and John Bloom quickly settled their differences, and Dell made plans to publish the collection in the form Bloom wanted it published. Joe Bob, in effect, belonged to John Bloom.

A lot of Bloom's old colleagues do not think he won a great asset. "What bothers me is that John Bloom is a significant talent who can endure, and Joe Bob is an ephemeral kind of thing," one of them said recently. "If John thinks no one else can kill Joe Bob, fine. Then at some point he should kill Joe Bob himself." The syndicated Joe Bob column is in fact a marginal operation. It appears in a few dozen newspapers, but a lot of them are college papers or alternative weeklies. The pattern, Bloom says, is that the feature editor buys the column, it runs once, and the executive editor cancels it. It's a difficult column to sell. The reason is partly the traditional cautiousness of newspapers—Bloom has always maintained that the only reason Joe Bob appears outrageous is that the material surrounding him is so bland—but it is also partly that the "We Are the Weird" controversy gave Joe Bob a reputation not simply for controversy but also for racism.

Joe Bob's one-man show has been polished considerably since its rather shaky start in Cleveland. He has even put out a video, called *Joe Bob Briggs Dead in Concert*. Like a lot of shy people who have to transform themselves into public characters, Bloom uses hats in the stage show—a cowboy hat, a feed hat, one of those caps that have horns extending from the sides. Joe Bob tells stories about bimbos and Baptists and a county where the major industry is dirt. He sings songs like "Dirt Mine Blues" and "We Are the Weird" (with the words significantly toned down). This fall, he used his column to recruit a troupe of seriously overweight young women, and in a Dallas appearance on the weekend of the Texas-Oklahoma game he worked them into the act as the Dancing Bovina Sisters, doing dances like the Frito Stomp. People who know John Bloom tend to be surprised that he's as fluid as he is onstage, but the act has received mixed reviews. One of the problems of Joe Bob's coming to life was pointed out a couple of years ago by Bloom himself, when he was explaining to Dennis Holder, in the *Washington Journalism Review,* why Joe Bob could never be on television: "This thing is so fragile that the last thing you'd want is to remove the mystery and magic through the cold reality of a camera. If you ever gave Joe Bob a specific face, or even a voice, some of the power would be lost." Onstage, Bloom plays a redneck who tells stories, but that may disappoint people who hope to see the real Joe Bob. A headline in the *San Francisco Chronicle* after Joe Bob's appearance in the Wimp Capital of the World said JOE BOB "LIVE" IS A PUSSYCAT. Molly Ivins says that even without having seen the act she knows that Bloom can't be very persuasive as Joe Bob Briggs. "For one thing, he's too good-looking," she said not long ago. "If he could act, he'd play the young Byron."

"I'm bothered that he's given up serious journalism for a cardboard cowboy," Will Jarrett said recently. In general, Bloom's former colleagues tend to talk about him the way a bunch of medievalists would talk about one of their number who had gone off to write potboilers. Their theories of just why Bloom is hanging on so hard to Joe Bob depend a bit on what they thought of him in the first place. Some people think it's just pure stubbornness. Some think that under Bloom's shy exterior was always a lust for show business; they point out that he became pals with some Hollywood types during his regular movie reviewing days, and that he has appeared in a scene (later cut) in the sequel to *The Texas Chainsaw Massacre*. Some people think that Bloom sees Joe Bob as a ticket to fame and fortune, and some people think that Bloom sat through so many splatter movies "his brain got fried." Some people think that John Bloom, no matter how enlightened and how educated, simply had a wild, racist redneck inside him, and that the redneck has finally surfaced; they tend to say, "John Bloom has become Joe Bob Briggs." Bloom himself says that he'll kill off Joe Bob when he gets tired of him. "Maybe I'll do it until I find the heart of Joe Bob, find out what about him disturbs people," he said recently. "When you see what a threat Joe Bob is to people, the issue becomes the integrity of Joe Bob."

Joe Bob Briggs is no longer much of a presence in Dallas. His column appears in a weekly paper, *The Observer,* and there are still plenty of hard-core Joe Bob fans. But the day is past when all Friday morning talk seemed to center on what Joe Bob had gone and said now. These days, on Friday morning or any other morning, the talk in Dallas's shiny new office buildings is likely to be about how many square feet of the building remain unleased; the people driving into the city in pickups are likely to be concerned about whether a job will still be there when they arrive. When Joe Bob's mentioned, it's often in the past tense. "The trouble with the character was that he had to push it further and further," Molly Ivins said not long ago. "The poor bastard just outlived his time." The talk about how Joe Bob's column ended sounds a bit like the talk that could be heard in some other American cities twenty years ago—some white people saying that militant blacks were simply looking for an issue, and militant blacks saying that *of course* they were looking for an issue. For a while, people like Willis Johnson thought that the success in galvanizing people around the issue of Joe Bob Briggs might awaken what was sometimes referred to as the sleeping giant of the Dallas black community. They thought that the victory in the *Times Herald* auditorium might serve as an impetus for a more confrontational approach in dealing with the white business community. But there is now a widespread feeling that the giant stretched and then went back to sleep. Johnson says that he and John Wiley Price have been subjected to some criticism among the traditional leadership for not trying to settle differences with the *Times Herald* in a quieter way. Charlotte Taft is still at the Routh Street Women's Clinic. One set of fundamentalists shows up to picket on Wednesday, another set pickets on Saturday, and the Catholics have set up next door in one of those operations whose advertising and name seem designed to attract young women who think they're going to an abortion clinic but find themselves in a place dedicated to talking them out of it. Sometimes, Charlotte Taft gets discouraged. When she ponders the difficulty of financing her operation through the usual fund-raising events, she said with a smile not long ago, she sometimes thinks she might have been too quick in rejecting Joe Bob's nude-mud-wrestling challenge.

The *Times Herald* now has the same problem every other daily newspaper has in figuring out how to cover trashy movies. The paper is under new management, and there has been a lot of turnover in staff. Some people on and off the paper say that the controversy over Joe Bob was what finally pushed the Times Mirror Company into giving up on the Dallas newspaper war. There were, of course, solid business reasons for selling the *Times Herald,* which had just dipped into the red after fifteen years of considerable profits. The Dallas boom had fizzled. The war with the *Morning News* had been lost. The resources of the Times Mirror Company could presumably be better invested elsewhere. Those who say that the Joe Bob episode was the last straw for Times Mirror—the experience that soured it forever on Dallas—seem to mean that more symbolically or spiritually than literally. In the words of Ron Smith, one of the people who brought Joe Bob into the world, dealing with the "We Are the Weird" controversy was for the Times Mirror Company "like biting into a bad clam."

The advertising campaign of the new management features a picture of the new editor saying, "Nobody wants to read a wimp newspaper." It is said that the use of a Joe Bobbian word is a coincidence, but there is a temptation to see some connection between the strong anti-wimp statement and the fact that the capitulation in the auditorium left some lingering taint of wimpiness in the building. It also left a new verb in Dallas—"to Joe Bob," meaning to march on an institution with an intimidating number of citizens and hope to buffalo that institution into changing some policy. When Jim Schutze wrote a column critical of one of the black ministers in Dallas some time ago, for instance, the response of one of the minister's supporters was the threat "We're going to come down there and Joe Bob your ass." Some people on the *Times Herald* resent the part played by both John Bloom and management in creating the situation that led to the verb's existence, and some of the same people miss the excitement of those Friday mornings when everyone turned to *Weekend* to see who had been called a communist French-fry head this week. Talking about the career of Joe Bob Briggs at *The Dallas Times Herald* recently, Ron Smith said that Shelby Coffey III, who was the editor of the paper at the time the Times Mirror Company sold it, once turned down an idea for a satirical feature by remarking, "This paper has a sorry history on satire"—an allusion, of course, to Joe Bob Briggs. "I took exception to that," Smith said. "I don't think it was sorry. I think it was a noble experiment that went awry."

Professionally, John Bloom transmogrified into Joe Bob Briggs—best known as the host of drive-in movie nights on various television networks. He does a traveling one-man show with titles like Joe Bob's Indoor Drive-In Geek-out. *Several decades after the split with the* Times Herald, *he was asked by an interviewer if John Bloom still existed. "Very rarely," he said. "Very rarely do I see him anymore."*

Negative and Controversial

1970

A year or so ago, I read that the daily paper of Nampa, Idaho—*The Idaho Free Press*—had been accused by a group of local businessmen of "emphasizing the negative and controversial." One of the unchallengeable premises of any American town is that the town is, as the brochure always says, A Friendly Place with Excellent Schools, Beautiful Parks, Progressive Government, and Fine Recreation Areas Nearby—an ideal place, in other words, for any company to build a factory. There is no room for the negative and controversial in that picture. In practice, a group of local businessmen is the decision-making body of a small town—the people who decide, often over their early-morning coffee at a downtown café, whether the town should have a new industrial park or a new tax levy—and businessmen always believe that the most constructive way to make decisions is quietly, without "stirring people up." In a small town in America, a man can still be damned by being called "controversial" without anybody's having to inquire which side of what controversy he is on.

This way of doing business might be thought to be offensive to a newspaper, but, as it happens, one of the businessmen having coffee at the café every morning is likely to be the newspaper publisher. Like the other businessmen, the publisher thinks of himself as a public-spirited citizen who tries to act "for the good of the town"—the most widely used indicator of "good" being retail sales. He can always cite instances of his paper's publishing the name of some prominent citizen arrested for drunken driving, but if the businessmen at the café think that it would be for the good of the town to wait for a while before saying anything about plans for a new industrial park or problems with the old one, the publisher is likely to cooperate. The editor is also likely to cooperate. He's a good citizen, too.

I first read about the Nampa paper's problems in the *Intermountain Observer,* an enterprising weekly that is published in Boise and circulated throughout the state. Not having a precise hometown, the *Observer* is not afflicted with the hometownism that comes with having coffee at downtown cafés or, in larger cities, lunch at downtown businessmen's clubs. A year after the first article, the *Observer* ran a piece by Oren Campbell, who had been the negative and controversial editor of *The Idaho Free Press,* on the occasion of his inevitable departure. In Nampa, the people who were irritated by Campbell's article were not surprised that the *Observer* was where it appeared. John Brandt, a real-estate man, who is the most influential businessman in Nampa, says of the *Observer,* "It's a dirty sheet if ever there was one." Adam J. Kalb, who publishes the *Free Press* for a chain called the Scripps League of Newspapers, refers to the *Observer* as "an offbeat publication"— which in terms of the Scripps League of Newspapers it is.

Campbell came to Nampa in 1966 from Wichita, where he had been a sports editor. Nampa, with about twenty thousand people, is the largest town in Canyon County, although the county seat is in Caldwell, six miles away—a town with which Nampa has always had a rivalry that includes not only high-school football games but also activities that would normally be considered the province of adults. A fertile agricultural area not far from Boise,

Canyon County now has a number of food-processing plants, which keep the economy healthy and on certain evenings make the clear Western air of Nampa smell like eighty-five million potato peels. Even by Idaho standards, Canyon County has always been particularly conservative. The letters column in the *Free Press* regularly runs letters with headlines like COMMUNISM IS CANCER OF MIND or CONSPIRACY DOES EXIST.

Campbell liked Nampa. He joined the Jaycees and the Optimists. He praised the school board for its fiscal responsibility. He worked relatively smoothly with Pete Hackworth, the editor of the Caldwell *News-Tribune*, which is published in conjunction with the *Free Press* in a financially profitable but editorially awkward arrangement that calls for some pages appearing in both papers. Campbell's editorials were routinely approved without change by Adam Kalb, who had encouraged him to write with some bite— the previous editor's having, in Kalb's opinion, carried noncontroversy almost too far. (That editor was made publisher of another Scripps League newspaper—one of the few publishers in the chain to have been selected from the editorial department rather than the advertising department.) The first serious disagreement between Campbell and Kalb didn't come until the senatorial campaign of 1968, when Senator Frank Church was being opposed by a Republican congressman named George Hansen; Kalb decided that the *Free Press* would endorse Hansen, and the endorsement was made. Campbell, who usually votes Republican himself, wanted to publish a personal letter taking exception to the endorsement, and Kalb refused to allow it. Campbell didn't challenge Kalb's right to decide on the endorsement or to refuse to print a letter from his editor that would have undercut it. In American journalism, no one seriously objects to the fact that the man who has final responsibility for advising the community on political matters is usually someone who prepared for that role by selling advertising space to department stores.

When the Woolworth store in Nampa closed, the *Free Press* quoted the manager as saying that downtown Nampa was no longer much of a place to do business, a conclusion that would seem fairly apparent even to a casual shopper, since about all the downtown merchants did to counter the new shopping centers was to declare that two dreary square blocks downtown were no longer two dreary square blocks downtown but "The Loop—Idaho's Largest Shopping Center," and put up a sign to prove it. The balanced way to have handled the Woolworth closing, one member of the business community later said, was demonstrated by the newspaper of another Idaho town that lost its Woolworth—a sentence or so about the closing of the store and then a paragraph about all the businesses that had recently moved into the town. Some downtown businessmen were beginning to think that *Free Press* photographers made a specialty of empty storefronts.

Campbell eventually made education his specialty and came to believe that fiscal responsibility had some limitations as an educational philosophy. A group of Nampa citizens—many of them people who had moved in from other places, and a remarkable number of them wives of doctors—were campaigning for changes in the schools, a campaign that was necessarily negative, being based on the premise that Nampa schools were badly in need of change. Campbell gave the campaign a lot of space in the news columns, and editorially the *Free Press* became an advocate of what the reformers called "innovations" and what some other citizens called "frills." There came a time when it seemed to John Brandt—who had served on the school board for eighteen years— that just about every headline in an issue of the *Free Press* announced something critical of Nampa.

The irritation of the business community came out in the open during a series on sanitation and housing problems in the spring of 1969. The articles included pictures of uncollected garbage and pictures of run-down housing—housing that, in the words of one businessman, "you could find in any town." The fourth piece in the series was headlined GHETTO-LIKE HOUSING EXISTS RIGHT HERE IN VALLEY. It included an interview with a former Canyon County health director, who, speaking in Caldwell, said, "I don't think the realtors here make a business of promoting cheap housing as much as they do in Nampa." The Nampa Board of Realtors wrote a formal letter to deny that charge, and some other citizens, expressing what was probably the prevailing viewpoint in Nampa, wrote letters that included statements like "Filthy conditions are developed by filthy people" and "No human being will live in a house not fit to live in." The real-estate people gathered signatures for a letter to Kalb about the paper's emphasis on the negative and the controversial. "This policy is harmful to our businesses and, in fact, has an adverse effect on advertising placed in the paper," the letter said. "We respectfully request that the editorial policy be changed to conform more nearly with the desires of the community, taking a more positive approach to promote Nampa and the benefits of living here." Brandt, an erect, straightforward man in his sixties, who often uses the word "wholesome" to describe conditions he considers beneficial to the town, sees the letter to Kalb as a matter of simple economics, a "veiled threat" to withdraw advertising. "If it's bad for our business, why should we advertise?" he now says. "If there's something wrong, we don't condone glossing it over, but suppose you were a person thinking about moving here and read the paper and read everything bad. It's our business to be optimistic about the community. The more people who come in here and buy farms or move businesses in here, the more we make." The people who had worked for educational reform sent a rebuttal letter that said, in part, "We believe it is crucial to the future life and progress of our community to have a newspaper unafraid to comment and to show us up, warts and all." Kalb was officially invited to the weekly meeting of the Chamber of Commerce board—the Friday breakfast meeting at the Hong Kong Cafe—to talk about the paper.

Those who attended the Chamber of Commerce meeting told Kalb that they weren't asking the paper to be totally uncritical but merely objective and balanced—so that, one man suggested, if it became necessary, for some extraordinary reason, to print a picture of a shack, the picture should be accompanied by a picture of some of Nampa's fine houses. What the businessmen said they objected to was, as Brandt put it, "always looking for the one percent negative instead of the ninety-nine percent positive." Kalb found himself in an odd position. He didn't want anybody telling him how to run his business, and he said so. He stated that the newspaper would continue to print the truth. On the other hand, he agreed that it had been bad taste to run the housing series on the front page—complete with pictures of dirty shacks. As a businessman who knew that problems should be handled quietly behind the scenes, he was less offended at the attack on the paper than at the method—the fact that the realtors had circulated a petition instead of merely coming into his office to talk matters over. "First it got local publicity and then state publicity and then national publicity," Kalb now says. "If they had handled it properly, it never would have gone that far." All the publicity resulted from the piece in the *Intermountain Observer*. In Nampa, neither the veiled threat to the publisher nor the letter of support from the reformers nor the confrontation at the Hong Kong Cafe made the paper.

Some businessmen thought the *Free Press* calmed down for a while after the meeting with Kalb, but no one thought it was likely to meet John Brandt's standards of wholesomeness as long as Campbell was the editor. When an issue of the Nampa highschool paper included, among other matters of controversy, a signed editorial advising students to refuse induction into the armed forces, Brandt withdrew his advertising, and Campbell defended the right of the high-school editor to state an opinion with which the *Free Press* did not happen to agree. The *Free Press* ran a two-part interview with a former Peace Corps volunteer from a nearby town who had gone to Cuba to cut sugar cane and had returned with impressions that most people in Nampa considered too controversial but not negative enough. With a referendum for a new school tax levy approaching, Campbell wrote a series of pieces on the schools that had headlines like SECONDARY CLASSES BULGING and GRADE SCHOOL NEED COSTLY. Campbell's advice had been ignored by the voters on a couple of previous school elections, and by the time of the voting on the tax levy some people in Nampa thought of it as Oren Campbell's personal crusade. It was overwhelmingly defeated. Campbell's reaction was to write a bad-tempered column headlined THEY TURNED AGAINST THE KIDS, which identified those he accused of putting personal prejudice above the welfare of the community's children. Brandt, who happened to be speaking that night at the retirement ceremony of some teachers and principals loyal to the old ways, said that the defeat had been a good thing for the town, and added that it had been caused by, among others, "certain busybodies in the community and doctors' wives" and "Oren Campbell and the *Free Press*."

By the time of Brandt's speech, communication between Kalb and Campbell had degenerated into an exchange of sarcastic memos. Kalb keeps a file of the outraged memos he sent Campbell—about the editorial department's not using dresses from local stores in the fall-fashion issue, about Campbell's showing him editorials only when it was too late to change them. One of Campbell's memos implied that Kalb was embarrassed by any story that his friends at the country club found offensive. The column about the referendum was looked upon by Kalb as the final act of insubordination—a way of getting around Kalb's check of the editorial page by sneaking something into the news columns. By the middle of the summer, Campbell had left to become managing editor of a paper in Bremerton, Washington.

Now that Campbell has been gone for a while, there are several theories in Nampa about why so many of the citizens found him irritating. Some believe that Campbell was seriously handicapped by being an outsider who had come in and started telling people to change the way they had always done things; Brandt sometimes refers to him as "that editor from Chicago," Campbell having spent a year and a half away from Kansas working for a Chicago paper. A lot of people believe that, particularly on the education issue, Campbell caused considerable irritation by a tendency to harp on a subject. Pete Hackworth, who has been the editor of the Caldwell *News-Tribune* for a number of years and is now the editorial director of both papers, says that the *News-Tribune* has been critical of Caldwell at times but has been careful not to dwell on a subject after the point has been made. Larry Gardner, the new editor of the *Free Press,* says that Campbell lost his objectivity and became personally involved in the referendum campaign. In his farewell piece in the *Observer,* Campbell said that he was silenced by "the crowd from the country club," and both Hackworth and Gardner resent what they believe to be the implication that those in charge now are willing to knuckle under. They say that the paper is as willing to print negative articles as it ever was, and Gardner points with some pride at the irritation of the local farmers over the *Free Press* coverage of efforts to organize farm workers during the summer.

Those in the community who were most actively working for change believe that the days of front-page crusades have passed for the *Free Press*. The businessmen believe they have won. A lot of them seem to look back on Campbell's editorship as a kind of aberration that has now ended. A businessman who tries to explain the aberration tends to speak in terms of economics, so he might say something like "I guess sensationalism sells more papers," and then shake his head in disappointment at somebody who would put his own commercial interests ahead of what is good for the town. "You see, we were spoiled by having a great editor here for many years," one of the businessmen told me. "He was one of the greatest editors in the West. He knew when to write a story and when to keep his damn mouth shut."

A Few Observations on the Zapping of the Inner Circle

1972

S ome New York Irish who always assumed that GAA stood for the Gaelic Athletic Association are now being told that it stands for the Gay Activists Alliance. A lot of them have not made the adjustment. The editorial page of the New York *Daily News,* which unofficially reflects the views of the New York Irish in the same way that *L'Osservatore Romano* unofficially reflects the views of the Vatican, seems to have been unaffected by all the talk in the last few years about the civil rights of homosexuals. A dozen years ago, when homosexuality was hardly ever discussed in print, other papers tried to hint at the homosexual relationship between two National Security Agency cryptographers who had defected to Russia by mentioning their shared lodgings or their constant companionship; the *News* settled the matter by referring to Nikita S. Khrushchev as "the Red fairy-snatcher." Just this spring, in an editorial expressing approval of the Supreme Court's refusal to consider the case of a man who was denied a job by a state government because of his homosexuality, the *News* broadened its views on the subject only to the extent of offering its readers a larger selection of sobriquets: "Fairies, nances, swishes, fags, lezzes—call 'em what you please." The editorial was headlined ANY OLD JOBS FOR HOMOS?

In the view of activist homosexuals, the hostility expressed in the *News* is typical of people tied to an ethnic culture that is strongly affected by religion. Some of the homosexuals who have been lobbying at City Hall for the passage of Intro. 475—a proposal to extend the city's anti-discrimination law to cover "sexual orientation"—say that one Jewish member of the City Council explained he could not vote for the bill because his rabbi had told him homosexuality was a sin. New Yorkers who consider themselves too sophisticated to hold views imposed by their ethnic or religious backgrounds read the *Times* instead of the *News* in the morning, but the Gay Activists Alliance claims that the *Times* engages in a form of "media oppression" that differs from the variety practiced by the *News* only in the matter of subtlety. Writing this March in *(MORE)*, a New York review of journalism, Merle Miller accused the *Times* of being unwilling (or perhaps unable) to recognize the significance of any events involving gay liberation—the significance, for instance, of the first fight that homosexuals put up against the police, during a raid in 1969 on a gay bar called the Stonewall. (Today, the battle at the Stonewall is accepted as the beginning of the gay-liberation movement in New York.) Homosexuals have accused the *Times* of ignoring or burying news about gay liberation, and of balancing what it does carry with pronouncements from the people whom homosexual activists consider much more dangerous enemies than the editorialists of the *News*—the psychiatrists who maintain that homosexuality is not an alternative way of life but a sickness. The Gay Activists Alliance has at times considered expressing its complaints against the *Times* by means of a demonstration—usually referred to among the members as a zap—and it did stage a demonstration at the *News* offices after the editorial on the right of homosexuals to job protection.

This April, the GAA decided to protest "media oppression" in general by zapping a formal press banquet—the annual Inner Circle show at the New York Hilton.

What now seems most surprising about the evening in the Hilton ballroom was that women's liberationists didn't get there first. The two official requirements for induction into the Inner Circle are having reported on City Hall politics for at least a year and being male. When the Inner Circle stages its annual show making fun of the city's politicians, the female roles are a burden borne by men who lack organizational seniority—giving the evening at the Hilton some resemblance to those scenes in Second World War movies in which the enlisted men in the German prison camp stage a burlesque for the entertainment of the officers. Until a couple of years ago, maleness was also a prerequisite for the guests who watched the show from banquet tables on the main floor of the ballroom; the main-floor tables are now open to female public officials who hold the rank of city commissioner or above. Non-officeholding female guests still have to eat in the balcony. Mary Lindsay, the mayor's wife, is apparently the first one of them to have thought of commenting on the seating arrangements by flicking peanuts at the men below.

A group called Media Women had, in fact, privately considered picketing the Inner Circle dinner this year, but the possibility of a demonstration of any kind had evidently not occurred to the people sitting in the Hilton ballroom. When Gay Activists Alliance demonstrators burst into the ballroom during the intermission between the second and third acts, some guests thought they were part of the show. The demonstrators handed the guests leaflets that quoted the *News* editorial as an example of press prejudice. They briefly captured the public-address system backstage. Eventually, after a minor scuffle or two, they were put out of the ballroom. But at the escalator in the foyer outside there was more than a scuffle. When the demonstrators left the Hilton, at least two of them had been badly beaten.

In the Sunday papers the following day, the GAA demonstration was hardly mentioned, but on Monday the *New York Post,* which has no Sunday edition, carried an angry and explicit column by Pete Hamill on the beatings. According to Hamill's sources, the most violent of the guests had been Michael Maye, the president of the firemen's union. That gave the evening a certain symmetry, since Mickey Maye is the personification of the *News* editorial page—a former Golden Gloves national heavyweight champion, a decorated firefighter, an ex-Ranger with combat service in Korea, a model of the tough, two-fisted Irish he-man whose voice the *News* editorialists always seem to be trying to reproduce. Hamill wrote that Maye had broken through the crowd to beat and stomp on a demonstrator who was on the escalator. Pursuing the story, the *Post* reported that three or four city officials had been eyewitnesses to the beating. Finally, a grand jury considered the case, but the charge it brought against Maye was not assault but harassment—a charge comparable in seriousness to a traffic violation.

In arguing that the press and the City Council should treat homosexuals like any other legitimate minority group, the Gay Activists Alliance is trying to persuade newspapermen and city councilmen who probably do not believe that homosexuals really *are* a legitimate minority group. A letter from the GAA to the staff of the *Times* said that the paper's extensive use of quotations from psychiatrists about the illness of homosexuals was "rather as if at the beginning of the black civil rights movement the *Times* had chosen to 'balance' any story of black life or political activity with interviews with those few Bible Belt zoologists who continued to believe in 'black inferiority.'" But the analogy holds only if the *Times* considers homosexuals a minority group rather than a lot of people who happen to be sick in the same way. Intro. 475 was voted down by the City Council's General Welfare Committee in January even though it had almost no organized opposition. Most of the councilmen who voted against it were presumably voting their consciences—refusing to grant the respectability of the law to a way of life they considered immoral. Intro. 475 has become the paramount issue of the gay-liberation movement in New York—not so much because it would offer a certain amount of job or housing protection to homosexuals as because it would legitimize homosexuality by placing homosexuals right there in the law with the other minority groups.

In a speech at New York University this year, Eldon Clingan, one of the co-sponsors of Intro. 475, told homosexual activists that they could not realistically expect their demonstrations to cause confrontations of conscience. (The Gay Activists Alliance has, in fact, used demonstrations almost strictly for strategic harassment—zapping the apartment house of the chairman of the General Welfare Committee late at night last fall, for instance, to persuade him to gain some peace by scheduling a vote on Intro. 475.) Clingan pointed out that an important element in the movement that set the style for modern American demonstrations—the black movement in the South—was the tension between what Americans supposedly believed in and what they knew about the way black people were treated. When the movement forced Americans to decide, say, whether black people had the right to vote, the only public defense left to Southern whites was to say that more time was needed to set things right in an orderly way. But there is no contradiction between popularly accepted American ideals and a contempt for homosexuals. The only tension, in fact, is likely to be found in liberals who try to maintain a position of tolerance toward something they have been brought up to believe is either an unfortunate disability or a willful perversion. When gay-liberation demonstrators zapped a fund-raising benefit for Mayor Lindsay—whose administration supports Intro. 475, although without unseemly fervor—none of them were beaten. But, according to Miller, the reaction of some of the well-off liberals to the disturbance was to shout "Faggot!" at the nearest demonstrator.

Around Room 9, the pressroom of City Hall, the dominant response to the demonstration has been irritation at the unfavorable publicity it brought the Inner Circle. Hamill and others have written that many of the members responsible for staging the annual show now earn their living as press agents rather than as reporters. *(MORE)* ran a piece by Terry Pristin saying that those Inner Circle regulars who are reporters spend most of their time in Room 9 "filing routine budget stories and gossiping to pass the time between City Council meetings." The hundred dollars a plate charged for the Inner Circle dinner goes to charity after expenses are deducted, but Pristin claimed there was little left for charity after the Inner Circle had paid for a lavish production and two or three months of boozy rehearsals. In a column in the *Post,* James Wechsler questioned the Inner Circle members' talent (although the demonstrators were obviously trespassing, he said, a reading of the show's lyrics indicated that "almost any diversionary performance should have been welcome"), and even their virility. "Avowed homosexuals are ancient targets for sadistic bullyism," Wechsler wrote. "In the age of Kinsey, however, it is reasonable to voice skepticism about those who must belligerently affirm their manhood by kicking around the vulnerable or laughing on the sidelines."

According to the talk in Room 9, such criticism obscured the fact that it was the Inner Circle that was harassed and the GAA that did the harassing. The Inner Circle, after all, was holding a private party, and no gay liberationists had been invited. Although the demonstrators say they had heard at the last minute that the show contained a scene ridiculing homosexuals, the demonstration had been organized to register complaints against the press in general rather than to protest any policies of the Inner Circle. No one has claimed that any Inner Circle members hit anyone. Joe Famm, a radio reporter who is this year's Inner Circle president, says that even the rumor about the show's having a sketch mocking homosexuals was untrue. In the scene in question, the leading opponent of Intro. 475 asks where he can find the bill's sponsor, and another councilman, mincing across the stage, says, "Kiss me and I'll tell you." Describing the exchange recently, Famm said, "What the hell's so offensive about that?"

Any newsdealer who saw the defense and the prosecution witnesses waiting to testify at the trial of Mickey Maye could have sized up the contest immediately—a bunch of *News* readers against a bunch of *Times* readers. For the defense, a group of firemen, all of them union officials, took the stand to offer testimony consistent with Maye's version of what had happened on the escalator—that he had merely run down to set a fellow firefighter on his feet, without hitting or stomping anyone. ("Look at the size of me! If I stomped on anybody, you think that fellow'd be walking around?") The firemen were Irish or Italian. They had short haircuts. A couple of them wore American-flag pins in their lapels. Of the dozens of people who must have seen some part of the violence at the Hilton, five city officials came forward to testify against Mickey Maye, and none of them had a short haircut or an American-flag pin. All of them were dressed in a way that would have made them inconspicuous in any gathering of the mod staff men of the Lindsay administration. Four of them were Jewish. The fifth was John Scanlon, who is in charge of public affairs for the Economic Development Administration. Scanlon is indisputably Irish—a former participant in the Gaelic Athletic Association, an organizer of the Northern Ireland Civil Rights League, a man who described his decision to come forward as the result of what the nuns had taught him in eighth grade civics—but he was described by GAA activists, with some wonder, as "a liberated Irishman." Scanlon wears a full beard and used to work in publishing and has appeared in a movie and associates with the kind of New York Irishmen who still put in a lot of saloon time but in literary saloons. (Hamill, in fact, first heard about the demonstration from

Scanlon over drinks at Elaine's.) But Scanlon, however sophisticated, was the witness culturally out of place. A fireman might not
be surprised at being turned in by a deculturated Jewish liberal
wearing a double-knit blazer and a wide tie; when Maye muttered
curses in the hall against his oppressors, it was Scanlon he muttered against.

On the stand, Maye assumed the kind of moral stance that
might be expected of anyone accused of tormenting people who
are generally considered a threat to morality. He and his friends
had decided to ask the demonstrators to leave, he said, only after
they began to use profanity. In answer to the prosecutor's question, Maye said he did not indulge in profanity himself. The prosecutor implied that Maye might have been a barroom brawler in
the past and might have once worked as a bouncer at a gay bar, but
Maye said he did not go into bars. Every day, when Maye left the
courtroom, GAA members—most of them wearing dungarees decorated with GAA patches or the Lambda sign of gay militancy—
would gather around him as the television cameras approached. A
brace of tiny defense lawyers who appeared to be hanging on
Maye's huge arms would shout "No comment! No comment!" But
Mickey Maye seemed to find a comment difficult to resist. When a
man from WCBS-TV approached after the first day in court, Maye
said, "I don't know what the hell I'm doing in a place like that—
queers, homosexuals, and every degenerate in the country." Then
he added that the complainants seemed to want to "kiss and make
up." Then he smiled—like the *News,* unrepentant.

Maye was found not guilty. The judge, mentioning the conflict-
ing testimony, said the prosecution had not proved the case beyond a reasonable doubt. The president of the Gay Activists
Alliance reacted by repeating his accusation that the District Attorney's office had never made a serious effort to prove the case at
all—the lesson being, he said, that "gay women and men have no
rights." After Maye had expressed his disgust at the whole affair to

television interviewers, he was asked what he now thought of Intro. 475, which is scheduled to come up for another vote in committee this month. "Anyone's entitled to advance himself in any field he's capable of doing," Maye said. "But I don't want to see them in the school system, because there's a moral question there. And I don't want them in the New York Fire Department, because my life depends on the *man* behind me."

The Truth Will Out

1978

As a lover of truth, I am naturally pleased to see the facts emerging about the prediction attributed to H. L. Mencken concerning the first president from the Deep South. I suppose what stirred interest in the passage from the start was that, by chance, the First Family Mencken envisioned seemed rather close to our very own Carter First Family: "The President's brother, a prime specimen of *Boobus Collumnus Rubericus,* will gather his loutish companions on the porch of the White House to swill beer from the bottle and snigger over whispered barnyard jokes about the darkies. The President's Cousin, LaVerne, will travel the Hallelujah circuit as one of Mrs. McPherson's soldiers in Christ, praying for the conversion of some Northern Sodom's most Satanic pornographer as she waves his work—well thumbed— for all the yokels to gasp at. The incumbent himself, shorn of his bumpkin ways by some of Grady's New South hucksters, will have a charm comparable to that of the leading undertaker of Dothan, Alabama." After the quote had been reprinted in a number of newspapers, Mencken scholars began saying that they had been unable to find it anywhere in Mencken's writings. At the time, I described their inability to come up with the passage as "yet another demonstration of the limitations of American scholarship."

Last spring, I reprinted the Mencken quotation in this column—reprinted it routinely, I might add, in the way that American newspapers once routinely reprinted the body count handed out each day by the U.S. Army spokesman in Saigon.

For a while, other publications reprinted the passage as routinely as I had. Then we were faced with what I can only call a backlash. It was led by Georgia state senator Julian Bond, whose statesmanlike exterior, I know, has masked a deep sense of frustration and rage ever since he managed, in 1961, to integrate the public tennis courts of Atlanta only to be beaten in straight sets by a female dietitian in her late fifties. Bond himself reprinted the Mencken passage in a column for the *Atlanta Gazette,* provoking a *Los Angeles Times* investigation of its origin which has not been matched for journalistic enterprise since my own investigation, in the early 1970s, uncovered a conspiracy between Richard M. Nixon and Willard Marriott to consolidate all of the cooking in this country into one gigantic kitchen, to be located somewhere in Virginia.

The *Los Angeles Times* reporter, Jeff Prugh, questioned a number of Mencken scholars, including Alistair Cooke, who put together *The Vintage Mencken.* According to Prugh's account, Cooke "pored voraciously" over his Mencken collection for nine days, and then concluded that the passage was a "mischievous parody." The tip-off, Cooke said, was the use of the word "pornographer," as in the president's cousin "praying for the conversion of some Northern Sodom's most Satanic pornographer as she waves his work—well thumbed—for all the yokels to gasp at." Informing Prugh that "pornographer" was little used in the 1920s, Cooke offered the opinion that the entire passage may have been invented by Julian Bond.

A few days later, Bond hastened to clear himself by telling the implacable Prugh that the passage may have originated in this column. I had to face up to the implication carried in Bond's words: there was a possibility that the person who passed the quotation on to me, a person I have refused to say was or was not Zbigniew Brzezinski, had taken advantage of my trusting nature. But Bond, like one of those fallen-away Stalinists who immediately start accusing everyone of being an agent of the Red Menace, began writing letters to the editor claiming that I was not what used to be dismissed as a "useful idiot" but the inventor of the quotation myself—a conscious hoaxer of the American people who had been caught at last by the wily Cooke. According to Bond's letters, I had been driven to the deed by my embarrassment at having been snookered many years before by "a story about 'seal boy,' a youth who fell off a boat in the Gulf of Mexico and was raised by porpoises." I was not so much angry as a little bit hurt.

Then, as so often happens in America these days, the truth began to emerge through the efforts of an accountant. Don Harvey, an accountant in Chicago, wrote me to say that "pornographer" was not only used in the twenties but had been used by Mencken himself in 1920 in a *New Republic* article called "Star Spangled Men." If I did not have access to back numbers of *The New Republic*, Harvey said, I could find the same essay reprinted in *The Vintage Mencken*, collected and with an introduction by Alistair Cooke.

This raises some questions about Cooke's role. If the Mencken quote is not genuine, why did Cooke try to shift the blame to Julian Bond? Does Cooke know Brzezinski? Does he know Don Harvey? Is it possible that Cooke had something to do with making up the quote and now fears he may be deported if discovered? Is Alistair Cooke an American citizen? If so, why does he talk so funny?

Once the truth began to emerge, it overwhelmed the naysayers and cynics. Only last month, in the course of interviewing a visiting specialist on the subject (me), *The Kansas City Star* finally printed the truth about the seal boy hoax. "The Seal Boy Hoax (a boy who supposedly lived with dolphins in the Gulf of Mexico) was a concoction Bond took for real," the *Star* article said. "He reported it, and then blamed Trillin when the truth was made known."

Recently, I received a letter about the Mencken quotation from John Givens, the news director of WAGF in Dothan, Alabama. "I could dismiss the quote as being a hoax," Mr. Givens wrote. "Instead of that, I asked around town and found that the piece reeks of Mencken's pen and may very well be authentic. Let me explain that H. L. Mencken was very much familiar with Dothan, Alabama. . . ." After listing some of Mencken's Dothan connections and reaffirming his own belief in the quotation, Mr. Givens ends by saying, "I would appreciate some insight to its authenticity." This, Mr. Givens, is it.

Part VI
NICHES

Beautiful Spot

1984

Reading the article *New York* ran on the multifaceted life of Malcolm Forbes—who manages to publish a magazine and captain transcontinental balloon flights and amass great collections and oversee vast real-estate holdings— I was interested mainly in his parking situation. We all have our own areas of specialty. Mine happens to be parking. I speak as the co-editor of *Beautiful Spot: A Magazine of Parking,* a pioneer publication in the parking media field. In fact, we are this very month celebrating the twenty-second anniversary of *Beautiful Spot*'s first issue—a celebration dampened in only the smallest way by the fact that the second issue has yet to appear.

It seems only yesterday that we were putting the first issue of *Beautiful Spot* to bed, but it was, as the diplomats say, many wars ago: the title of one piece was "The Algerian Problem (Parking in Algiers)." Time flies when you have production difficulties. My co-editor, Gerald Jonas, was then in his heyday as perhaps the finest parallel parker on the West Side of Manhattan—a multi-talented man, in the Forbes mold, who could back in well enough to be known as Two Turns Jonas and could also unearth for our premiere issue a moving poem on parking tickets (usually credited to the noted Brooklyn sonneteer L. M. Bensky):

The smalla the space the smalla the fella
Sez my cop, who puts the green things
Happy and stringy like angels' bright wings
On the cars nearest the thingamajig
Which can't be parked within fifteen feet of.

Jonas and I no longer work steadily on *Beautiful Spots*, but naturally I like to keep a hand in. That's why a passage in the article on Malcolm Forbes caught my eye: "He had begun his working day seated beside the chauffeur-bodyguard in the leather seat of his bronze Maserati, which is equipped with a telephone, New York Press plates—" Stop right there! New York Press plates? Although *Beautiful Spot* did not deal with New York Press plates in its first issue, that subject was on our list of future stories, along with "Parking and the Jewish Question" and a polemic called "Let's Put the Park Back in Park Avenue." I bring the list of future stories up to date now and then, just in case our production difficulties clear up, and I have just put at the top of the list a piece to be called "What Is Malcolm Forbes Doing with New York Press Plates?"

Is it possible that he covers those fast-breaking stories that require a reporter to screech to a halt in front of a burning building and leap out of his car, with no time to search for a parking spot? I tried to picture the action in the *Forbes* newsroom as word of a fire in a Bronx chicken-feather warehouse comes over the police radio, and Forbes is assigned the story by the gruff city editor (also named Forbes). "Forbes!" Forbes shouts. "Get on your roller skates and get out to that two-alarmer in the Bronx. If that joint burns down, the chicken-feather market's going to go through the roof, and we'll have a scoop. If Max Fortune of *Fortune* beats you out there, don't bother to come back."

I should say right here that "Get on your roller skates" is a figure of speech, peculiar to city editors. A man who has a bronze Maserati with a chauffeur-bodyguard does not roller-skate to the Bronx.

But wouldn't covering a fire present special problems for someone with a three-million-dollar car? I can imagine some sooty spray falling dangerously near the Maserati as firemen desperately soak down the warehouse. The chauffeur-bodyguard instructs the fire department lieutenant in charge to redirect the hoses, using that turn of speech peculiar to chauffeur-bodyguards: "Watch the paint job, creep."

So, as we say in the trade, I made a few calls. I asked a few questions. Why, for instance, are the stretches of curb reserved by "NYP Plates Only" signs so far from the police headquarters and so convenient to the theater district? Do newspaper editors who leave their cars in Larchmont during business hours really need NYP spaces near midtown restaurants, where they like to spend long evenings congratulating one another on exposés of congressmen who pull rank to bump decent folks off airplanes? It must be clear by now that the delay of *Beautiful Spot's* second issue has not been caused by any lack of aggressive, hardnosed reporting. We've had production difficulties.

Here is what I uncovered: The State Department of Motor Vehicles, which has nothing at all to do with the "NYP Plates Only" signs, certifies certain organizations as news-gathering organizations but leaves it to them to provide the names of those employees in need of NYP plates. (If the person who provides the list would rather include a police reporter in Queens than the man who pays his salary, fine.) The Bureau of Traffic Operations puts up the "NYP Plates Only" signs but has nothing to do with assigning the plates that make it possible to park in front of them. In other words, if you can find out precisely who is responsible for giving magazine publishers special parking privileges in New York, you can probably find out precisely who was responsible for involving this country in the Vietnam War—a war, I regret to say, which production difficulties caused *Beautiful Spot* to miss completely, much to the disappointment of readers who were looking forward to an article we had promised on the exotic parking meters of Hue.

Here is what worries me: When other influential people in New York realize that NYP plates have virtually nothing to do with gathering the news, they'll want special plates of their own. The garment industry will demand NYSB plates for designated shmatta barons, and that will bring a demand for NYRES plates from the real-estate sharks. The average parker—*Beautiful Spot*'s loyal reader—will see all these special plate signs going up as he circles the block again and again, looking for a spot. Malcolm Forbes will have nothing to worry about: he'll have his New York Big-Time Collector plates and his New York Transcontinental Ballooner plates, among others. *Beautiful Spot* will do an article on his multifaceted parking life, as soon as our production difficulties are cleared up.

By Meat Alone

2008

approached *Texas Monthly*'s cover story on "The Top 50 BBQ Joints in Texas" this summer the way a regular reader of *People* might approach that magazine's annual "Sexiest Man Alive" feature—with the expectation of seeing some familiar names. There was no reason to think that the list's top tier—the five restaurants judged to be the best in the state—would look much different than it had the last time a survey was published, in 2003. In recent years, Hollywood may have seen some advances in physical training and cosmetic surgery, but barbecue restaurants still tend to retain their luster much longer than male heartthrobs do. In fact, I've heard it argued that, absent some slippage in management, a barbecue restaurant can only get better over time: many Texas barbecue fanatics have a strong belief in the beneficial properties of accumulated grease.

In discussions of Texas barbecue, the equivalent of Matt Damon and George Clooney and Brad Pitt would be establishments like Kreuz Market and Smitty's Market, in Lockhart; City Market, in Luling; and Louie Mueller Barbecue, in Taylor—places that reflect the barbecue tradition that developed during the nineteenth century out of German and Czech meat markets in the Hill Country of central Texas. (In fact, the title of *Texas Monthly*'s first article on barbecue—it was published in 1973, shortly after the magazine's founding—was "The World's Best Barbecue Is in Taylor, Texas. Or Is It Lockhart?") Those restaurants, all of which had been in the top tier in 2003, were indeed there again in this summer's survey. For the first time, though, a No. 1 had been named, and it was not one of the old familiars. "The best barbecue in Texas," the article said, "is currently being served at Snow's BBQ, in Lexington."

I had never heard of Snow's. That surprised me. Although I grew up in Kansas City, which has a completely different style of barbecue, I have always kept au courant of Texas barbecue, like a sports fan who is almost monomaniacally obsessed with basketball but glances over at the NHL standings now and then just to see how things are going. Reading that the best barbecue in Texas was at a place I'd never heard of, I felt like a *People* subscriber who had picked up the "Sexiest Man Alive" issue and discovered that the sexiest man alive was Sheldon Ludnick, an insurance adjuster from Terre Haute, Indiana, with Clooney as the runner-up.

An accompanying story on how a Numero Uno had emerged, from three hundred and forty-one spots visited by the staff, revealed that before work began on the 2008 survey nobody at *Texas Monthly* had heard of Snow's, either. Lexington, a trading town of twelve hundred people in Lee County, is only about fifty miles from Austin, where *Texas Monthly* is published, and Texans think nothing of driving that far for lunch—particularly if the lunch consists of brisket that has been subjected to slow heat since the early hours of the morning. *Texas Monthly* has had a strong posse of barbecue enthusiasts since its early days. Griffin Smith, Jr., who wrote the 1973 barbecue article and is now the executive editor of the *Arkansas Democrat-Gazette*, in Little Rock, was known for keeping a map of the state on his wall with pushpins marking barbecue joints he had been to, the way General Patton might have kept a map marked with spots where night patrols had probed the

German line. I could imagine the staffers not knowing about a superior barbecue restaurant in East Texas; the Southern style of barbecue served there, often on a bun, has never held much interest for Austin connoisseurs. But their being unaware of a top-tier establishment less than an hour's drive away astonished me.

I know some of the *Texas Monthly* crowd. In fact, I once joined Greg Curtis, the former editor, and Steve Harrigan, a novelist who's had a long association with the magazine, on a pilgrimage to Lockhart, which some barbecue fans visit the way the devout of another sort walk the Camino de Santiago. I know Evan Smith, who was the editor of the magazine when this latest barbecue survey was published and has since been promoted to a position that might be described as boss of bosses. I couldn't imagine Smith jiggering the results for nefarious purposes—say, telling his staff to declare a totally unknown barbecue place the best in Texas simply as a way of doing what some magazine editors call "juicing up the story." I took him at his word when, a few months after the list was published, he told me how Snow's had been found. His staff had gone through the letters written after the 2003 survey complaining about the neglect of a superior specialist in pork ribs or the inclusion of a place whose smoked sausage wasn't fit for pets—what Smith, who's from Queens, refers to as "Dear Schmuck letters."

He did acknowledge that his decision to name a No. 1—rather than just a top tier, as in the previous barbecue surveys—came about partly because everyone was so enthusiastic about Snow's product but partly because its story was so compelling. Smith himself was not in a position to confirm the quality of the product. Being from Queens is not the only handicap he has had to surmount in his rise through the ranks of Texas journalism: he has been a vegetarian for nearly twenty-five years. (The fact that he can resist the temptation presented by the aroma of Texas pit barbecue, he has said, is a strong indication that he will never "return to the dark side.") As a longtime editor, though, he knew a Cinderella story when he saw one. It wasn't just that Snow's had been unknown to a Texas barbecue fancy that is notably mobile. Snow's proprietor, Kerry Bexley, was a former rodeo clown who worked as a blending-facility operator at a coal mine. Snow's pit master, Tootsie Tomanetz, was a woman in her early seventies who worked as the custodian of the middle school in Giddings, Texas—the Lee County seat, eighteen miles to the south. After five years of operating Snow's, both still had their day jobs. Also, Snow's was open only on Saturday mornings, from eight until the meat ran out.

My conversation with Evan Smith took place in a Chevrolet Suburban traveling from Austin toward Lexington. I'd been picked up at my hotel at 7:20 A.M. The *Texas Monthly* rankings had attracted large crowds to Snow's, and, even four months later, we weren't taking any chances. Greg Curtis and Steve Harrigan were with Smith in the back seats. Harrigan was one of the people who, having been tipped off between the time the feature was completed and the time the magazine came out, hurried over to Snow's like inside traders in possession of material information not available to the public. He seemed completely unrepentant. "I took my brother and brother-in-law and son-in-law and nephew," he said, smiling slyly. Next to me in the front seat, Paul Burka was doing the driving. Greg Curtis once reminded me that "all barbecue experts are self-proclaimed," but *Texas Monthly* had enough faith in Burka's expertise to send him to Snow's late in the selection process as what Smith calls "the closer." It was up to Burka to confirm or dismiss the judgment of the staffer whose assigned territory for the survey included Lexington, and of Patricia Sharpe, the editor in charge of the project, and of a second staffer sent in as a triple-check. Some people at the magazine had predicted that Burka wouldn't like Snow's barbecue simply because it bore Pat Sharpe's imprimatur. "Paul thinks Pat's judgment of restaurants is fancy and white tablecloth and Pat thinks Paul is a philistine," I heard from the back seat. "And they're both right."

When I spoke to Pat Sharpe a couple of days later, she bristled at the accusation that she is a person of elevated taste. "I'll eat barbecue in the rattiest joint there is," she said in her own defense. Burka, on the other hand, seemed unconcerned about being called a philistine. He is a large man with a white mustache and a midsection that reflects a forty-year interest in Texas barbecue. Having grown up in Galveston, which is not a barbecue center, he innocently started eating what he now describes as "'barbecue' that was one step removed from roast beef" while he was a student at Rice, in Houston; he had his true conversion experience on a trip to Lockhart with Griffin Smith in 1967, when they were both in law school at the University of Texas. Burka, who worked for five years in the Texas state legislature, writes about politics for *Texas Monthly*. Speaking to him as the Suburban rolled toward Lexington, I was reminded of the Austin brought to life in *The Gay Place*, Billy Lee Brammer's marvelous 1961 novel about an LBJ-like governor called Arthur (Goddam) Fenstermaker. That Austin was essentially a two-company town—the university and the state government—and I always pictured those connected with both companies sharing irreverent observations of the passing scene while consuming a lot of beer in the back of Scholz's beer garden. It is an Austin that is sometimes difficult to discern in a much larger city of slick office buildings and computer-company headquarters and the mother church of Whole Foods, which offers barbecue in the meat department of its Austin stores. ("Organic barbecue," Burka muttered, when somebody brought that up.)

The first time Burka went to Lexington to check out Snow's, he arrived just before noon. "It looked like it had never been open," he said. "It was deserted." When he finally got there at a time when meat was still available, he was convinced. In fact, he was rhapsodic, particularly concerning the brisket ("as soft and sweet as cookie dough") and the pork butt. Smith believed that Burka's description of the latter—"the butt was tender and yielding"—was in need of some editing, but without having to consume any critters personally, he was persuaded by Burka's report. Snow's was to be named the best barbecue in Texas, and Evan Smith never had any doubt about what would happen as soon as that designation was on the newsstands. "I basically said, 'Congratulations and I'm sorry,'" he told me, "because I knew what would happen."

"That brings up the subject of remorse," I said.

"You mean remorse on their part?" Smith asked.

"No, remorse on your part—remorse for having turned the place into an ugly scene."

"We don't publish *Best-Kept Secrets Monthly,*" Smith said, as he got out of Burka's Suburban. He sniffed confidently, presumably to reassure himself that, despite the aroma, he would have no trouble limiting himself to coleslaw and potato salad. Then he marched across the street toward Snow's BBQ.

Regular consumers of Hill Country style Texas barbecue know what to expect when they walk into an establishment that is said to offer the real article. I had never been to Louie Mueller's, in Taylor, before this trip, but when Greg Curtis and I went there the day before the Snow's outing for what we referred to as some warmup barbecue, the place looked familiar. At a Texas barbecue joint, you normally pick up a tray at the counter and order meat from one person and sides from another. The person doling out the meat removes it from the smoker and carves it himself. It is sold by the pound—often brisket and pork ribs and sausage and beef ribs and chicken and, in some places, clod (beef shoulder). The carver serves it on some variety of butcher paper. If, despite having worked with smoke in his eyes for many years, he is of a generous nature, as the carvers at Mueller's are known to be, he might slice off a piece of a brisket's darkened outside—what would be called in Kansas City a burnt end—and, before you've ordered anything, place it on your tray as a small gesture. (Given the quality of Mueller's brisket, it is a gesture that can make a traveler feel immensely pleased about being back in Texas.) A couple of slices of packaged white bread are also included. Usually, the only way to have a brisket sandwich in central Texas is to make your own.

A Texas barbecue joint is likely to have neon beer signs on the walls, and those walls are likely to have been darkened by years of smoke. At Mueller's, a cavernous place in a former school gym, there is a large bulletin board festooned with business cards, and most of the cards by now look like specks of brownish parchment. In a restaurant serving Hill Country barbecue, there may be bottles of sauce on the tables, but the meat does not come out of the pits slathered in sauce. I remember a sign at Kreuz Market announcing that the management provided neither sauce nor salads nor forks. In central Texas, you don't hear a lot of people talking about the piquancy of a restaurant's sauce or the tastiness of its beans; discussions are what a scholar of the culture might call meat-driven.

Geographically, Lexington is not in the Hill Country—it's in ranch land, northeast of Austin—but ethnically it is. Burka told me that a politician from Lee County once said to him, "It's the Germans against the Czechs, and the Americans are the swing vote." Snow's BBQ turned out to have the sort of layout found in a place like Kreuz Market, except in miniature. It's a small dark-red building that has room for a counter and six tables—with a few more tables outside, near the cast-iron smokers that in Texas are referred to as pits, even if they're not in the ground. A sign listed what meats were available, all for $8.45 a pound: sausage, brisket, pork, pork ribs, and chicken. The sides offered were "Mrs. Patschke's homemade coleslaw and potato salad," plus free beans. There were only a couple of people ahead of us in line. Burka stepped up to the counter to order.

"Are there five of you?" the young woman slicing the meat asked, as Burka tried to figure out how many pounds we needed.

"Well," Burka said, glancing at Evan Smith. "Four, really. One is . . . he has a big meal coming up."

"You're ashamed of your friend," I whispered to Burka. "You've abandoned him."

"I just couldn't say the V-word," Burka said. He looked sheepish—not, I would guess, a normal look for him.

I had warned the *Texas Monthly* crowd that if they were looking for confirmation of their ranking by an objective outlander, someone from Kansas City was not likely to provide it. A jazz fan taken to a rock concert might admire the musical technique, but he probably wouldn't make an ecstatic rush to the stage. As we sat down at one of the outside tables, under a galvanized-tin covering, I told them that they could expect the sort of response that a proud young father I know has received during the past year or so whenever he e-mails me pictures of his firstborn: "A perfectly adequate child." Still, what Burka had ordered was good enough to make me forget that we were eating a huge meal of barbecue at a time on Saturday morning when most people were starting to wonder what they might rustle up for breakfast once they bestirred themselves. I particularly liked the brisket, although I couldn't attest that it was as soft and sweet as cookie dough. In Kansas City, it is not customary to eat cookie dough.

Although Snow's hours may seem odd to a city dweller, they seem normal in Lexington. Saturday is traditionally when farmers and ranchers from the surrounding area come into town, and at twelve-thirty every Saturday there is a cattle auction in yards that are just down the street from Snow's. From 1976 to 1996, in fact, Tootsie Tomanetz, who is known far and wide in Lee County as Miss Tootsie, served barbecue every Saturday at a meat market that she and her husband ran in Lexington. Miss Tootsie's husband is half-Czech and half-German. She was born Norma Frances Otto, German on both sides, and her father liked to say that when she married she went from having a last name that could be spelled backward or forward to having one that couldn't be spelled at all. Before the Tomanetzes opened their store, Miss Tootsie had put in ten years tending the pits at City Meat Market, in Giddings. In other words, Kerry Bexley, who's forty-one, could have a certainty about Miss Tootsie's gift that was based on having eaten her barbecue virtually all his life.

After lunch, if that's what you call a large meal of meat that you finish just before 9 A.M., I had a chat about Snow's origins with its management team. We talked near the pits, so Miss Tootsie could pull off sausage links now and then. "I felt like with her name and barbecue and my personality with people we could make it work," Bexley told me. He's a short, outgoing man whose résumé includes—in addition to rodeo clown—prison guard, auctioneer, real-estate agent, and shopkeeper. He already had the location— a place where he'd run a farm and ranch store in 1992. The name came from a nickname he'd had since before he was born. According to the family story, his brother, then four years old, was asked whether he was hoping for the new baby to be a boy or a girl, and he replied, not unreasonably, that he would prefer a snowman. Kerry (Snowman) Bexley and Miss Tootsie opened Snow's in March of 2003—Bexley had built the pits—and it did well from the start. "For the most part, we cooked two to three hundred pounds of meat," Bexley told me. "We sold out by noon."

In the weeks after the *Texas Monthly* feature was published, Snow's went from serving three hundred pounds of meat every Saturday to serving more than a thousand pounds. At eight in the morning—six or seven hours after Miss Tootsie had arrived to begin tending the pits—there was already a line of customers, some of whom had left home before dawn. Bexley said that one Saturday morning, when there were ninety people waiting outside, a local resident asked permission to gather signatures along the line for a petition, only to return a few minutes later with the information that there wasn't one person there from Lee County. Some locals expressed irritation at being shut out of their own barbecue joint. At times, Bexley and Miss Tootsie felt overwhelmed. There were moments, they say, when they wished that the tasters from *Texas Monthly* had never shown up. Then Bexley added three brisket pits, Miss Tootsie got some help, Snow's for a time quit taking pre-orders by phone except for locals, and the amount of meat prepared every Saturday leveled off to about eight hundred pounds.

Most of the time, Bexley and Miss Tootsie are grateful for the additional business. Not long after the survey appeared, Snow's BBQ started selling T-shirts that had on them not only "Voted #1 BBQ in Texas" but a motto that Bexley's wife had suggested— "Smokin' the good stuff." Looking around for a way to extend the newly famous Snow's brand without sacrificing the quality of the product, Bexley has hit on mail order, and is hoping to have that under way soon. Snow's already has a website. Bexley and Miss Tootsie are also pleased by the personal recognition. They've worked hard. Most people in Lee County work hard without anybody's noticing. Whether or not Kerry Bexley and Tootsie Tomanetz ever feel able to give up their day jobs, they have received the sort of pure validation that doesn't come to many people, no matter what their field of endeavor.

"Miss Tootsie gets some recognition now for what she's actually done all her life," Bexley said. "She's now"—he turned to Miss Tootsie—"seventy-four? Excuse me for asking."

"No, I'm just seventy-three," Miss Tootsie said, smiling. "You add a year every time."

"What did you do when you heard that you were No. 1?" I asked.

"When we found out we were No. 1," Bexley said, "we just set there in each other's arms and we bawled."

No Gossip in Russia

1988

n a recent newspaper story, there was a quote from Liz Smith, the gossip columnist of the New York *Daily News,* that I couldn't get out of my mind: "Remember, they don't have gossip in Russia."

This was said in the context of trying to get some perspective on a widely publicized feud between two other gossip columnists—in these grim times, Ms. Smith pointed out, being able to devote a lot of attention to something so frivolous could be seen as a luxury—but it had a different effect on me. It made me realize that there are 262 million Russians who don't know the first thing about Elizabeth Taylor.

Once I began thinking about those Russians, I envisioned them in every part of their daily routines. I could see them at the tractor factory, where they're under a lot of pressure because their previous efforts to meet higher production quotas resulted in sending out tractors whose motors tended to fall out at inopportune moments. (There is actually no opportune moment for a tractor's motor to fall out; I'm just trying to be diplomatic.) I could see them at the market, buying beets and cabbage and potatoes—or maybe, now that Gorbachev has begun to restructure the entire society, instant borscht. I could see them settling down after dinner in comfortable armchairs to read *Pravda* or watch the Soviet State Television's weekly prime-time family drama based on the technical operation of a hydroelectric plant in Sredne Kolymsk. All that time, they're wondering about Elizabeth Taylor. "What's with Liz?" they say to one another. "Is she keeping her weight down? Who's she married to these days? What ever happened to Eddie Fisher?"

The questions draw only shrugs. Nobody knows. *Pravda* doesn't have a gossip columnist. It runs editorials now and then saying that gossip is a symptom of bourgeois decadence. Thousands of people secretly listen to the Voice of America on shortwave radio, hoping to hear some news of Elizabeth Taylor, but all they hear is reports of atrocities by Russian troops in Afghanistan.

Some gossip seeps in, of course. Packages sent by Russian immigrants in Brooklyn to their relatives back home in Tbilisi and Kislovodsk contain economy-size bottles of diet root beer wrapped in old copies of New York tabloids. Western tourists who pass through Leningrad may leave behind a copy of *People* magazine that the chambermaid recovers from the wastebasket, painstakingly irons, and then passes around, hidden behind the cover of *Soviet Agricultural Pioneer News.*

What little gossip there is, though, is often old and inaccurate. People who are separating the wheat from the chaff on a collective farm in the Ukraine pass the time by arguing about whether Barbara Hutton is going to leave Ali Khan. Old men in Bashkir think Elizabeth Taylor is still married to Nicky Hilton. When all is said and done, they don't have any gossip in Russia.

When I finally came to grips with that fact, it made me realize that there are a lot of other things they don't have in Russia—TV game shows and miniature golf and takeout Chinese food and drive-in banks and commercials for bran cereals. No wonder they don't seem to understand what we're talking about when we try to negotiate with them. As Lenin himself used to say, they don't know where we're coming from.

All of this made me think that we may be on the wrong track with cultural exchange programs that send the Cleveland Symphony to Russia and the Kirov Ballet here. The Russians are familiar with symphonies. We're familiar with ballets. Maybe it would be better if we were both sent things we'd otherwise know nothing about. I don't know what the Russians could send us—that's the whole point—but we could send them something like gossip.

We'd start with a program to teach them how to have a domestic gossip industry. It would fit right in with glasnost. First, we train a lot of press agents, reminding the Soviet authorities of an old Russian proverb: a gossip columnist without press agents is a dairy farmer without cows. Then the Soviet columnists start doing some local items ("The soulful tête-à-tête between Minsk party heavy Vladimir Selomentsky and Ukrainian harvest committee Deputy First Secretary Tanya Gunestkov at Boris Karputsky's après–May Day Parade bash has tongues wagging all over Zvenigorodka"). Gradually they begin including items about American gossip-column regulars—the usual charity-ball trotters and previously owned debutantes. Then Frank Sinatra. Then, precisely on the schedule laid out in the new cultural exchange treaty, Elizabeth Taylor.

Alternatives

1978

The alternative press is now respectable enough to be edgy about being called alternative. Apparently, the word was an attempt at respectability in the first place—a way for proprietors of certain weeklies to distinguish their papers from the underground press—but when it is uttered out loud inside of a bank or an advertising agency it still seems to give off little puffs of incense and marijuana smoke. Representatives of about thirty alternative weeklies met recently in Seattle to discuss, among other matters, the possibility of forming a sort of trade association— a notably respectable goal in itself—and, almost without discussion, they decided against describing their papers as "alternative." That left them temporarily at a loss for word. When an alternative weekly is mentioned in the national press—usually as the source for a story that the local daily, through ignorance or exceedingly good manners, failed to print—it is customarily described as "lively" or "sprightly," but I can't imagine a trade association's calling itself the National Association of Sprightly Weeklies.

Although the Seattle conference was announced as a gathering of "metropolitan weeklies," a couple of statewide papers were represented, and one that was not, *Maine Times,* is considered a prototype for the entire field. The *Pacific Sun,* whose editor played a prominent role in the conference, serves neither a city nor a state but the kinky exurbia of Marin County, California. The gathering in Seattle provided an exception to any single definition. Almost all alternative weeklies are tabloids that use their front page as a sort of two-color magazine cover; *Willamette Week,* of Portland, Oregon, is about the shape, if not the thickness, of *The New York Times.* Although almost all are small independent businesses, the three *Advocate* papers in Connecticut and Massachusetts constitute a small chain. Just about all alternative weeklies are directed at readers who were born after the Second World War, but the Seattle paper that organized the conference, the *Weekly,* has a readership with a median age of thirty-six. Some alternative weeklies and some of their staffs did evolve from the underground press; names like *Steppin' Out* or *Creative Loafing* remain, like vestigial plumage, from the sixties. But some of them, like *The San Francisco Bay Guardian* and *Maine Times* and the *Pacific Sun,* were founded ten or fifteen years ago by people who spent the early sixties as daily newspapermen rather than as graduate students—people who took the plunge newspaper reporters have always spoken of in boozy fantasies on days when the assignment seemed particularly boring or the deskmen particularly thickheaded. The working title that the Seattle conferees finally decided on was the National Association of Newsweeklies, which sounds to me like the managing editor of *Time* meeting the managing editor of *Newsweek* for lunch to talk about why their covers so often turn out to have the same person on them. It also fails to describe one of the most successful papers at the conference—the *Reader,* of Chicago, which considers itself more of a features weekly and is particularly proud of having run a nineteen-thousand-word piece on beekeeping in the Chicago area.

As reluctant as I am to give up the word "alternative," I can sympathize with the efforts of any journalistic enterprise to put as much distance as possible between itself and the underground press. With one or two exceptions, I found the underground weeklies I once read to be sloppy collections of rock glop and drug fantasies and political-conspiracy theories—all of which had the appearance of being both undependable and likely to come off on your hands. Five years ago, when a number of weekly newspaper proprietors attended a meeting in Boulder, Colorado, it was already customary to say that what remained of the underground press was evolving into newspapers run by people who thought of themselves as journalists rather than revolutionaries or harbingers of the New Zonked-Out Millennium.

But the survivors of the Boulder meeting who made it to Seattle, editors of *Straight Creek Journal,* of Denver, and *New Times Weekly,* of Phoenix, remember it as being so dominated by the rhetoric of the period—angry speeches by women about to form their own caucus, philosophical arguments pitting people committed to keeping their bodies free of all chemicals against people who had too many chemicals in their bodies to put up much of an argument, long discussions about whether the true goal of journalism was overthrow of the government or getting one's head together—that those few conferees who wanted to exchange information on how to put out a newspaper had to sneak off to the coffee shop for informal discussions. In the past five years, though, an increasing number of American cities have found themselves with a weekly paper that is not so much the source for news of an alternative way of life as the alternative source for news of subjects the daily papers are or should be dealing with. It is the paper that is likely to treat, say, a neighborhood dispute over the opening of an X-rated movie theater with what amounts to a magazine piece—without a daily paper's restrictions on space or a daily paper's version of objectivity. It is the paper that is likely to carry the sort of unsparing analysis of the new stadium's financial implications which the daily paper might not carry even if its publisher were not one of the stadium's most active boosters.

In Seattle, everybody wanted to exchange information about putting out a newspaper. Just about everyone wanted to talk about taking market surveys and collecting accounts receivable and figuring out the hideous problems of distribution. ("Is there anyone here who has a wholesale distributor who isn't a rotten, monopolistic son of a bitch?") Most alternative newspapers are still small, financially precarious operations, but there are alternative weeklies well enough established to have their own public-relations man or even their own labor strife. On the rare occasion when someone at the Seattle meeting raised the sort of moral question that would have presumably set off a two-hour discussion and several caucuses in Boulder—when, for instance, someone from the *Alaska Advocate* asked whether alternative papers really differed corporatively from the monopolistic daily press they all abhorred—the answer was a quick return to the business at hand. One of the prominent participants in the Boulder conference—the proprietor of an underground press service—showed up with a friend at the Seattle conference for an appearance that was considered significantly brief. Looking like a retired punk rocker and his manager, they made their entrance into a room where forty or fifty respectable-looking people, some of them in tweed sports coats, were discussing such subjects as circulation acquisition. The newsservice proprietor and his companion sat down for a few minutes and then quietly took their leave—like a couple of massage parlor operators who had rushed over to work the largest convention in town without having first bothered to find out that it was a conference of Lutheran liturgists. For the remainder of the conference, they were referred to as "the two gentlemen in costume."

Among the demographic analyses offered in Seattle to explain who reads alternative weeklies, the one I was particularly taken with was what is sometimes called the Rat Through a Python Theory. It is based on the belief that people who were born in the baby boom that started in the late forties and were educated in the late sixties are moving in a self-contained lump through American society, like a rat moving through the body of a python. According to a strict Rat Through Python analysis, underground papers have tended to fade away and the sort of papers represented in Seattle have tended to proliferate simply because people in what is sometimes called "the demographic bulge" have outgrown rock glop and are now ready for analytical news features—meaning, presumably, that in a few years they will want to read even less about Elton John and much more about how to put hanging plants to the best decorating use. The publisher of an alternative weekly whose readership survey two years ago showed an average age of twenty-six is likely to assume that the average age of his readers is now twenty-eight. The Rat Through Python explanation of why the staff of *Straight Creek Journal* has felt a growing acceptance from the respectable citizens of Denver in the past year is not that people in Denver are beginning to become aware of the sort of reporting *Straight Creek* has been doing—a series of investigations into the financing of the Denver Center for the Performing Arts, for instance—but merely that many of its core readers have reached the age of being respectable citizens.

According to the theory, the boom babies provide a strong core readership within what is sometimes called "the upper half of the eighteen-to-thirty-five market" not just because of their numbers but also because of their habits. A lot of them remain in the city—or, at least, in certain cities—instead of settling down in the suburbs, which are considered more the territory of the slick city magazines. (The ability of Boston to support two of the strongest alternative weeklies, *The Real Paper* and the *Phoenix,* is normally explained by the fact that Boston has several hundred thousand residents under the age of thirty-five.) A lot of them remain single, or at least childless. The readers of *The Real Paper* have an average age of twenty-eight, and only fourteen percent of them are married people with children. (The readership survey of an alternative paper is likely to come close to describing its staff: of the seventy-five people working in one way or another for *The Real Paper,* only one is both married and living with children.) Having resisted the temptation to toss away their disposable income on mortgages and baby carriages, readers of alternative weeklies have a lot of it to spend on films and restaurants and stereo sets. The results are visible not just in advertisements but in the amount of space alternative weeklies devote to arts and entertainment. The skimpier weeklies represented at the Seattle meeting have not gone much beyond being an entertainment listing; even those that have can tell from surveys that their principal appeal for a lot of readers remains entertainment listings or even entertainment advertisements. The customary way for an established daily to strike back at an alternative weekly that seems to have reached the point of costing it some business is not to begin running longer and livelier features but to publish a weekly entertainment calendar.

These days, most editors of alternative weeklies—even editors who may have once had visions of energizing the proletariat—have accepted the fact that they are putting out what one editor in Seattle described as a special-interest publication for a minority audience. ("Each of us is the FM newspaper in our community.") "The upper half of the eighteen-to-thirty-five market" includes people still in college, of course, but proprietors of alternative weeklies tend to talk more about reaching "urban sophisticates." It is not unusual to hear an editor of an alternative weekly describe the age and education and purchasing power of his readership by saying that his paper has "upscale demographics."

Around the college daily I worked on, the editorial department was always referred to as Upstairs; the people who handled advertising and business matters were Downstairs. The separation was strict, reinforced Upstairs by that weirdly contradictory system of values common to liberal-arts colleges in a capitalist society—the notion that a business career is acceptable for people not quite bright enough for writing and scholarship. Although observers of

American press lords may have been puzzled as to why Henry Luce, who was, in effect, the chief executive of a huge corporation, bore only the title of editor-in-chief at Time Inc., the reason was never in doubt to anyone who shared with Luce the experience of working on that college daily: He obviously couldn't bear to think of himself as Downstairs. Magazines are sometimes started by Downstairs types—a number of the city monthlies, in fact, were started by the local Chambers of Commerce—but Upstairs people start weekly newspapers.

The place to start them used to be a small town. The motivation usually had something to do with liberation from the constraints of a big-city daily. But a lot of irritations connected with a big-city daily are also present on a small-town weekly. City dailies are weighed down with the baggage of being the newspaper of record—the United Fund drive results and the routine economic statistics from Washington—but, for its own territory, a weekly in a small town is just as much a newspaper of record as *The New York Times*. A small-town weekly is likely to be thought of by its readers as a receptacle for more or less official notices rather than as an independent news-gathering organization—so that people in small towns, whether discussing a visit by out-of-town grand-children or a potentially controversial real-estate transaction, may ask one another, "Are you going to put it in the paper?" There are a few small-town weeklies whose editors manage, in the tradition of Hollywood films, to battle the entrenched interests and print the social notes from outlying hamlets at the same time—*The Mountain Eagle,* of Letcher County, Kentucky, is probably the best known—but most of the small-town weeklies I have seen across the country turn out to be routine appendages to a small printing business.

John Cole, the co-founder of *Maine Times,* once told me that one of the greatest freedoms he felt running a statewide weekly was freedom from the stories he did not have to print. The metropolitan weeklies that have developed in the past five years or so have found the same sort of freedom: They are not the newspaper of record or a stalwart of the Chamber of Commerce, but, like a statewide weekly, they exist in a place large enough to provide plenty to write about. They can exist in a large city partly because offset printing has made it easier to start a newspaper from scratch—only one of the thirty newspapers represented in Seattle owns a printing press—and partly because "the upper half of the eighteen-to-thirty-five market" provides definable readership with special interests. It may be that the baby boom, among its other cultural effects, has made the traditional fantasy of disaffected reporters a practical possibility—without, of course, changing the traditional long hours and the traditional threat of bankruptcy.

The reporter involved, people at the Seattle meeting seemed to agree, has to be willing to spend a lot of time running what one of them summed up as "a small business with a limited access to capital." When a few of the conference participants were interviewed on public television in Seattle, Bruce Brugmann, the editor of *The San Francisco Bay Guardian,* was asked how he accounted for the success of his newspaper—a weekly that recently forced the withdrawal of a presidential appointment and has over the years persuaded a significant number of San Franciscans that what was happening to their business district was not economically stimulating redevelopment but destructive "Manhattanization." Brugmann's explanation of the *Bay Guardian*'s success was direct: he had a view of commerce inherited from a father and grandfather who ran a small-town pharmacy in Iowa, he said, and his wife happens to be a first-rate businesswoman. In three days of discussions by editors whose newspapers have published some remarkable prose, the only passage I can remember hearing quoted was from a lawyer's letter that *Gris Gris,* a weekly in Baton Rouge, sends to advertisers who have not paid for their ads. (The lawyer threatens the deadbeats with legal actions "that will amaze and astound you.") The editorial workshop at the conference seemed to turn rather quickly in the direction of editorial payrolls. The participants seemed untroubled about paying their writers less than their advertising salesmen, on the theory that a lot of people will write articles for fun or glory, but nobody will sell advertisements for any reason other than money. In a small business, how much of the budget to spend for freelance articles is a decision roughly the same as how much to spend for office rental. The person who makes it, even if he is also the person who writes the editorials, is Downstairs.

A 2014 study by the nonpartisan Pew Research Center indicated that since the 1978 Seattle meeting the combined circulation for the top twenty alternative weeklies in the United States had declined by six percent. Some of the more prominent weeklies had folded. Some alternative weeklies had been sold to the established dailies they once regarded as their competition.

Part VII
CLOSINGS

Meeting My Subjects

2000

Around the time Steve Forbes dropped out of the presidential race, I imagined myself walking into a New York dinner party a bit early and finding him to be the only other guest on hand. That pasted-on grin of his, I notice right away, seems even more maniacal in person than on TV; I half expect him to break out any moment in a crazed cackle, like the Mozart character in *Amadeus*. "I've got just a few things to check in the kitchen," the hostess says after introducing us. "I'm sure you two have a lot to talk about." As she leaves the room, Forbes suddenly quits smiling. (*So he doesn't actually have to smile if he doesn't want to,* I think to myself. *Isn't that interesting!*) He starts glaring at me. His glare is easily as maniacal as his smile, and much more malevolent. "Well," I say as cheerfully as I can manage, "I suppose you might be wondering why I referred to you in *Time* as a dork robot."

Forbes, still glaring, doesn't say anything. "And I should say that I might have used the same phrase later in *Brill's Content,* just as a reference," I go on. "And, yes, it was quoted in *The New Yorker* by a completely different writer—someone I don't really know all that well, by the way. Well, I'd just like to say that, for what it's worth, that phrase. . . ." But Forbes has turned around and is fumbling around amid the dishes and silver on the sideboard behind us. It occurs to me that he is looking for a weapon.

In my role as a jester among the jackals of the press—as opposed to my role as a serious (well, all right, moderately serious) reporter who usually writes about people nobody has ever heard of—I've been making rude comments about public figures for more than twenty years, and it used to be that I never thought much about running into any of them. After all, most of them live in Washington, and I live in New York—only a few blocks from the Forbes building, now that I think of it, although I go over there only to look at the toy soldier collection in that dandy little Forbes gallery I was intending to compliment Steve Forbes on as soon as he put that steak knife back where he'd found it.

Beat reporters—the beat could be a police precinct or the United States Senate—mix with the people they write about all the time, of course, and that can have the effect of maintaining a sort of governor on how nasty their reporting gets. On the day the paper comes out with their piece on what happened that fateful night at the station house, they may run into the desk sergeant in question and may even be in a position of having to ask him for a favor. A similar constraint is one reason people in small towns are less likely than people in New York to say something terminally vicious to someone who, say, cuts in front of them in a line: They're aware that they're going to see that person again the next day or the day after that. Those of us jackals who hurl our gobs from afar, on the other hand, like to feel that we're free of the unfortunate limitations placed on irresponsible invective by the niceties of civilized human interaction.

The possibility that our insulation is a bit frayed was brought home to me last fall when I took part in a panel in New York on political humor. During the discussion, I'd mentioned that the Bush administration was a grim period for people in the political humor game—no indictments to speak of, a cabinetful of over-poweringly respectable Protestant gentlemen of the sort the president might have met at Andover. For that reason, I said, we tended to concentrate our attention on John Sununu, who had a characteristic that attracts us faster than free drinks: he was, to use the Irish phrase, full of his wee self. I told the audience that Sununu's manner had led Ed Rollins, the Republican political consultant, to describe him as a lesson in the perils of telling your child that he has a high IQ and that his manner and splendidly euphonious name had inspired me to begin writing deadline poetry for *The Nation* with a piece of verse entitled "If You Knew What Sununu." During the question period, the moderator called on a woman in the back of the auditorium, and she began by saying, "I'm John Sununu's sister. . . ." That got by far the biggest laugh of the night.

Sununu's sister, who teaches Spanish and French and Italian, turned out to be so good-humored that I didn't have to follow my first instinct, which was to jump up, shout "I just realized I left something on the stove," and bolt from the stage. I assume from the discussion that night that she is a broad-minded person who can take a joke about her own family—although I suppose there is also the possibility that she, too, sees her brother as a lesson in the perils of telling your child that he has a high IQ. Still, the encounter got me thinking. If Sununu's sister and I have crossed paths, can Sununu himself be far behind?

In fact, I now find myself wondering at odd moments if he's the portly man who has just bustled past Forbes and me at that dinner party, making a beeline for the hors d'oeuvres. He's not the only new arrival. Although I've managed to detach myself from Forbes, I've been backed into the corner by Billy Graham, who is literally thumping on his pocket Bible as he presses me on where I could have gotten the idea that his own vision of hell is a world in which he doesn't get to play golf with the president.

"I'd just like to say. . . ." I begin.

"You call that poetry!" Alfonse D'Amato interrupts, as he suddenly appears in our conversation. "You putzhead!"

"I think I can explain, Senator," I say. "It just happens that 'D'Amato,' which doesn't rhyme with much, does rhyme with 'sleazeball obbligato.'"

"It doesn't rhyme with the sleazeball part!" D'Amato shouts, pushing up against me like a manager expressing his outrage to an umpire.

That strikes me as a pretty good point, but before I can say so Al Gore is upon me, delivering in that wooden manner of his an excruciatingly boring lecture on why it was irresponsible of me to refer to him as a "manlike object." As I try to get a word in—making sure that the fevered D'Amato doesn't make me spill my drink on the vice president, because I know how those earth tones hold a stain—I see, to my horror, that Donald Trump and Dan Quayle and Ron Perelman and Henry Kissinger have entered the room and are bearing down on me. Henry Kissinger! Could that one little war-criminal joke in 1981 still be troubling him? Talk about hypersensitive! Desperately, I look around for an escape route. There is only the window.

It turns out that the war-criminal joke isn't what bothered Kissinger. He's angry because, when I tried to figure out why George Shultz, another Republican secretary of state, is always referred to as Mr. Shultz but Kissinger is always called Dr. Kissinger, I came up with the possibility that Kissinger has a podiatry practice on the side.

Suddenly, a commanding voice says, "Settle down everyone." The voice, it turns out, belongs to John Sununu's sister. People stop moving toward me. D'Amato and Graham and Gore back off. It occurs to me that anyone with extensive teaching experience knows how to handle unruly behavior. "He was just joking, so take it easy," Sununu's sister says. "Don't be so full of your wee selves."

After a beat or two of complete silence, everybody begins chattering as if nothing had happened, and then we all go in to dinner. Before we can sit down, Sununu's sister, like a no-nonsense nanny confiscating a pack of bubble gum, walks over to Forbes's place setting and removes the knife.

Check It Out

n light of the revelations about *Boston Globe* columnists describing people and events whose existence couldn't be confirmed, I decided to go back through columns I have written to see if there might be even the slightest cause for concern. I owed that much to my readers, I told my wife, although I couldn't quite put my finger on what they'd ever done for me.

"All of the columns you've written?" my wife asked. Her tone was not completely enthusiastic. Over the years, my wife has come to believe that I will use almost any excuse to reread my own prose. She claims that she has occasionally heard me in my office late at night cackling away at some ancient witticism of my own, occasionally bursting out with "That's a good one!" or "Now there's a fellow who knows how to write!"

I have tried to explain to her that it's perfectly natural for writers to have a healthy curiosity about how their work holds up over the years. You could consider it after-the-fact quality control. According to a *New Yorker* article that described people reading aloud to E. B. White during his final illness, even White, a man widely admired for his modesty, wanted to hear only his own writing. That made perfect sense to me. If you have limited time, why waste it on strangers?

I had, in fact, decided to restrict my examination to the columns I have written since February 1996, when, after seven years in *The Nation* and ten years in newspaper syndication, the column began appearing in *Time*. I made that decision despite the risk that some might interpret it as a way of avoiding a discussion I had with the *Nation*'s then-editor, the wily and parsimonious Victor S. Navasky, whose existence, by the way, is beyond question. Navasky, concerned about some of the quotes I'd been using, asked me if John Foster Dulles had really said "You can't fool all of the people all of the time, but you might as well give it your best shot," and I replied, according to a widely circulated story, "Victor, at these rates, you can't expect real quotes."

After my examination and rechecking of the *Time* columns, I can report the following:

In a column on June 10, 1996, the following sentence appeared: "As Immanuel Kant used to say, 'It don't make me no never mind.'" I now believe, to the point of moral certainty, that Immanuel Kant never said those words, although it should be noted that I have not yet reread all his work. I regret having assured the people at *Time* that they needn't bother to check the quote.

On July 15, 1996, in a column on Manhattan restaurants being filled with packs of Wall Street types who wear red suspenders and smoke cigars and argue loudly about brands of single malt scotch, I mentioned "studies indicating that wearing red suspenders, instead of a belt, lowers your sperm count." I have not been able to confirm the existence of such studies, although I feel constrained to point out that the Wall Street people in red suspenders who have been observed by me in restaurants have never been accompanied by children.

In a February 16, 1998, column on Hillary Clinton's statement that a "vast right-wing conspiracy" was behind the accusations about her husband and Monica Lewinsky, I quoted "my friend Hobart, the conspiracy connoisseur," as saying, "If she had changed that to 'creepy little cabal,' I might have gone for it." I have not been able to confirm that I have a friend named Hobart, although the creepy little cabal does check out.

A column dated March 2, 1998, says that Rudolph Giuliani "may be the only Italian-American in the Greater New York area with absolutely no personal charm." This conclusion, while probably true, appears to have been based on no more than anecdotal evidence.

Frankly, what surprised me in this reexamination of my columns was how much of what sounds like it was invented turned out to be true. For instance, Molly, the eleven-year-old girl who first stirred my interest in the so-called V-chip by confessing to her parents that she had been watching Martha Stewart while they were at work, does exist, and witnesses confirm that Molly did say, when asked about her impression of Martha Stewart, "She seems to have a lot of time on her hands." It was easy to confirm that a sport called kabaddi, which requires a player to chant "kabaddi-kabaddikabaddi . . ." as long as he is on his opponents' side of the court, was indeed played in the Asian Games in Japan in 1994. There was also no difficulty confirming the existence of a *Washington Post*–ABC News survey that same year indicating that fifty-nine percent of people who have reported encounters with flying saucers preferred Ross Perot to Bill Clinton or Bob Dole in the 1996 presidential election. It almost goes without saying that, as I mentioned in an August 5, 1996, column, Torrington, Alberta, does, in fact, have a museum that seeks to portray scenes of everyday life in Torrington through displays of stuffed gophers.

My wife was not overly impressed by how many unlikely facts in my columns turned out to be true. "Nobody is meant to take the column seriously anyway," she said.

"Well," I said. That seemed to be the best response for the time being. It's true that when it comes to claims of factual accuracy, I have always made a distinction between pieces based on reporting and columns that are designed to provide a chuckle or two. Still, everyone makes mistakes. Is it possible that factual errors have crept into my reporting pieces?

It's difficult to know that, of course, without rereading all the reporting pieces. Yes, all the reporting pieces. I'm doing that now. I'm having a splendid time.

Internetfactchecking.com

2014

Dear Internet Fact Checking:

I spend a lot of time in a genealogical chat room called whos-yourgranny.com. Recently, it carried a post suggesting that the Koch brothers, the right-wing billionaires from Wichita, Kansas, were distantly related to the late Ed Koch, the former Democratic mayor of New York, despite the fact that their names are pronounced differently. It sounds right to me, but someone I work with told me that you can't believe everything you read on the Internet.

High Flier, Torrance, Calif.

Dear High Flier:

Whoever told you that you can't believe everything you read on the Internet is a deeply cynical and untrustworthy person. Both the mayor and the billionaires from Wichita flatly denied any family connection, and flat denials are, of course, the next best thing to an admission. According to kissincousins.com, the mayor and the Koch brothers discussed the matter in 2008, during a reception honoring David Koch for his donation to what became the David H. Koch Theater, at Lincoln Center— although Mayor Koch had privately referred to the donation and the renaming as "yet another reputation-laundering operation" (dishmonger.com). At the reception, the Wichita Kochs dismissed a family relationship with Ed Koch as ridiculous, and spent twenty minutes trying to explain why without mentioning the word "Jewish" (knishdish.com). Finally, Mayor Koch ended the conversation by saying, "I'm not related to any out-of-towners" (whosyourgranny.com).

Dear Internet Fact Checking:

Now that every product on the shelves claims to be gluten-free, I started to wonder what happened to all of that gluten that used to be in everything. Then I read on cashgab.com that someone has been buying up gluten (at bargain-basement prices) and storing it in caves in Utah, on the theory that—like eggs, which used to be considered unhealthy and now are considered OK to eat— gluten will someday be found to be perfectly healthy, food companies will want to put gluten back in their products, and buyers will find that one person has cornered the world's gluten supply. Is this true?

Ravioliron, Rock Springs, Wyo.

Dear Ravioliron:

As usual, cashgab.com is, if we may put it this way, on the money. Where has all the gluten gone? Is it just a coincidence that the same question was raised (hidingstuff.com) about the eventual destination of the trans fats that so many products claimed to have rid themselves of? What about reports (photosquashed.com) that astronauts took pictures from space of quivering mountains of trans fats in the Chihuahuan Desert, and that the pictures were suppressed because of pressure from the Trilateral Commission? As if this weren't proof enough, trucks have definitely been seen driving through Utah (eyeballer.com). Why else would trucks drive through Utah? Is it just a coincidence that Utah ranks fourteenth among the states for number of usable caves? It is hardly insignificant that when George Soros was asked whether he was trying to corner the gluten market, he said, and we quote, "What a stupid question!" (cashgab.com).

Dear Internet Fact Checking:

I read on the Internet (I think it was on starschmutz.com) that some London bookmakers are taking odds on whether Vladimir Putin or Kate Winslet will appear the most times without a shirt in front of a camera during any given month. A friend of mine read the same thing, which makes me think it's true.

Sixpacker, Chillicothe, Mo.

Dear Sixpacker:

The report on the London betting was indeed by starschmutz.com, and you can take their reporting to the bank. In fact, the story, we're told by a reliable media outlet (gossipedia.com), goes farther: London, where you can legally bet on almost anything, is a city that has proved very attractive to billionaire Russian oligarchs, all of whom have an intense interest in Vladimir Putin. According to russoblab.com (significantly, the site that had the exclusive on Putin and Madonna's love child), the oligarchs sometimes refer to Putin as the Bare-Naked Boychik. No less an authority than moviedirt.com reports that the oligarchs are suspected of having been behind the fact that Kate Winslet, who was heavily favored to win against Putin for December 2008, because of the release that month of *Revolutionary Road,* managed to complete two sex scenes in that film without removing her shirt. See the post on celebritybreasts.com (significantly, the same site that had the exclusive on Putin and Prince Harry's love child) entitled "Was the Editing Room Locked?" At the same time, we have reports that a December 2008 photo will soon emerge showing Putin—whose shirtless pictures have usually been of some outdoor activity like horseback riding or fishing—appearing naked from the waist up in a formal meeting with His Holiness Kirill I, Patriarch of Moscow and Primate of the Russian Orthodox Church. The Patriarch was fully clothed, according to a source who was nearly there (starschmutz.com).

New Grub Street

2001

I n Chinatown not long ago, on the corner of East Broadway and Forsyth Street, a sandwich that I bought from a street vendor started me wondering whether I could consider myself a chowhound. Did I, that is, conform to the standards of the breed set forth by a website called chowhound.com, which describes its devotees as people who "blaze trails, combing gleefully through neighborhoods for hidden culinary treasure," people who "spurn trends and established opinion and sniff out secret deliciousness on their own"? The sandwich did possess deliciousness, and you could say that it kept at least one secret even from me: since the vendor didn't speak English, I wasn't able to figure out precisely what was in it. Chowhoundishly (on the website, the word can be morphed into just about any part of speech), I do regularly comb through at least one neighborhood, Chinatown—two, if you count the neighborhood I live in, Greenwich Village, which is only a short bike ride away. I've always spent a certain amount of time in such wanderings, most of it with my mouth full. It should be said that when I began my visits to Chinatown, forty years ago, there wasn't much to buy from a street vendor, unless your craving was for firecrackers. At that time, Chinatown was a small island below

Little Italy—a small island that seemed to be getting smaller, as if it were being eroded by the constant lapping of olive oil and Chianti at its borders.

Chinatown then had only a single, small dim-sum parlor and not many other restaurants whose menus varied significantly from the sort of Americanized fare being served by descendants of Chinese railroad workers in Denver or Chinese fruit pickers in Sacramento; what was available was mostly the Chinese equivalent of the red sauce and pasta that defined Italian restaurants in the years before most New Yorkers had heard the word "trattoria." At one of the more culinarily advanced places we frequented in Chinatown, what we considered a particularly exotic dish was, upon reflection, exotic mainly for the way it was listed on the menu: Shredded Three Kinds Meat.

This was prior to the Immigration Act of 1965, in the years when this country's immigration policy, based on a system of national quotas, reflected not simply bigotry but the sort of bigotry that seemed to equate desirable immigrants with blandness in cooking. The quota for the United Kingdom was so high that it was never filled. Asians were, in effect, excluded. Thirty-second Street, a couple of blocks from Herald Square, hadn't begun to resemble a bustling commercial street in Seoul. Carroll Gardens did not yet offer its residents a choice of Yemeni cafés. Travelers to Coney Island expected to find Nathan's hot dogs but not Azerbaijani *kufta-bozbash*. Although I am perfectly aware that only a person lacking in sensitivity would compare the problem of living in a place that offered a narrow range of truly interesting restaurants with the horrors of involuntary servitude, I have to say that some serious eaters think of the Immigration Act of 1965 as their very own Emancipation Proclamation.

Once the effects of the 1965 changes began to kick in, a burgeoning Chinatown swallowed great chunks of what had been Little Italy. We eventually had a profusion of not just Peking duck but duck tongues and deboned duck feet with jellyfish. These days, I find that I can eat splendidly in Chinatown without leaving my bike. It was on the way home from one of those Chinatown rambles that I stopped my bike at East Broadway and Forsyth, where vendors were selling several unfamiliar items. What caught my eye was a sandwich, tightly wrapped in clear plastic. It consisted of an ordinary Western-style bun with something green peeking out of the middle. I risked a dollar for a taste. Inside the bun was a chopped vegetable that might have been bok choy or mustard greens, flavored with something that tasted like horseradish. I loved it. Whenever I was in Chinatown during the next few weeks, I'd pick up a few greens sandwiches and hand them out when I got back to the Village, like trophies from an adventure abroad. When a recipient of my largesse gobbled up the sandwich with great enthusiasm, I beamed with pride. When someone took a couple of bites, thanked me with elaborate courtesy, and carefully folded the plastic around the remains, I made an instantaneous diagnosis: Wooden Palate Syndrome. It turns out that you don't have to know what's in a sandwich to feel proprietary about it.

Then a thought occurred to me: this is chowhound stuff. I couldn't help thinking of the Arepa Lady. Jim Leff, who presides over chowhound.com and sometimes refers to himself as the Alpha Dog, has called the Arepa Lady "pretty much my signature 'find.'" Although Leff's site is basically a collection of message boards for the food-obsessed, it also includes such features as "What Jim Had for Dinner" and "When Bad Food Happens to Good People," plus an occasional special report. The Arepa Lady of Jackson Heights, Queens, rated a special report. Late on weekend evenings, Leff wrote, she grills the Colombian corn cakes called *arepas* at Seventy-ninth and Roosevelt Avenue. This is underneath the elevated tracks used by the No. 7 subway train as it passes over the cooking odors of several dozen countries on its route from Times Square to a booming second Chinatown that has developed since 1965 in Flushing. Because of the rumble of the No. 7, you often have to shout to be heard on Roosevelt Avenue, and what you're likely to be shouting is "What a *samosa!*" or "That's the best *taco al carbon* I've had outside of Mexico!" Roosevelt Avenue is the sort of place where someone who has just downed some Filipino barbecue may emerge from the restaurant and, in the next block or two, be tempted to follow that up with an Afghan shish kebab, a Mexican *torta,* an Indian *dosa,* and a Tibetan *momo* before making the decision about whether to go with Korean or Uruguayan baked goods.

On this almost sacred ground, Leff cautions, you have to search among the vendors for "the tiny, ageless woman with the beatific smile"—the Arepa Lady, serving what Leff has called his favorite food in New York. "The arepas themselves are snacks from heaven," his special report says. "You try one, and your first reaction is 'mmm, this is delicious.' But before that thought can fully form, waves of progressively deeper feelings begin crashing, and you are finally left silently nodding your head. You understand things. You have been loved." When the Alpha Dog finds something he likes, he eschews restraint.

Compared to the Arepa Lady, the vendor I'd just patronized did lack a certain remoteness. There wasn't any question in my mind that her very convenience made the experience less chowhoundish than it might have been. New Yorkers who revel in chowhoundry tend to do most of their eating in the outer boroughs—particularly Queens and Brooklyn, where a lot of the people admitted in the place of all those Englishmen have congregated. Judged by the standards of people who post messages on chowhound.com, I am a stranger to the boroughs. Given the variety and quality of food available within walking distance of my house, I'm reluctant to leave lower Manhattan at mealtime. A vendor of exotic foodstuffs is not likely to be discovered in an obscure neighborhood by someone who doesn't even like to go uptown.

My vicarious experience in outer-borough eating, on the other hand, has been quite extensive. About ten years ago, before the Internet made chowhound.com possible, I'd begun to follow the travels of a food critic named Robert Sietsema, whose dispatches I read first in an occasional newsletter he puts out called *Down the Hatch* and then in *The Village Voice*. Although *Down the Hatch* began with a concentration on Manhattan, Sietsema was soon spending a lot of his time in places like a Haitian night club on Flatbush Avenue or a Portuguese *churrasqueira* off the Jericho Turnpike or an Arab diner in Astoria or a Ghanaian seafood restaurant in the Bronx. At the time, I hadn't met Sietsema, but I took to calling him "my man Sietsema." As my wife and I perused different publications over breakfast, she would occasionally comment on the news—"Looks like they've got another truce in Northern Ireland," say, or "The Fed is apparently going to cut the interest rate"—and I would say, "My man Sietsema's been eating at an Egyptian fish joint in Brooklyn," or "My man Sietsema has visited the best Oaxacan restaurant in New Brunswick." You might say that I followed Sietsema's adventures to the outer boroughs and beyond the way some sedentary Victorian burgher in Manchester or Leeds must have followed the travels of Henry Stanley in Africa.

Eventually, my man Sietsema was not the only adventurer I followed. A handful of professional food writers in New York spend enough time in out-of-the-way restaurants to be able to disagree among themselves—sometimes via the message boards of chowhound.com—about where to find the best Salvadoran *pupusa* or a superior Albanian *burek*. (Both of these turn out to be versions of meat or cheese inside dough; anyone who spends a lot of time trying unfamiliar cuisines in the boroughs may come away with the impression that most things turn out to be versions of meat or cheese inside dough.) Writers who concentrate on what is sometimes called ethnic eating or alternative eating or offbeat eating form a small, occasionally bickering community, like a community of drama critics who concentrate on Off Broadway. Or maybe Off Off Broadway.

Some of them—Myra Alperson, for instance, who publishes a newsletter called *NoshNews* ("Nosh your way from Odessa to Bombay. . . . And never leave New York")—are virtually full time in the neighborhoods. Others, like Eric Asimov, who writes the "$25 and Under" column for the *Times,* make occasional forays as part of their assignment to review inexpensive restaurants. They have produced several guidebooks, including Sietsema's *The Food Lover's Guide to the Best Ethnic Eating in New York City* and Leff's *The Eclectic Gourmet Guide to Greater New York City.* The Los Angeles equivalent would be Jonathan Gold's *Counter Intelligence.* Members of the community do not limit themselves to the cooking of new immigrants. On chowhound.com, Leff insists that a true chowhound's lust for "hyperdeliciousness in all forms" includes foie gras and Château Margaux. Still, an adventurous eater in New York is not likely to spend his time in the latest chic Manhattan bistro while there are Nigerian yam-porridge outposts in Brooklyn left to explore.

Over the years, I've come to know several members of this community, and when I've talked to, say, Sietsema, or to Sylvia Carter, who began writing the "Eats" column for *Newsday* in 1980 and is sometimes referred to as the den mother of the alternative eaters, or to Ed Levine, who became familiar with the boroughs when he began his food-writing career searching out places to shop, I feel positively sedentary by comparison. It has occurred to me that, despite the hymns I have sung for years to the 1965 Immigration Act, I may not be completely emancipated. Eventually, I decided to get in touch with Jim Leff, and when I phoned him he asked if we should get together for a meal.

"Sure," I said.

"Great," Leff said. "You want to go to Danbury for goulash?"

That, I thought, was the Alpha Dog talking.

On chowhound.com, a battalion of food crazies stands ready to respond promptly and forthrightly if a complete stranger wants to know where to obtain the best version of a certain Vietnamese sandwich, or asks if there are any modestly priced restaurants his parents might like when they come from Moline for a visit, or seeks opinions on whether her friend's birthday splurge this year should be at Eleven Madison Park rather than at the Gramercy Tavern, or demonstrates an obvious need to be corrected by a more knowledgeable person on what to order in some new Chinese restaurant in Sunnyside. In fact, Leff assured me that if I posted news of my Chinatown sandwich, I would know within a few hours not only its precise ingredients but maybe even where to get a better one. Eric Asimov has said that chowhound.com, with its generous exchange of information by people who are similarly obsessed, is just what a website was meant to be, which may be another way of saying that it doesn't make money.

Although food has been a passion for Jim Leff at least since high school, when he started sending restaurant tips to Sylvia Carter at *Newsday,* he makes his living in large part as a musician—a trombonist with a leaning toward jazz and a willingness to play Hasidic dance music if that's what the gig calls for. According to Sietsema, who played in a rock band himself for a number of years while making his living at the typing and book designing and photo editing he refers to as "urban roustabout work," Leff is a "bizarrely talented" trombonist. Asimov is a guitarist, and Jonathan Gold spent years playing the amplified cello in a punk-rock band. Ed Levine used to manage a jazz club in the Village. Someone might be able to put together a theory about a part of the brain that controls both offbeat food yearnings and an ear for rock or jazz music, but the way Sietsema explains it is that once you make the sound check late in the afternoon you've got nothing to do for four or five hours but search around in a strange neighborhood for someplace to get dinner.

Leff might be picked out of a crowded restaurant by someone told to look for the musician. A bearded, informally dressed man in his late thirties, he has dark hair pulled back into a knot. I've heard Leff and Sietsema and Gold and some members of what Leff calls his Fress Team—the *fressers* (Yiddish for eaters, or maybe trenchermen) who sometimes accompany him to a new restaurant he's trying—described as looking like "guys who stayed in graduate school too long." (Leff, in fact, did some graduate work, and Sietsema actually spent five years in graduate school at the University of Wisconsin, apparently without displaying any unseemly interest in a degree. Gold's "Counter Intelligence" begins, "For a while in my early twenties, my only clearly articulated ambition was to eat at least once at every restaurant on Pico Boulevard, starting with the fried yuca dish served at a *pupuseria* near where the street began in downtown Los Angeles, and working methodically westward toward the chili fries at Tom's #5 near the beach. It seemed a reasonable enough alternative to graduate school at the time.") If they showed up anonymously to review a fancy French restaurant on the Upper East Side, the question might be not whether the headwaiter would recognize them but whether he would be willing to seat them. The answer is presumably yes: Gold, who might be considered the alternative eater's first crossover act, now reviews mainstream New York restaurants for *Gourmet.*

My first glimpse of Leff did not turn out to be in a goulash restaurant in Danbury. Danbury seemed a long way to go for goulash, although Leff assured me that it was only an hour away, that the journey would include a stop at a homemade-yogurt place in East Elmhurst which also does great spinach pie, and that eating the Danbury goulash would almost certainly be an experience that transformed my life. He was also quick to say that the goulash place had not been discovered by him but by Jane and Michael Stern, who have been sniffing out unpretentious restaurants around the country for years—although he was willing to take credit for discovering, in a manner of speaking, that the Sterns had underrated it.

Leff's eagerness to take me to what was, in effect, someone else's restaurant seemed to refute what other alternative eaters had told me about his singular attachment to restaurants that he has himself discovered. Most food writers who report on the offbeat pay at least lip service to the notion that it's of no real importance who happened to write about a restaurant first. Leff seems unembarrassed about using "Major Discovery" as a headline or referring to a restaurant as "my greatest discovery ever." He is exquisitely conscious of which restaurants were mentioned first on chowhound.com, reflecting the territorial instincts you might expect to encounter in an alpha dog. Jonathan Gold—who, like Robert Sietsema, has at times felt unwelcome on chowhound.com—has called Leff "the premier proponent of the paranoid school of restaurant criticism."

On the other hand, I can understand taking some pride in a signature pick. Witness how I feel about my greens sandwich. Discovery is part of the game. Also, discovery is hard work. Sietsema wears out a copy of *Hagstrom's New York City 5 Borough Atlas* every year as he prowls the streets, becoming particularly alert when he goes through a neighborhood in which, as he has put it, "the hipster coefficient is zero." When Sietsema reads in a neighborhood newspaper about a homicide in some bar described as a place frequented by West Africans, he finds himself wondering not about the victim or the crime but about whether the bar happens to be the sort of bar that serves food.

Sietsema says that, once a writer discovers a place, he may feel the necessity to "defend it against all comers." If others are unimpressed with it, after all, it wasn't much of a discovery. When I accompanied Ed Levine one day for a lunchtime outing in Queens—we'd started on Roosevelt Avenue with a Cuban sandwich at El Sitio and some *picaditas con carne* at a *taquería* called

El Grano de Oro 2000, then finished up in Corona with an empa-
nada at El Palacio de las Empanadas and a sublime eggplant-
parmigiana sandwich at the Corona Heights Pork Store, those two
treats separated by what you might call a palate cleanser of old-
fashioned Italian lemon ice in a paper cup at Benfaremo, the
"Lemon Ice King of Corona"—he did his impression of Jim Leff's
response to hearing another eater's disappointment in, say, a Salvadoran *pupuseria* Leff had discovered: "But the cook went back to
El Salvador. You didn't *know?* The mama's only in the kitchen on
Thursday. You went on a Tuesday? You didn't *know?*"

The moment a restaurant is discovered, of course, it stands
exposed to the danger of going downhill. It might indeed lose
its cook to the constant back-and-forth of modern immigration.
It might become self-conscious from having attracted what Leff
refers to with great contempt as "Zagat-clutching foodies"—
a foodie being in his lexicon precisely what a chowhound is not.
Chowhound.com has a department called "Downhill Alert!" I once
heard Leff say that the entire route of the No. 7 was going downhill. This was not long after the route, which has often been mentioned in the mainstream press, became the subject of a piece by
Jonathan Gold in *Gourmet,* foodie central. In the piece, Gold, perhaps innocently, mentioned that he'd never been able to find the
Arepa Lady.

All the offbeat eaters are, of course, aware that what seems
breathtakingly exotic and authentic and even quaint could be a
trap—that they could be so smitten by the palpably unspoiled
granny bustling around the tiny kitchen in her babushka that they
overlook the rocklike quality of her dumplings. If pressed, they
will sadly report one another's propensity for falling into the trap.
Leff has said that if a place selling astonishing blueberry muffins
were next door to a so-so Mozambican place, Robert Sietsema
would write about the Mozambican place and followers of "What
Jim Had for Dinner" would hear about the blueberry muffins, the

chowhoundian way being never to "ingest anything undelicious," whether it's exotic or not.

Sietsema, who believes he adheres to the nothing-undelicious principle of chowhoundishness himself, acknowledges that he takes an almost anthropological approach, even though anthropology was not one of the subjects he got around to studying during his academic career. He once told me, for instance, that he has spent some time trying to find out why all the Uzbekistani restaurants he's tried seem to have a dish called Korean carrots. The subject came up while we were having the second leg of lunch one day at an Uzbekistani restaurant in Forest Hills called Salute. We had started in Ridgewood with a Frisbee-size hamburger sandwich (a *pljeskavica,* actually) at a stand called Bosna Express Corp.—we ate on an automobile seat that had been propped against the wall across from two folding chairs to create the sort of sidewalk café one might expect to find in an area of the Balkans that had seen its share of trouble—and we would finish off with a *masala dosa* in a tiny café called Dosa Hutt, next to an ornate Hindu temple in Flushing. One theory he has come across about Korean carrots, Sietsema said, is that one of the conditions the Japanese imposed upon Russia after winning the Russo-Japanese War was that Russia accept some of Japan's unassimilated Koreans, who were then sent to Uzbekistan. On the other hand, Sietsema, who has a penchant for irony that is rare among the food-obsessed, finds it difficult to part with the notion that the name comes from the fact that Uzbeks, like everyone else in New York, buy their carrots from fruit-and-vegetable stands run by Koreans. I should say that the Korean carrots were not so-so. They were quite good. Not as good as a sort of vegetable-noodle soup called *lagman,* which we'd eaten just before the carrots arrived— the *lagman* was what Leff would have called hyperdelicious—but still quite good.

One Tuesday evening I accompanied Leff and his Fress Team to

a place near Sheepshead Bay that he'd heard was "the end-all and
be-all of Georgian food." It won out as our destination over the
restaurant in a Russian *shvitz* called Wall St. Bath & Spa. The Fress
Team outing had started me thinking about how strenuous chowhounding is—strenuous, I mean, beyond just the strain of eating
two or three lunches. On the way to Sheepshead Bay, Leff had out-
lined some of the problems we might face. For one thing, given
the language difficulties he'd encountered when he phoned the
restaurant, it could turn out to be closed on Tuesdays. In case we
found ourselves in need of a fallback, he'd brought along a thick
printout that listed, in tiny type, all the restaurants in his reper-
toire, arranged by neighborhood. Some of the restaurants were
listed by name only, and some not even by name ("Irish place in
back of Ping's"). Some of them included comments or favorite
dishes. On the upper left-hand corner of the first page was typed
3281, the number of restaurants on the list. Leafing through the
printout, I told Leff that it looked like the life list of a particularly
maniacal birder.

He ticked off some other potential problems: maybe Tuesday
was such a slow night they'd have nothing available beyond
chicken and *pelmeni,* which he has referred to as "the ubiquitous
Russian tortellini." Or maybe the menus would be in Cyrillic characters only, meaning that the glossary he'd taken the trouble to
assemble that afternoon, partly from research on the Internet,
would do him no good at all.

In chowhounding, the language problem is ever present. So is
the danger of being ensnared in the quaint-granny trap. So is the
difficulty of familiarizing yourself with dozens of different cuisines. When we finally did get to the Georgian restaurant and
managed to order, Leff, who says that he has eaten in every decent
Georgian restaurant in New York, was confident that the *khacha-
puri* (as it happens, a version of cheese inside dough) was insufficiently flaky, given its startling resemblance to quesadillas; as

someone who has traveled extensively as a musician, he is in a position to compare, say, *salgadinhos* he tries in Astoria to the *salgadinhos* he has had in Brazil. But, given the rate and variety of immigration, there is a limit to everyone's experience. At a Brooklyn spot called Olympic Pita, we'd had an Iraqi Jewish mango hot sauce called *amba* that Leff had pronounced both authentic and extremely rare. But had we been eating a superior *amba* or only a run-of-the-mill *amba*? If I did ever meet an Iraqi Jew and proudly escorted him to Olympic Pita for a little surprise, would he say derisively, after a quick taste, "They told you that was *amba*?"

Robert Sietsema, who happens to live only a few blocks from me in the Village, dropped in one day with some early issues of *Down the Hatch* that I'd asked to see, and we talked a bit about the restaurants we liked in the Village. I reminded him how fortunate we were to live in an area that offered such remarkable food only a stroll away. I'd told him about a restaurant in Hoboken, and I realized that I liked the thought of my man Sietsema, armed with a street atlas of Hudson County, checking it out, maybe on one of those mild fall evenings when my wife and I enjoy walking to a pizza parlor on Spring Street which we treasure for its clam pie. Maybe he'd happen across a fabulous purveyor of Guyanese *rotis* or Dominican fritters on the way. Thinking about a walk downtown reminded me of my greens sandwich. I had posted it on chowhound.com, but nobody seemed interested in enlightening me about its origin or telling me where I could get a better one— although only a few days later there was, coincidentally, a spirited discussion about the steamed buns in the place I patronize on Mott Street. I happened to have a greens sandwich in the fridge, and I offered it to Sietsema. I like to think that I hadn't prepared myself to respond to an unenthusiastic reception by saying that refrigeration is known to deaden the taste of Chinese greens or that I'd heard rumors that the regular sandwich maker had recently been picked up by Immigration.

Sietsema loved it. "It's a real find," he said. "A totally unique entity."

"Did you say 'totally unique entity'?" I said.

He had.

"Well, thank you," I said. "Thank you very much."

Sabbath Gasbags,
Speak Up

2013

Nearly a week after the television news coverage of Memorial Day, I'm still thinking about how much I envy Tom Brokaw for having managed to slip a phrase into the language. He slipped in "the greatest generation." I've never slipped in anything.

Slipping a phrase into the language means inserting it so firmly that it no longer carries your name. Sure, Brokaw must be pleased when a correspondent, covering a program that brings World War II veterans to visit monuments in Washington, identifies them as "members of what Tom Brokaw called the greatest generation." But the real kick has to be hearing the phrase stand alone, as if it's some commonly used, modern-sounding phrase that only the editors of the Oxford English Dictionary know was first heard in a play by Christopher Marlowe in 1589.

When I first referred to the people who pontificate on Sunday morning talk shows from Washington as the "Sabbath gasbags," it was part of a plan to systematically insinuate the phrase into the language. I first used it in a newspaper column. Then I used it in a book. Then I used it on television shows, gradually trying to drop modifiers like "the people I refer to as." Still nothing. Oh, sure, I've seen "Sabbath gasbags" mentioned occasionally with my name attached, but that's not slipping it into the language. I wanted to see it used routinely—say, "In addition to his newspaper work he appears as a Sabbath gasbag on ABC."

I suppose you could say that "Sabbath gasbags" is too, well, judgmental to be slipped into the language. But my luck has been no better when I try to slip in a practical phrase like R.N.A. Placed at the end of a letter, R.N.A. means Reply Not Anticipated: you can reply if you want to, but the other person involved in this interchange is perfectly happy with things as they stand. R.N.A. didn't catch on even after the advent of the Internet. When I put those initials at the bottom of e-mails, people tended to write back, "What does R.N.A. mean?" In other words, their response to Reply Not Anticipated was to reply.

All this time, I've thought that the best conduit to carry a phrase into the language was *The New York Times*. It is, after all, called the newspaper of record. My first attempt was unsuccessful. Many years ago, in discussing boosters who were intent on fitting out their hometowns with international airports and domed stadiums and the other trappings of "a major league city," I said such people were suffering from rubaphobia—not fear of rubes but fear of being thought a rube. The *Times* editor said I'd misspelled "rubaphobia."

"But I made it up," I said. "It's my word."

"It's not *Times* style," he said.

So, the spelling was changed. The word not only didn't make it into the language, it didn't make it into the newspaper.

Recently, I tried the *Times* again. Describing the tendency of older men's hindquarters to flatten out, I spoke of a condition called D.T.S.—Disappearing Tush Syndrome—and mentioned that it could cause an otherwise respectable senior citizen to walk right out of his pants. So far, nobody else has mentioned D.T.S. Still, there's time. In my optimistic moments, I envision NBC calling Tom Brokaw back to lead its Memorial Day coverage in Washington next year. "As I said on one of the Sabbath gasbag shows yesterday," Brokaw says, "when I see these World War II veterans returning to the nation's capital for this ceremony, I know that— though stooped, though gray, though suffering from D.T.S.—they remain the greatest generation."

As I envision it, I write Brokaw a note complimenting him on his performance, and put at the end "R.N.A." Brokaw, catching on immediately, does not reply.

It may be too late to slip "Sabbath gasbags" into the language. Thanks to cable news, there are gasbags opining every day of the week.

Back on the Bus

2011

Last fall, at a gathering in Santa Fe on the subject of storytelling, I met a woman whose name sounded familiar. It turned out that I had last encountered her precisely fifty years before. She was then a six-year-old African American girl, Ruby Bridges, being escorted into William Frantz School, in New Orleans, by federal marshals every morning, and I was a reporter standing across the street from the school, observing a gang of women who were spewing obscenities and racial epithets at her. I remember "black ape" as one of the phrases they were particularly fond of. Morning after morning, I stood amidst those women, some of whom seemed to have settled comfortably into their role as featured players on the evening news. When I approached one of them with a question during the second week, her response was "I only speak to Martin Agronsky"—then a well-known correspondent for NBC. Ever since, I've had on the wall of my office a photograph, taken by a *Life* photographer, of a worried-looking little girl flanked by two men wearing U.S. Marshal armbands. In Santa Fe, I told Ruby that it was nice to see her all grown up.

The desegregation of the New Orleans schools took place toward the beginning of a year I spent in the South, in the Atlanta bureau of *Time*—from the fall of 1960 to the fall of 1961. It's a period now being recalled in any number of half-century commemorations, because a lot happened in that twelve-month span. The public schools of New Orleans and Atlanta were desegregated. A federal judge ordered two black students, Charlayne Hunter and Hamilton Holmes, into the University of Georgia. Sit-in movements succeeded in desegregating lunch counters and other public facilities in Atlanta and Nashville. Freedom Riders made their way through the South to demonstrate that Supreme Court decisions desegregating interstate transportation were routinely flouted on buses and in waiting rooms. Both before and after those twelve months, there were extended periods—from the Montgomery bus boycott, in the mid-fifties, until the first sit-in, in 1960, for instance—when the civil rights story faded from the front pages. The country had not yet begun to see segregation as a moral wrong that had to be addressed rather than as a regrettable regional peculiarity. The reporter I replaced as the junior man in the two-man Atlanta bureau had left six months before I arrived; the reporter in that position when I returned to Atlanta early in 1963, just before the brutal response of police dogs and fire hoses to demonstrations in Birmingham shocked the nation, told me that, as far as he could tell, the civil rights story had pretty much petered out.

During the year I was in the South, I occasionally worked on something other than civil rights. During the first burst of national coverage of the John Birch Society, whose founder famously believed that Dwight D. Eisenhower was an agent of the Communist conspiracy, I was dispatched to Macon, Georgia, to look into the early life of the man the society was named after. (I concluded that it had probably been named appropriately: as an undergraduate at Mercer University, a Southern Baptist school, Birch had managed to provoke a heresy trial of several professors.) Now and then, I was assigned to contribute to what was called a "business roundup"—phoning around to bankers to hear what they had to say about interest rates or inflation or the housing market. Mostly, though, I'd be at the airport early in the week for a flight to some-place where Jim Crow was being threatened. (Air transportation was one reason for the bureau's location: it used to be said that when you die in the South you might go to Heaven, but you'd have to change planes in Atlanta.) Atlanta itself was going through sit-ins, boycotts, mass meetings, and an impending school desegrega-tion. Even on weekends, I was on what we sometimes called the Seg Beat.

I wonder whether I would have remained in reporting if I had spent twelve months in the South when the civil rights story was in one of its dormant periods—twelve months of nothing more exciting than the occasional folksy conversation about interest rates with Mills B. Lane, Jr., of the Citizens and Southern National Bank. *Time* was then practicing what was called "group journal-ism," so that the correspondent in the field filed a long report for the writer in New York, who used it (among other sources) to write for a senior editor, who sometimes rewrote the piece with the flu-idity available to someone who is working without the encum-brance of having read the original file. It was said that *Time* was a great place for a reporter to work unless he read the magazine. But I never felt that I'd been wasting my time on reporting that didn't show up in the finished product, because I found myself building knowledge on a single subject: race. Any writing requires a leap of confidence—you have to convince yourself that somebody is going to be interested in what you put down on the page—and believing that you know more about the subject than most of your readers do can work wonders for your confidence.

Once I'd accepted the job, I had, of course, done some reading. I knew from W. J. Cash's *The Mind of the South* that the scene then conjured up by the phrase "antebellum South"—a cultivated plan-tation owner composes poetry at his Louis XIV desk while dozens of his slaves sing in the cotton fields—was drawn from Hollywood rather than from history, even if most white Southerners accepted it as gospel. I knew from C. Vann Woodward's *The Strange Career of Jim Crow* that physical separation of the races was not something that had always been part of the fabric of life in the South but a system that had been installed in the eighteen-nineties, after Reconstruction. Mainly, though, what confidence I had came from dealing with the subject week after week. I heard so many sermons in black churches that I began holding what I called the Martin Luther King Extended Metaphor Contest. (King himself was ineligible, since he would have won in a walk every week.) I knew all the verses to "We Shall Overcome." My expense account included items like "trousers torn in racial dispute" and "after prayer-meeting snack, Tuskegee, $3.75." I could calibrate a white Southerner's racial views by the way he pronounced the word "Negro." I'd been exposed to enough Ku Klux Klan terminology to know a kleagle from a klaxon from a klavern. I had watched ordinary people make momentous moral decisions—a white mother in New Orleans deciding that she had to walk her first grader past that gang of screaming women outside William Frantz School in defiance of a white boycott, a Greek-immigrant diner owner with tears in his eyes telling black sit-in students in Atlanta that, as much as he sympathized with their cause, serving them would mean the end of his business. I was deeply immersed in what my daughters call my Boy Reporter Mode. I loved it.

A remarkable number of white people I met in the South—not just obvious bigots but respectable, decent people who may themselves have even thought that change had to come—believed racial incidents occurred only because of meddling by outsiders. Yankee reporters were, of course, part of the meddling process. ("Where you from?" was the first question asked of a reporter who encountered a deputy sheriff. "I work out of the Atlanta bureau" was not considered a satisfactory answer.) If resistance to change included violence, the press was not just resented but targeted—

particularly members of the press who were recording the violence in pictures. In Atlanta, *Time* shared an office with *Life,* and I used to say to Donald Uhrbrock, a *Life* contract photographer, "When we get in one of those situations, at best I don't know you. At worst, I'm one of the people chasing you." Even in the relatively progressive confines of Atlanta, where I had college friends who were natives and where there was an abundance of Yankees in southeastern branch offices, my presence at a social gathering could cause some strained questions or an argument or, worst of all, an attempt to enlighten me about "the Negro" with what I came to think of as yard-sale anthropology.

There were two major commemorations of the Freedom Rides anniversary this spring, one in Jackson, Mississippi, and one in Chicago. (The Chicago event had originally been set for Washington, D.C., where the Freedom Rides had begun. But Oprah Winfrey, who wanted as many Freedom Riders as possible to be either in the audience or onstage for the taping of a show dedicated to the anniversary, offered to fly everyone to Chicago and pay for two nights in the convention-center hotel.) In simplest terms, the Jackson gathering—which was officially co-hosted by Governor Haley Barbour and Bennie Thompson, a black congressman from Mississippi—was a commemoration of a historical period, in the spirit of reconciliation and even apology. The Chicago gathering was a reunion organized by people who believe that the struggle is still going on. One of its organizers, the Reverend Jim Lawson, who fifty years ago had instructed the students of the Nashville movement on the principles of nonviolence, still gives classes in nonviolence. Two others, Diane Nash, a leader of the Nashville movement, and C. T. Vivian, a minister who was active in Martin Luther King's Southern Christian Leadership Conference, are still working with a project in Neshoba County, Mississippi. A fourth, Ralph D. Fertig, was recently the plaintiff in a Supreme Court case challenging the constitutionality of the Patriot Act. I wasn't surprised to hear that those four organizers of the Chicago gathering had distributed a letter explaining, in strong language, why they wouldn't be attending the Jackson event. Even within the movement, the Freedom Rides were contentious from the start.

They came along at a time when the civil rights story in the South was shifting. Before the sit-ins gained traction, the story was often covered from the white side of the street. There were a few black lawyers, like Constance Motley, bringing legal cases, mostly in school desegregation; there were a few black students involved in desegregating the schools. But the story was mainly about how white people would respond to pressure to change. Would the governor who had campaigned on a platform of "not one, no not one" close the University of Georgia if Charlayne Hunter and Hamilton Holmes were ordered in by a federal judge? Would business leaders in Atlanta or New Orleans find some peaceful accommodation to school desegregation and thus avoid the turmoil that could lead to the economic stagnation expressed as "another Little Rock"? Increasingly, during the year I was in the South, the impetus moved to the black side of the street.

In Montgomery, during the Freedom Rides, I heard Martin Luther King say that while *Brown v. Board of Education* had been the legal turning point in the movement, the Montgomery bus boycott and the sit-ins were the psychological turning point. With hundreds of black students from local universities risking injury by sitting nonviolently at whites-only lunch counters, it had become more and more difficult to claim that both white and black people would be content with the Southern Way of Life if outsiders would just stop interfering. To put it another way, black people—particularly, young black people—got tired of waiting and took matters into their own hands.

King said that the Freedom Rides were an extension of that psychological turning point. Under the sponsorship of the Congress of Racial Equality, the campaign had begun on May 4, 1961, when two buses embarked from Washington, D.C.; it was abandoned ten days later, in Birmingham, after the riders on one bus were attacked by a mob there and the other bus was firebombed in Anniston, sixty miles or so to the east. Within days, students from the Nashville movement appeared in Birmingham to take up where CORE had left off—riding from there to Montgomery and eventually on to Jackson. But at the beginning many black leaders in the South had not, in fact, seen the Freedom Rides as an extension of the Montgomery bus boycott and the sit-in movements. Privately, people like Medgar Evers, the field secretary for the NAACP in Mississippi, expressed serious reservations or even outright hostility.

CORE, which had its headquarters in New York, was not unknown in the South. Jim Lawson was a member. John Lewis, a leader of the Nashville sit-in movement, was on both a CORE bus from Washington and the bus that Nashville students rode from Birmingham to Montgomery. There was a CORE chapter in New Orleans. By and large, though, those of us on the Seg Beat thought of CORE as a Northern organization. It was led at the time by James Farmer, an imposing man with a mellifluous voice, and the most cynical view of the Freedom Ride was that it was an attempt by Farmer to gain some standing for CORE in the South, where there was jockeying for influence among the NAACP and the Student Nonviolent Coordinating Committee and the Southern Christian Leadership Conference.

As many critics within the movement saw the Freedom Rides, a group of outsiders had come up with a way of reinvigorating the old lie about a peaceful South being beset by outside agitators— leaving the locals to deal with whatever repercussions were left behind. White liberals were particularly incensed. In Montgomery, where first the press and then the Freedom Riders were set upon by a mob when the bus from Birmingham arrived at the Trailways station, a local man I thought of as open to the proposition that black people ought to be treated as full citizens said to me, "I was sickened today. For the first time, I was ashamed of being from this town. But this is not sympathy for those nuts. I hate them." It occurs to me now (it didn't then) that if people were going to demonstrate that Supreme Court decisions on desegregating interstate waiting rooms had been ignored in the South, those people would have to be outsiders either where they got on the bus or where they got off the bus. Most of the people on those first CORE buses did live in the North, but Farmer rejected the outsider label from the start. "We don't believe we're outsiders," he said, "because we're Americans."

A Gallup poll in the spring of 1961 found that only one in four Americans approved of the Freedom Ride. (The Kennedy administration, for a variety of reasons, simply wanted it to go away; one of the speakers at the Chicago gathering referred to John and Robert Kennedy as "the brothers grim.") There had been a similar pattern with the sit-ins. Partly because sitting in at a department-store lunch counter involved consciously breaking the law—and in a privately owned establishment where the proprietor presumably had a right to decide whom he would serve—it had been opposed by some people in the movement, not to speak of many people outside the movement. (The same poll indicated, at a time when the Nashville sit-in movement had pretty much completed the desegregation of the city, that fifty-seven percent of Americans believed the sit-ins and other demonstrations would hurt rather than help the chances of Negroes being integrated in the South.) The sit-in movement, though, had an almost romantic appeal—polite, well-dressed black college students sitting peacefully at a lunch counter while hooligans harassed or even attacked them. Once, when I was allowed in the Atlanta jail to interview some students who had been arrested at a sit-in, I could hear the faint sound of singing grow louder as a guard and I walked toward the cell where they were being held; by the time we reached the cell, the freedom songs, echoing off the jailhouse walls, sounded like a full church choir. I can still conjure up the scene in my mind; I can still hear the singing.

The Freedom Ride was a tougher sell, even after the baton was passed in Birmingham from CORE to the Nashville movement. It appeared that the South's disregard of Supreme Court rulings on interstate transportation could be dramatically demonstrated only if the Freedom Riders who integrated bus stations were met with violence—whether the violence was described by Southern politicians as "looking for trouble" or by nonviolent theoreticians as "cleansing the soul with blood." A number of places in Virginia and the Carolinas and Georgia had simply allowed the Freedom Riders to mill about in the whites-only waiting room until their bus left, and then returned to segregated business as usual. Jim Lawson was blunt about the violence. "Chances are that without people being hurt you cannot solve the problem," he said.

By the time the Freedom Ride was stalled for a few days in Montgomery, a united front had formed, but there remained differences in how to proceed. While people like Martin Luther King were trying to convince Attorney General Robert Kennedy that the federal government was obligated to provide protection for the Freedom Rides, people like Jim Lawson, who had volunteered to be on the first bus into Jackson himself, were arguing that protection should be declined, since the issue was not whether black people could use desegregated facilities if they traveled in a heavily armed caravan. I had witnessed what would happen without protection. We'd followed the bus by car from Birmingham to Montgomery, where the police escort melted away at the city limits and the Freedom Riders arrived at a station that didn't have a policeman in sight. (Yes, Don Uhrbrock, the *Life* photographer, was among the first to be assaulted; when the attackers went for his camera, he had the presence of mind to give them a blank roll of film that he had palmed, keeping the roll that provided *Life* with a full-page picture of one of them pulling back his foot to kick a TV cameraman who had been knocked to the ground.) At a mass meeting in Ralph Abernathy's church during the Montgomery hiatus, it was, in the opinion of many, only an unorganized but eventually effective perimeter of U.S. marshals that prevented the mob from storming the church or burning it down.

In Chicago, fifty years later, Lawson, who has spent much of the intervening time as the pastor of a United Methodist church in Los Angeles, sounded unchanged in attitude. "We did not desegregate America," he said. "We did not dismantle the system." The letter that he and three other organizers of the Chicago event sent to explain why they wouldn't be attending the Jackson commemoration argued, in effect, that the struggle needed especially to be continued in Mississippi ("A lot has changed in the state, but be assured, racism is alive and well in Mississippi"). The signatories said that the Jackson commemoration was part of an effort in Mississippi that amounted to "stealing the legacy of the civil rights movement so they can profit from tourism." Some dismal statistics in living standards and education and criminal justice were presented.

At the time, Haley Barbour was still thought of as a potential presidential candidate. Although that candidacy wasn't mentioned, the letter tapped into a widespread concern that Barbour could use the commemoration as a cover with those minority voters who suspect that he is not truly reconstructed. A few months later, that would have become a particular necessity for him because of an interview in which he credited the Citizens Council with keeping the peace in his hometown of Yazoo City during the times of trouble. The Citizens Council, which was founded specifically to resist desegregation, kept the peace in the sense that it favored economic intimidation over violence—having a potential troublemaker fired, say, or kicking his family off land they'd farmed for generations. Barbour made it sound like some benign United Fund committee. Others called it the uptown Klan.

In 1961, Mississippi was thought of as the most intransigent of the Southern states. A few years later, Nina Simone, who could exude a level of anger that made someone like Jim Lawson seem rather accommodating, started singing a song called "Mississippi Goddam." Ray Arsenault, who has written the definitive history of the Freedom Rides, and who spoke at both commemorative gatherings, likes to tell the joke about the 1964 Freedom Summer volunteer from the North who has finished his training in Ohio and finds himself terrified on the night before he's supposed to leave for Jackson. He kneels and says, "God, please send me a sign that you'll go with me to Mississippi." Finally, after a long pause, a deep voice from above says, "I'll go as far as Memphis."

Actually, I felt physically safer in Mississippi than I did in Alabama. In 1961, Mississippi's approach was still dominated by the Citizens Council, which was conscious of how violence could mar the image of a state that was sending speakers north to present itself as a peaceful place to do business. That approach was backed up by the State Sovereignty Commission—a government agency that had evolved into a sort of cornpone Stasi, with investigators who monitored people's writings and contacts and even their love lives. For a Yankee reporter in Mississippi in 1961, there was a feeling of being watched rather than pursued. Once, when I'd arranged an interview with the mayor of Jackson, I arrived at his office to find that local reporters were there as observers; so were the chief of police, the chief of detectives, the city attorney, a city councilman, and the mayor's secretary (to make a transcript). The story in the next day's paper began, "Mayor Allen Thompson told a *Time* magazine reporter yesterday. . . ." I felt relatively safe in Mississippi, but also uneasy. I wondered if I was imagining that people I didn't know seemed to recognize me on the street. When I was ready to file a story overnight, I tried to do it from Memphis or New Orleans; I'd phone my office and say, "I've slipped over the border." After the Freedom Ride finally left Montgomery, I wrote in my *Time* file, "The brutal, chaotic bumbling of Alabama gave way to the well-oiled, kid-glove, image-conscious performance possible only in a monolithic police state."

As the first bus was about to pull out of Montgomery for Jackson, Claude Sitton, the Southern correspondent for the *Times,* and I were standing in the Trailways station discussing whether it was appropriate for reporters to be on it. In questions about when a reporter would be crossing the line from reporting on to participating in the civil rights struggle, I tended to take my cues from Claude, whose sympathy was expressed in the fairness and scrupulousness of his reporting. I didn't pretend that we were covering a struggle in which all sides—the side that thought, for instance, that all American citizens had the right to vote and the side that thought that people who acted on such a belief should have their houses burned down—had an equally compelling case to make. It wasn't like trying to remain objective while covering the Michigan–Ohio State game. But at mass meetings I would never have put any money in the collection cup. When, at the invariable end of the meeting, people in the congregation locked arms to sing "We Shall Overcome," I always edged away toward the exit. Still, I thought we should be on that bus. I reasoned that it was a public bus and we had a right to buy tickets. Also, other reporters were buying tickets. Claude agreed that we should be on the bus, and we sat down just a couple of seats behind the driver. When the bus finally left the station, there were more reporters on board than Freedom Riders. The passengers also included a small contingent of Alabama National Guardsmen. The bus moved out in a caravan of seventeen state-police cars.

At the Mississippi line, the Alabama escort withdrew. We were joined on the bus by some Mississippi National Guardsmen under the command of Lieutenant Colonel G. V. (Sonny) Montgomery, who later had a long career in Congress. Montgomery said that his orders were to take the bus directly to Jackson without stopping. In what I suppose was a reflection of my confidence that Mississippi was going to handle things in a Citizens Council rather than a Klan manner, I fell asleep. Then I felt Claude poking me. Reverend C. T. Vivian had asked for a rest stop, and Colonel Montgomery was answering in the negative. Vivian, who was sitting right across the aisle from us, began asking how Montgomery rationalized the acts he had to perform every day. I still remember snatches of the speech almost word for word. "What do you tell your wife when you get home?" Vivian said. "What do you say to your child? What do you say to your God when you pray? Or do you pray?" I'd never imagined that a request to leave the room could be made with such eloquence. A Canadian reporter was so moved that he stood up and began shouting at Montgomery to stop the bus. Claude spoke sharply to the Canadian reporter. As I remember his words, he said, "Sit down and shut up. You're a reporter."

A photograph that was prominently displayed this spring at the Mississippi gathering shows a bus moving through downtown Jackson. Except for a policeman every ten or fifteen feet, the street is virtually empty. The bus is framed in the foreground by two policemen with German shepherds—presumably Rebel and Happy, the dogs that the Jackson police department borrowed on such occasions from the Vicksburg police department. (When Jackson police broke up a gathering of black people outside a courthouse a month before the Freedom Rides—the crowd had gathered in support of some Tougaloo College students who'd been arrested in Mississippi's first sit-in—it was alleged that a minister named S. Leon Whitney had been bitten, an allegation that the Jackson police vigorously denied.) The police contingent inside the Trailways station was under the command of Chief of Police Detectives M. B. Pierce, whom I'd dealt with before. I suspected that Pierce had been chosen for his unflappability; he would just smile whenever I said to him, "I forget, Chief: was it Rebel that didn't bite Reverend Whitney or was it Happy that didn't bite Reverend Whitney?" When the Freedom Riders went into the whites-only waiting room, they were asked politely by the police to move on, and when they refused, they were, just as politely, arrested—a policy that was also followed when a second bus pulled into the Greyhound station a few hours later, and followed for the next few months as people from all over the country showed their support by taking a bus to Jackson and serving ninety days in Parchman Prison. There were three black reporters on our bus, but when they came into the whites-only waiting room they were not bothered. Chief Pierce called that to my attention. "Professional courtesy," he said.

In Jackson this May, the Freedom Riders were praised for their bravery and their effectiveness. (The wrong they sought to demonstrate had indeed been corrected: under pressure from Robert Kennedy's Justice Department, the Interstate Commerce Commission, in September of 1961, mandated that "Whites Only" signs be removed from interstate facilities.) Haley Barbour's speeches were cordial and complimentary and, in at least one case, apologetic. The speakers who shared the podium with Barbour at one event or the other included Jackson's black mayor and its second black female chief of police. As the commemoration began, an article in the Jackson *Clarion-Ledger* recalled some of the smears against the Freedom Riders in 1961. Senator James Eastland had called one CORE rider "a Communist agitator and organizer of the most dangerous kind." The editor of the *Jackson Daily News,* the *Clarion-Ledger*'s sister paper, had referred in his column to the Freedom Riders as "deranged mammals." The *Clarion-Ledger* article about the smears was written by Jerry Mitchell, who over the past twenty years has won renown (and a MacArthur Fellowship) for stories that brought to justice civil rights–era criminals like Byron De La Beckwith, the murderer of Medgar Evers. The Jackson airport now bears Evers's name.

Fifty years before, Ross Barnett, then the governor of Mississippi, had called the Freedom Riders "outside agitators trying to stir up our people for no good cause whatsoever," but in his deal-ings with the press at the time he'd sounded just as cordial as Haley Barbour. On the day after our bus's arrival, Barnett began his press conference by saying, "I'm pleased to say we're grateful indeed for your presence here. I extend a most cordial welcome to the great and sovereign state of Mississippi." For the reporters who were in Jackson to cover the Freedom Rides in 1961, Mayor Thompson had arranged a tour of the city—including what were then sometimes called "Supreme Court schools," schools built after *Brown v. Board of Education* for black children in an effort to dem-onstrate that "separate but equal" was something other than a joke. Thompson also gave us badges indicating that we were honorary members of the Jackson, Mississippi, police force.

One of Barbour's speeches was at the unveiling of a plaque that marked the old Greyhound station (now restored as an architect's office) as a stop on what the state is calling the Mississippi Free-dom Trail—a tourism scheme that is joining the Mississippi Blues Trail and the Mississippi Country Music Trail. "We have to put our past in front of us if we're going to put our past behind us," Bar-bour said. Civil rights history buffs can soon be guided to, among thirty or so other places, the university where Clyde Kennard ap-plied for admission in the fifties, only to be framed and thrown into jail. They can see where Medgar Evers was shot, in 1963, and where another NAACP leader, Vernon Dahmer, was killed, in 1966, when the Klan firebombed his house. Barbour said that he has also managed to get the legislature to appropriate twenty million dollars for a civil rights museum in Jackson—there is already such a museum in Birmingham—and he promised that it would be "a sensationally popular attraction." Presumably, this is the sort of thing that the Chicago-reunion organizers had in mind when they wrote, "Mississippi white racists have discovered the millions of dollars that can be derived from tourism pertaining to the legacy of the civil rights movement." Another way to look at it, of course, is as evidence that Mississippi, after half a century, is definitely part of America: it has figured out how to turn its history, even its horrific history, into an industry.

In both Chicago and Jackson, some of those in attendance were carrying around a large book called *Breach of Peace: Portraits of the 1961 Mississippi Freedom Riders,* by Eric Etheridge, one of the organizers of the Jackson commemoration. They were trying to get as many signatures of Freedom Riders as they could. Occasionally, one of them would approach me and say, "Were you a Freedom Rider?"

"No, I was just a reporter who was on the bus," I'd say.

Some of them insisted that I sign anyway, and eventually I decided that they were probably right in assuming that, after fifty years, the line between reporter and participant was not as bright as I thought it was when I worked in the South. In Chicago, I greeted, say, John Lewis, a sharecropper's son who had grown up to be a congressman, more like an old comrade-in-arms than like someone I'd mentioned in a couple of articles. We had been together at the Trailways bus station in Montgomery, where there was a distinct absence of what Chief Pierce called "professional courtesy."

I'm no longer as certain as I once was about how bright the line was even back then. During Charlayne Hunter's first semester at the University of Georgia, she was isolated in a dorm full of hostile coeds, and we spoke on the telephone from time to time. Once, she was talking about an uncomfortable train ride she'd just had from Savannah to Atlanta, and I said that I'd always heard that the train she'd been on—a well-known train called the Nancy Hanks—was particularly luxurious. "Not where we have to sit," she said. What flashed through my mind had nothing to do with the knowledge I had built up about segregation in interstate versus intrastate transportation and how long it would take to desegregate the latter. What flashed through my mind was, "They can't make *her* sit back there."

When one of the sessions in Chicago ended with people linking arms and singing "We Shall Overcome," I made my usual quiet move toward the door. Suddenly, I felt someone lock arms with me. Instinctively, I started to pull my arm away while looking around to see who it was. It was an older woman in a wheelchair. Was I really going to wrest my arm away from an older woman in a wheelchair? I stayed. Then I joined in. It turns out that I still know most of the verses.

About the Author

CALVIN TRILLIN, a longtime staff writer at *The New Yorker,* has also been a columnist for *Time* and *The Nation.* He lives in New York City.

About the Type

This book was set in Celeste, a typeface that its designer, Chris Burke (b. 1967), classifies as a modern humanistic typeface. Celeste was influenced by Bodoni and Waldman, but the strokeweight contrast is less pronounced. The serifs tend toward the triangular, and the italics harmonize well with the roman in tone and width. It is a robust and readable text face that is less stark and modular than many of the modern fonts, and has many of the friendlier old-face features.